We Saved the Best for You

D1545710

Imagination and Praxis: Criticality and Creativity in Education and Educational Research
Volume 1

SERIES EDITORS

Tricia M. Kress
The University of Massachusetts Boston, 100 Morrissey Blvd, W-1-77D, Boston, MA, USA 02125

Robert Lake
Georgia Southern University, College of Education, Box 8144, Statesboro, GA, USA 30460

SCOPE

Current educational reform rhetoric around the globe repeatedly invokes the language of 21st century learning and innovative thinking while contrarily re-enforcing, through government policy, high stakes testing and international competition, standardization of education that is exceedingly reminiscent of 19th century Taylorism and scientific management. Yet, as the steam engines of educational "progress" continue down an increasingly narrow, linear, and unified track, it is becoming increasingly apparent that the students in our classrooms are inheriting real world problems of economic instability, ecological damage, social inequality, and human suffering. If young people are to address these social problems, they will need to activate complex, interconnected, empathetic and multiple ways of thinking about the ways in which peoples of the world are interconnected as a global community in the living ecosystem of the world. Seeing the world as simultaneously local, global, political, economic, ecological, cultural and interconnected is far removed from the Enlightenment's objectivist and mechanistic legacy that presently saturates the status quo of contemporary schooling. If we are to derail this positivist educational train and teach our students to see and be in the world differently, the educational community needs a serious dose of imagination. The goal of this book series is to assist students, practitioners, leaders, and researchers in looking beyond what they take for granted, questioning the normal, and amplifying our multiplicities of knowing, seeing, being and feeling to, ultimately, envision and create possibilities for positive social and educational change. The books featured in this series will explore ways of seeing, knowing, being, and learning that are frequently excluded in this global climate of standardized practices in the field of education. In particular, they will illuminate the ways in which imagination permeates every aspect of life and helps develop personal and political awareness. Featured works will be written in forms that range from academic to artistic, including original research in traditional scholarly format that addresses unconventional topics (e.g., play, gaming, ecopedagogy, aesthetics), as well as works that approach traditional and unconventional topics in unconventional formats (e.g., graphic novels, fiction, narrative forms, and multi-genre texts). Inspired by the work of Maxine Greene, this series will showcase works that "break through the limits of the conventional" and provoke readers to continue arousing themselves and their students to "begin again" (Greene, 1995, p. 109).

EDITORIAL ADVISORY BOARD

Peter Appelbaum- Arcadia University, Philadelphia, PA, USA
Roslyn Arnold-University of Sydney, Australia
Patty Bode-Tufts University- Boston, MA, USA
Cathrene Connery-Ithaca College. Ithaca, NY, USA
Clyde Coreil- New Jersey City University, Jersey City, NJ,USA
Michelle Fine- CUNY Graduate Center, New York, NY, USA
Sandy Grande-Connecticut College, New London, CT, USA
Awad Ibrihim- University of Ottawa- Ottawa, ON, Canada
Wendy Kohli-Fairfield University- Fairfield, CT, USA
Carl Leggo- University of British Columbia, Vancouver, BC, Canada
Pepi Leistyna-University of Massachusetts Boston, MA, USA
Donaldo Macedo-University of Massachusetts Boston, MA, USA
Martha McKenna-Lesley University, Boston, MA, USA
Ernest Morrell- Columbia University- New York, NY, USA
William Reynolds-Georgia Southern University- Statesboro, GA, USA
Pauline Sameshima- Washington State University, Pullman, WA, USA
Vera John-Steiner-University of New Mexico, Albuquerque, NM, USA

REFERENCE

Greene, M. (1995). *Releasing the imagination: Essays on education, the arts and social change*. San Francisco, CA. Jossey-Bass.

We Saved the Best for You

Letters of Hope, Imagination and Wisdom for 21st Century Educators

Edited by

Tricia M. Kress
The University of Massachusetts Boston, USA

and

Robert Lake
Georgia Southern University, USA

SENSE PUBLISHERS
ROTTERDAM/BOSTON/TAIPEI

A C.I.P. record for this book is available from the Library of Congress.

ISBN: 978-94-6209-120-7 (paperback)
ISBN: 978-94-6209-121-4 (hardback)
ISBN: 978-94-6209-122-1 (e-book)

Published by: Sense Publishers,
P.O. Box 21858,
3001 AW Rotterdam,
The Netherlands
https://www.sensepublishers.com/

Printed on acid-free paper

All Rights Reserved © 2013 Sense Publishers

No part of this work may be reproduced, stored in a retrieval system, or transmitted in any form or by any means, electronic, mechanical, photocopying, microfilming, recording or otherwise, without written permission from the Publisher, with the exception of any material supplied specifically for the purpose of being entered and executed on a computer system, for exclusive use by the purchaser of the work.

CONTENTS

CONTENTS

ACKNOWLEDGEMENTS

First of all we want to thank all of the contributors to this book. We are keenly aware that you had to take time away from other projects, deadlines, family responsibilities, and so many other commitments to write for this project. We also want to thank Peter de Liefde and Michel Lokhorst at Sense Publishers for your innovative vision of publishing that makes a project like this possible. We also thank Melissa Winchell, a doctoral candidate at the University of Massachusetts- Boston and Amber Bryan a former graduate assistant at Georgia Southern University for their marvelous help with proofreading the first drafts of the letters. We also are also very grateful for the help in formatting and proofreading that we received from Sean Fretwell, a doctoral candidate at Georgia Southern University. Thank-you Wendy Chambers a colleague at Georgia Southern for allowing us to use her stunning photograph for the cover of this book. We wish to also thank our family members for the support and understanding showed us while working on this manuscript for many nights, off days and weekends. And finally, we wish to thank our students, the future teachers, whose brilliance and commitment to the education of future generations have inspired us to put together this collection.

TRICIA M. KRESS AND ROBERT LAKE

INTRODUCTION

Reigniting Radical Hope and Social Imagination in "Dark Times"

Those who have never despaired have neither lived nor loved. Hope is inseparable from despair. Those of us who truly hope make despair a constant companion whom we outwrestle every day owing to our commitment to justice, love, and hope (West, 2008, p. 185).

Dear readers

Let us begin by introducing ourselves. I (Tricia Kress) am an assistant professor at the University of Massachusetts Boston. I have been a teacher educator for about twelve years, and I am product of and advocate for urban public schools. I fancy myself to be an urbanite, a New Yorker cum Bostonian, who has just enough moxie to press against commonsense thinking that binds the purpose of education and just enough big city humility to know that I need to consistently re-evaluate my own stance on the matter; in the grand scheme of things, I can only ever know a tiny fraction of what it means to be in the world. I (Robert) grew up in a working class home in a small town in the Midwest and work as an assistant professor at Georgia Southern University. I am also a former guitar and harmonica player for a garage band who came to the field of education by using music to teach English to refugees from Vietnam and later Bosnia. Before I began my current position in teacher preparation, I taught Adult Education classes for a number of years. For many years I have been fascinated with theories of creativity and imagination and how they might be used in educational settings. About two years ago, I discovered Tricia's work when I read a piece she had written that was inspired by *Tommy,* the rock opera. In this article she wrote about how we can understand public education by thinking of teaching as playing a perpetual game of pinball (Kress, 2010). I was struck in particular by her use of "tilting the machine" as a metaphor and immediately after reading this article, I asked if she would write a piece for another book I was editing at the time (Lake, 2012). Through many conversations, mostly via email and telephone and (a few) face-to-face, we have discovered that we share an academic kinship, a lineage if you will, that can be traced back by following the historical roots of our shared desire for education that is humanizing and set ablaze by hope and imagination. Since you have picked up this book and opened its cover, we are hoping that this means you share this lineage too.

The origins of this collection lie in our discomforts with the ways in which, in the present ethos, the discipline of education and the practice of teaching are being conceived of by society. There seems to be a big black cloud hanging over our profession these days that can best be described by what Vinson and Ross (2003) describe as "surveillance-spectacle" (p. 243). As teachers and teacher educators, increasingly we find ourselves doubly scrutinized: we are the many who are gazed upon by the few (i.e., administrators and policy-makers) ostensibly for reasons of "accountability," and at the same time, we are also the few who are gazed upon by the many (i.e., the general public) via media spectacles. A prime example of how surveillance and spectacle collide in the lives of educators is the recent publicizing of all K-12 public teachers' students' test scores in New York City. Another is the publicizing of all public higher education professors' salaries in the state of Massachusetts. Alongside this type of scrutiny, there has also been a rash of media critiques of the public sphere and public workers in general, in which educators are frequently sensationalized as leeches who receive "Cadillac pensions" and exorbitant salaries without actually working, or as predators who abuse and/or take advantage of their students. Thus, imagination and creativity in the classroom are curbed as taking risks and making mistakes in teaching and learning becomes dangerous. What results from this is a corp of teachers and learners who need to somehow carve out a space for humanizing education amidst a climate of fear and resentment.

In response, well-respected scholars have begun referring to this contemporary moment as "dark times" (e.g., Butin, 2007; Giroux, 2005). Dialectically speaking, in our perspective, this seems to imply a longing for "the good ol' days" of the pre-Reagan era of the 1960's and '70s. This nostalgia indicates despair and loss, a mourning of sorts, that a) fails to recognize that, if you really examine history, the "good ol' days" really weren't all that good; and b) despite the contemporary pressure-cooker climate of education, good things still can and do happen in public schools. Quite frankly, we are disturbed when we hear people who (purportedly) are among the finest education scholars in the U.S. (and the world) saying things like, "We're toast," to their audience at the annual meeting of the American Educational Research Association (AERA). Furthermore, we are deeply saddened when the notions of "hope" and "imagination" are regarded as, at best, naive, and, at worst, dangerous. Where would we be if the great educators and social justice workers of the world had not hoped for and imagined a different future? Where would we be if they had settled for and simply coped with the "what is" reality? Our dissatisfaction with the way things are and the way things are being responded to have implored us to begin questioning what this means for those who choose to enter into the teaching profession. What are the messages we are sending; what messes are we leaving; and what damages are we perpetuating by thinking about and speaking this way to the inheritors of the world we are creating? Thus, our hope is that this volume illustrates the ways in which despair and desire (which we believe are parts of the same whole) can enable us to catalyze new visions of and possibilities for education as a facilitator for social change.

FANNING THE EMBERS OF HOPE AND IMAGINATION

When we first sent out the call for contributors for this volume, the outpouring of positive responses we received was humbling. Leading names in the field of education, emerging scholars of education, and practitioners in schools all expressed an enthusiasm for the message we were putting forth. As a result, we wound up with over 50 contributors. When we planned the edition, we knew that we felt a deep desire to bring hope and imagination back into the conversation around education "in dark times," but we did not expect there to be so many fine educators and scholars who equally shared this same desire. As the list of letters grew, we decided that we should put together a symposium for the AERA annual meeting. We contacted a number of our contributors and designed a session in which we would collectively share our letters of hope, imagination, and wisdom for future educators. Our session proposal for AERA, however, did not receive quite the same warm reception as our call for the volume. The reviews were polarized, in fact, with one reviewer expressing great enthusiasm and the other quite a bit of cynicism. Notably, the cynical reviewer wrote, "I personally don't buy into the usefulness of the 'hope' concept... Hope was the last thing out of Pandora's box, not to help us contend with all of the evils, but as the WORST evil of them all: hope keeps us always hoping, as in, accepting the present – accepting the nightmare that is the present? In curriculum studies, I really HOPE NOT!" (emphasis original). Upon receiving this feedback, we knew that we needed to think deeply about what "hope" means to us because, clearly, the way we think of hope and the way the reviewer thinks of hope are not the same.

Like Kincheloe (1999), we recognize that "All language is mulitaccentual, meaning that it can be both spoken and heard, written and read in ways that reflect different meanings and different relationships to different social groups and power formations" (p. 63). The story of Pandora resonates with us too, albeit, in quite a different manner than it did with our reviewer. While he/she took the myth to be a story of the dangers of hope, we see the myth of Pandora as having a much more positive connotation that conveys the dangers of hopelessness. Our interpretation is much more aligned with Govier (2011) who says, "When all the bad things were out, hope remained, with its potential of consoling and assisting mankind in coping with the evils of the world. The Pandora story may be interpreted as warning that to ignore hope is to ignore something of value, something that remains even in the aftermath of dire events" (p. 243). Furthermore, while our reviewer construed hope as passive, deterministic, and rooted in the present, we do not see hope as such. Rather, we draw our notion of hope from Freire (1995) and Fromm (2010) who see hope as active, dynamic, and forward-looking. In fact, for Fromm, hope that is not acted upon is not hope at all. And for Freire (1995), hope is so essential to what it means to be human that he describes it as an "ontological need" (p. 9). However, he goes on to say that, "Hope needs practice in order to become historical concreteness. The hoped-for is not attained by dint of raw hoping" (ibid).

If we think of "hope" as a source of power and the impetus for social change, it becomes clear there is a need to reclaim hope and redirect it toward action because if we don't, others surely will, although probably not in a way that will be productive for alleviating human suffering. As Carolyne Ali-Khan so eloquently observed,

> Today corporatized values spew through the feel good spectacles that flood my every moment. I often feel that this place in time is one where venture philanthropy is the new opiate, the solution to all that ails us. And in this brave new world 'hope' is a word much abused. It is a word on a bracelet that I buy at K-Mart, knowing that some portion of the profit goes to something good. Encircled in my rubber halo I can sleep at night, for I have fought the good fight. Hope is stripped from forests and pressed tight in Chinese sweatshops; it is a noose of platitudes, proudly brought to me by the sponsors of X (C. Ali-Khan, personal communication, April 24, 2012).

With this same sense of urgency, our conceptualization of hope is not naive; it is vigilant, strategic, and under-girded by the staunch belief that people have made the world what it is, therefore, people can remake the world to be something different.

A radical hope such as ours is decidedly *not* deterministic, and it represents a *refusal* to accept the world, with all its pain and ugliness, as it is. Yet, at the same time, it carries with it a responsibility to act upon our desire for a different future, otherwise, hope risks morphing into despair and stagnation (i.e., hopelessness). Here, is where Maxine Greene's (1995) notion of social imagination becomes a crucial part of our framework. It is not enough to simply hope that the world will change, we must develop our own vision of possible futures by *imagining* what this change might look like. And then, we must act upon the world to begin achieving our vision. We cannot sit idly by and wait for the world to change around us. For both Freire and Greene, social change begins with education by catalyzing conscientizaçao and wide-awakeness in ourselves and our students. While they use different terminology, they both emphasize the role of critical consciousness in social movement. Freire stresses the importance of reading the word and the world and developing a sense of historicity and self/other awareness. Similarly, Greene illustrates the importance of seeing the world both big and small, meaning seeing social actors close up in context (seeing things big) and seeing broad social trends that cut across contexts over time (seeing things small).

SHARED KNOWING VIA THE EPISTOLARY GENRE

In gathering a collection of letters written by scholar-practitioners who are currently in the field to pre-service practitioners who will be in the field in the future, we aim to illuminate experiential connections and continuity across space and time, while also allowing for each author's unique vantage point to take center stage. In this regard, the epistolary genre is appropriate for Freire's and Greene's goals of self/ other/world awareness and the catalyzing of social change. Each author's words are fundamentally human, addressed to a specific audience, and yet the content is also scholarly and pensive. This is akin to Moffett's (1968) concept of the discourse of conversation "which makes the existential, rhetorical, and behavioural features of I-you most keenly felt" (p. 41). Similarly, Bakhtin's (1986) notion of the dialogical nature of utterance sheds light on this genre as well.

> The utterance is filled with dialogic overtones, and they must be taken into account in order to fully understand the style of the utterance. After all, our thought itself – philosophical, scientific, artistic – is born and shaped in the process of interaction and struggle with others' thought, and this cannot but be reflected in the forms that verbally express our thought as well (p. 92).

Through the epistolary medium, spaces are created for conscientization, wide-awakeness, and seeing things both big and small as writer and recipient engage in an imagined dialogue.

We have arranged the letters in this collection into chapters entitled Hope, Imagination, Wisdom, The Praxis of Teaching, and Voices from the Past. They are primarily categories of convenience, and we recognize that they are rather artificial. Most of these letters could easily fit into another one or two of the chapters because hope, imagination, wisdom, praxis, and history are not separate; they are interchangeable and cumulative. As you read each of these heart-felt letters, we hope you take away the message that to hope and to imagine are not passive acts. They are choices based on action. Freire, Zinn, Fromm and many other great thinkers too numerous to list, all emphasized that the world we make is based on choice. Likewise, Marx stressed that we "become" by the work we do. Just as in Marx's economic theory, which posited that the Bourgeois take people away from their work and make them into machines, we see the present conversation around education and what it means to be an educator as parallel. If the work of being an educator is to cultivate citizens, as we believe it is, we need to reconnect teachers (ourselves included) to their work. We believe this connection is found in our hopeful actions for creating the future. Thus, we choose to initiate this connection and catalyze action via our letters of hope, imagination, and wisdom to you, our future educators. As we enter into our classrooms, as we walk through school building corridors, as we overhear our students' conversations in the cafeteria, each and every day we encounter sources of hope. The actions we choose to take as we move through our worlds and engage with others will steer us toward the future. And this, dear readers, is why we say, "We saved the best for you," because as nightmarish as the present may be, as dark as times may seem, "the best" is yet to come. In your connections with your future students, "the best" is the world you will create.

Yours truly,
Tricia Kress & Robert Lake

REFERENCES

Bakhtin, M. (1986). *Speech Genres and Other Late Essays*. (V. W. McGee, Trans.). Austin, TX: University of Texas Press.

Butin, D. W. (2007). Dark times indeed: NCATE, social Justice, and the marginalization of multicultural foundations. *The Journal of Educational Controversy, 2*(2).

Giroux, H. (2005). Cutlural studies in dark times: Public pedagogy and the challenge of neoliberalism. *Fast Capitalism, 1*(2).

Govier, T. (2011). Hope and Its Opposites. *Journal of Social Philosophy, 42*, 239–253. doi: 10.1111/j.1467-9833.2011.01532.x

Greene, M. (1995). *Releasing the imagination: Essays on education, the arts and social change*. San Francisco: Jossey-Bass.

Freire, P. (1995). *Pedagogy of Hope: Reliving the pedagogy of the oppressed*. New York, NY. Continuum Publishers.

Fromm, E. (2010). *The revolution of hope: Toward a humanized technology*. Riverdale N.Y. American Mental Health Foundation Books.

Kincheloe, J. L. (1999). Fiction formulas: Critical constructivism and the representation of reality. In William G Tierney and Yvonna S. Lincoln, (Eds.), *Representation and the Text: Re-framing the narrative voice* (pp. 57–79). Albany, NY: State University of New York Press.

Kress, T. (2010). *Tilting the machine: A critique of one teacher's attempts at using art forms to create postformal, democratic learning environments. The Journal of Educational Controversy, 5*(1).

Lake, R. L. (2012). *Dear Nel: Opening the circles of care. (Letters to Nel Noddings)* New York, NY: Teachers College Press.

Moffett, J. (1968). *Teaching the universe of discourse*. Boston, MA: Houghton Mifflin.

Vinson, K. D., & Ross, E. W. (2003). Controlling images: Surveillance, spectacle, and the power of high-stakes testing. In K. J. Saltman & D. Gabbard (Eds.), *Education as enforcement* (pp. 241–257). New York: Routledge.

West, C. (2008). *Hope on a tightrope: Words and wisdom*. Carlsbad, CA. Hay House Publishing.

PART I

LETTERS OF HOPE

TRICIA M. KRESS

1. TILTING AT WINDMILLS

Hope as an Ontological Need when Tilting the Machine

Dear Students,

Any educator will tell you that teaching is *hard;* it is exhausting, painful, frustrating and, at times, seemingly thankless. The difficulty of being a critical democratic educator who teaches with the desire of furthering social justice is tenfold. In previous articles (see Kress, 2010 and Kress, 2012) I have described the process of being and becoming a critical democratic educator as similar to playing a perpetual game of pinball. It is exhilarating and rewarding but frustrating and never-ending. Here, in my letter to you, the next generation of educators, I feel it is important that I am forthcoming in telling you: in addition to being "pinball wizards" who strive to beat the system at its own game, as we continually attempt to tilt the machine, we are simultaneously "tilting at windmills," that is, striving toward a noble goal that a) others may not recognize as noble, and b) is likely unattainable, at least in our lifetime. Like Cervantes' Don Quixote the ragtag "knight" who sought to slay windmills that he imagined were dragons, we may be scoffed at, pushed down, or degraded for undertaking a quest that others deem merely foolish and not rooted in reality. Consequently, we will, each of us, feel moments of despair and hopelessness as we fight constantly against the anti-imagination currents of the "what is" reality (Joyce, 2008). This is why I believe that nurturing hope is of the utmost importance for those of us who strive to live as critical democratic educators. To do so, we must begin to understand hope not as a thing, but as an energy that is generated over time and flows through and among us as we continue our practice as critical democratic educators.

In *Pedagogy of Hope,* Freire (2006) explains hope is an ontological need. People need hope in order to simply *be* in the world. As we live our daily lives, we envision our futures stretching out before us, and in that foresight lay our belief in a world yet to come. Along these same lines, we need hope to simply *be* as educators who wish to see our students and ourselves grow intellectually and emotionally and to contribute to making the world a better place. It is easy to see the obstacles before us as insurmountable—violence and war, increasing wealth disparity around the world, shrinking resources in the public sphere, increased accountability and standardization of the work we do, and the list goes on and on…

T. M. Kress and R. Lake (Eds.), We Saved the Best for You: Letters of Hope, Imagination and Wisdom for 21st Century Educators, 3–6.
© *2013 Sense Publishers. All rights reserved.*

Under these conditions, if we allow it to, hopelessness "paralyzes us, immobilizes us. We succumb to fatalism, and then it becomes impossible to muster the strength we absolutely need for a fierce struggle that will re-create the world" (Freire, 2006, p. 2). To combat this despair, it is necessary that we recognize hope as the fuel for being democratic teachers and continuing our practice. Without hope, without the belief that the world can be different and that we can help to bring about that difference despite what others may think, there will be times when it will be difficult to find the nerve and energy to keep fighting. But, as Freire (2000) so aptly states, "As long as I fight, I am moved by hope; and if I fight with hope, then I can wait" (pp. 91–92). Hope is what will sustain us when we face our most difficult battles and we cannot see the future on the horizon.

I am well aware that hope can be elusive because it is not so much a thing in itself, as it is a byproduct of the processes and relationships that we engage in as we strive towards our goal of making education and humanity more humane. At the same time, while hope is a product of our work, hope is also the sustenance for our work. If we accept the notion that being a critical democratic teacher means always being in process (i.e., continuously striving to tilt the machine), then our practice can be understood as cyclical and cumulative, as hope begets hope, and through our practice we continue to generate the fuel we need to keep going (and growing). As such, "hope, as an ontological need, demands an anchoring in practice. As an ontological need, hope needs practice in order to become historical concreteness" (Freire, 2006, p. 2). In other words, as with tilting the machine, as educators we must continuously work at regenerating hope through the act of critical democratic teaching, especially when we're tired and especially when we're exasperated and ready to give up, because it is hope that will revive us again. Once we recognize that hope is not a thing, but rather is an energy that is activated as a result of our practice and our relationships, our practice and relationships become the source of our hope. Hope, then, is not an object to be acquired and worn as a symbol or a shield. Hope is not something we can see or touch; it is an aching in our very core, and we know it exists because we can feel it rising up from inside us like adrenaline coursing through our veins as we experience moments of heightened emotion.

For three months, I have been starting and restarting this letter, trying on different voices, wanting to "sound" hopeful, to exude hope to you through my words, to embody hope in my writing. Upon reflection, I think I have felt the need to model "hope" for you in my practice right here on these pages. I have sought out sources of hope, trying to pin down where hope resides, and I kept searching outside of myself as I did so. I searched for hope in music, particularly the blues and classic rock n' roll; I gazed at artwork, and I read the works of great philosophers and creative writers.

Throughout this process, I had been feeling an increasing ache inside because I was unable to pin down how I truly experience the essence of hope as part of my being. And, quite ironically, there were moments where this seeking out of hope had itself made me feel quite hopeless because hope continued to idle in my peripheral vision, and every time I turned my head to fix on it, it was gone. Herein lies my final point: the very act of seeking out hope can be excruciating and exhausting, especially in those times when we feel we need it most to keep going because hope is not something we can simply find, as if it is a ripe fruit waiting to be picked from a tree. Rather, "Hope is rooted in men's incompletion, from which they move out in constant search—a search which can be carried out only in communion with others" (Freire, 2000, p. 91).

After weeks of sitting in front of my computer, trying so hard to describe how I experienced hope, like a withered and defeated Don Quixote, I finally gave up searching and simply let myself "be" in the moment. It was then I realized that hope cannot be rushed; it ferments inside us after we have spent long spells growing alongside others, often feeling stifled under the pressures of inhospitable conditions. Bound up in dark places hidden from the world, hope reveals itself to us only when it and we are ready. At that moment, what flowed from my fingers, my embodiment of hope, was not a narrative at all but a poem that I share with you now in solidarity.

> Hope twists inside me,
> a piercing corkscrew opening
> a bottle of ripe-aged wine.
> Spirits spilling in my body,
> intoxicating from the inside out,
> and I see the world differently:
> Circled by auras and shimmers.
> Hope the music of life.
> Me a drunken patron.
> Life a seedy blues bar.
> Twist, pain, sway again as
> hope echoes back.

REFERENCES

Freire, P. (2006). *Pedagogy of hope: Reliving pedagogy of the oppressed.* New York, NY: Continuum.
Freire, P. (2000). *Pedagogy of the oppressed.* New York, NY: *Continuum.*
Freire, P. (1981). *Education for critical consciousness.* New York, NY: *Continuum.*
Kress, T. (2012). Tilting to care in the academy. In Lake, R. (Ed.), *Letters to Nel Noddings* (pp. 55–57). New York, NY: *Teachers College Press.*
Kress, T. (2010). Tilting the machine: A critique of one teacher's attempts at creating postformal democratic learning environments. *The Journal of Educational Controversy, 5*(1).

AFFILIATION

Tricia M. Kress
Department of Leadership in Education
The University of Massachusetts Boston

CAROLYNE ALI-KHAN

2. CHALLENGING INEXORABILITY

A Journey of Critical Optimism

Dear Future Educators,

I want you to know that education can be the place where inexorability is conquered by hope. I ground this belief in the work of Paulo Freire, who states, "One of the most important tasks for progressive intellectuals is to demystify postmodern discourses with respect to the inexorability of (the) situation" (1998, p. 36).

Allow me an introduction: I have always been an optimist. I have reason to be: I have led a charmed life (one with enough struggle to let me know how lucky I am, but not enough to cripple me). I have crossed paths with amazing people. I have been blessed with nutritious food, clean water, love, health, shelter; in other words, all of those basics that should be (but are not) afforded to us all. But the icing on the cake is that in addition to these layers of privilege, I have another reason for optimism: I teach for a living! Despite all of its pressures and frustrations, to teach is to journey through hope. Teaching has afforded me the simple joy of being around youth (whose contagious energy exudes life), and in addition it has been a crystal ball, affording me a glimpse into the years ahead. I have spent my professional life with those who will craft the world. So I have, in the words of the artist once again known as Prince (1989), "*seen the future…and it works!*"

A WORKING FUTURE

But optimism without criticality is blind. In 2012 there is cause for concern. After more than two decades in K-12 classrooms I now teach teachers at a time of great upheaval and professional turmoil. The screws of "accountability" have tightened to squeeze the very soul of teaching and learning. I worry about my student teachers who must survive the political machines that truncate knowledge (rendering it a slave to metricians and statisticians). They enter a profession at a time when neoliberal attacks on the public sector threaten teachers and students alike. I worry about the questions these new teachers can ask as they form their careers under the scrutiny of edutrepreneurs (whose interests it serves to crush all but the most superficial definitions of knowledge). These teachers are under attack as professionals; they must face the encroaching monsters of charter schools, vouchers, scripted curriculum, stripped funds and nonsense standards. They must survive being told to

T. M. Kress and R. Lake (Eds.), We Saved the Best for You: Letters of Hope, Imagination and Wisdom for 21st Century Educators, 7–10.
© *2013 Sense Publishers. All rights reserved.*

sacrifice children's needs on the altar of standardized testing and emerge from all of these pressures (and more) with their souls intact.

Yet despite all the threats to public education (and the peace of mind of those who work in it), my students stand strong and undaunted! They work each day in schools and when they come to classes at night they do not look away from difficult questions about education. Instead, they seek to understand and remedy them. They bring to my college classes a great curiosity, passion and eagerness to address what it means to educate a child. I am humbled by them. *"Why?" "To what end?"* and *"Good for whom?"* are the questions they ask, while knowing full well that these are not permissible instructional questions in an era in which, "How high shall we jump?" (which in eduspeak is, "How much can we improve our reading scores?") is the only official mantra. As I think of the future in these new teachers hands, I know that "the situation is not inexorable." *I see the future and it works.*

INEXORABILITY UNRAVELING

The situation is no longer inexorable in public education and in the world beyond it. I write this as the crowds swell and are beaten back in Occupy Sites across the world, as social and economic injustice is being challenged in public space. "We are at the 99%!" The protestor's cry has been echoed on social media sites and (finally) in the press. The protestors are singing, marching, drumming, writing, blogging. They are beaten and maced by armed police (whose plastic makeshift handcuffs tell us that they were not ready for this push-back on the established regime). As one Occupy Site is crushed, another springs up. Naomi Klein speaks about disaster capitalism and shock doctrine (2007). She outlines how *crisis*, as a concept, has been manipulated to the benefit of the political right and their desire to corporatize and privatize. Then she reminds us that inevitably, the shock wears off, and when it does, people rise up to defeat injustice. I agree with her. I believe that time has come.

Teachers unions are on the streets in this movement, and are counted among the "99%" who had enough of exploitation, corporate greed, and predatory capitalism's brutal viciousness. These voices demand that governments take real steps toward environmental sustainability, equitable wealth distribution, job creation, decent schools, healthcare, and emergency services. It is no longer acceptable to believe that widening inequity is the natural outcome of a world always already there. (Not even in New York City, where relentless images of glamour have endlessly reiterated the fairytale of meritocracy while rendering invisible the working poor whose labor in sweatshops and kitchens have silently made "the dream" possible for the few). The cat is out of the bag; in Freire's terms *the discourses of inexorability have been demystified.* And while this moment may shift, it will not disappear.

"HOPE" REWOVEN

Surprisingly, hope and change did not come from expected avenues. Despite Obama's promises and the euphoria of bumper sticker rhetoric, hope did not "trickle down" through the feel-good platitudes of the powerful. It was not lovingly tossed to the crowds as scraps from the tables of the oligarchy, emblazoned on T-shirts and buttons. As Ken Tobin (in press) points out, *Yes we can!* rang hollow and "three years later and one year before the next election the political rhetoric and our lived reality is 'No he didn't!'...The futility of heroic individuals transforming society was never more apparent in the past few years." Against the odds and in spite of the propaganda machines, real hope is a grassroots affair, evident in every generation.

INEXORABILITY AND THE NEXT GENERATION

The "Me Generation" joined those who are taking a stand. I am not surprised. They have been reared in a society that hates children, particularly poor children (Giroux, 2003). Youth have suffered in this economic moment in which they are chronically unemployed, or employed in bleak jobs while the costs of a college education have skyrocketed; in which our public discourses drip with outdated sentimental narratives of "childhood innocence" that are not supported by care. They face a future in which the American dream has collapsed and they are the first generation not destined to be better off than their parents. They navigate a world dominated by relentless right-wing propaganda aimed at blaming the poor while simultaneously crippling them economically. Children now come of age in a moment saturated with infotainment and predatory advertising. Vast numbers of children go to school each day visibly aching with the weight of adult responsibilities, compounded by the strain of having internalized a multiplicity of deficit perspectives. These children were my students. Hegemony is perhaps the most heartbreaking when it gouges the souls and bodies of the young.

Yet, these youth fight back. I have known *countless* ordinary children with extraordinary strength. I have met many hundreds of youth who did not buy the despair, the self-blame, or the shallow lullabies of consumerism and who bear no resemblance to the self-absorbed dolts that the media commonly portrays teenagers to be. These young men and women struggle to see wisely, to hear clearly, to learn to speak with care, and to be heard. They are politically aware, engaged, passionate and compassionate; they are hardworking and loving and funny, savvy, smart and deeply resilient.

In my many years of working with youth I have encountered the future as it is written in those who have experienced life from the bottom of every hierarchy (race, class, gender, and age) and who have had to battle against a system of entrenched classism and racism with little or no support. Indeed some of these youth do "fall" and become incarcerated, addicted, consumed, and spiritually beaten. *But against what are no less than insurmountable odds, very many do not.* In all of them lies hope.

I TEACH, THEREFORE I AM AN OPTIMIST.

Paulo Freire asks us to challenge inexorability by exposing the fallacy of an immutable world. I believe in a better future, because I work with those who hold it. In the lives of the educators, future educators and youth, I have seen a world that replaces inexorability with resistance. I know there is reason for optimism.

Carolyne Ali-Khan

REFERENCES

Freire, P. (1998). *Pedagogy of the heart.* New York: Continuum International Publishing Group.
Giroux, H. A. (2003). *The abandoned generation: Democracy beyond the culture of fear.* New York, NY: Palgrave Macmillan.
Klein, N. (2007). *The Shock Doctrine.* Canadian Centre for Policy Alternatives. Retrieved 30 Oct. 2011 from http://www.youtube.com/watch?v=Ka3Pb_StJn4
Prince. (1989). *The future.* Retrieved 10 Oct. 2011 from http://www.lyricsmania.com/the_future_lyrics_prince.html
Tobin, K. (in press). Afterword: We can enact change. In B. Down and J. Smyth (Eds.), *Critical voices in teacher education: Teaching for social justice in conservative times.* Dordrecht, The Netherlands: Springer.

AFFILIATION

Carolyne Ali-Khan
Department of Foundations and Secondary Education
University of North Florida

EVE TUCK

3. LOCATING THE HOPE IN BONE-DEEP PARTICIPATION

Dear Sweet Honey Coated Readers,

(I once read a letter addressed in this way, and have since wanted to do the same).
I am going to use the space of this letter trying to describe something in writing
that I have only ever been able to capture in person, over the dinner table or while
on a long walk or subway ride. For you, *A}alikingan aqaangin*, our future, I'd like
to articulate where the hope resides in participatory pedagogy and participatory
research. Participatory pedagogy and research are generally regarded to have
change-making capacities, but I think it is important to try to understand why and
how such praxes can be transformative, to locate the hope in deep participation.

As I write this letter, schools and society can be characterized by what we might
call shallow participation. Shallow participation involves raising one's hand to
answer a question in class, volunteering for a few hours of community service,
voting in government elections, answering questions in a focus group or survey,
even shopping, or what some people call "voting with our dollars." These activities
are examples of shallow participation not because they are not worthwhile, but
because they invite people to take part in something in very defined and determined
ways. That is, people can answer, but not contribute to the framing of the questions;
students can share only portions of what they know; voters can support a candidate,
but not put their own concerns up for public discussion. Shallow participation is
occasional and is designed to have little structural impact. It permits participants
to respond to the terms set forth by others, and bypasses opportunities to craft and
reshape the stage of discussion. The possibilities for change are somewhat limited
by the parameters set by others in shallow participation, and participants, knowing
this, can be reluctant to pitch in. This can explain silence in the classroom when
a teacher poses a question about a book that students have really read, and why
some don't turn up at the voting polls, complaining that their votes don't count
anyway.

Deep participation, by contrast, invites people to help define the scope of
discussion, the rules of engagement, and the structure of relationships. Deep
participation yields opportunities for change that can be sustained, and impact
everyday life. Unfortunately, deep participation is a rare experience for youth and
adults. As an educator, I have collaboratively constructed some opportunities for deep

*T. M. Kress and R. Lake (Eds.), We Saved the Best for You: Letters of Hope, Imagination and Wisdom
for 21st Century Educators, 11–14.*
© 2013 Sense Publishers. All rights reserved.

participation. In a community organization in the South Bronx, I worked with youth and staff to collectively design curriculum for a summer program. We developed our own processes of brainstorming, decision making, and assessment that we then implemented to develop summer workshops that were innovative, inspirational, and downright juicy with ideas.

As a researcher, I have conducted participatory action research with urban youth on the lived value of the General Educational Development (GED) credential, school pushout, mayoral control, and education policy. In my work with the Collective of Researchers on Educational Disappointment and Desire (CREDD), we designed a comprehensive study on the use and misuse of the GED to push unwanted students out of their public high schools. Several youth researchers in our collective had been pushed out of their former schools, so our research was very personal to them. At the same time, we were creating our collective as a space for collaboration and learning. We were trying to create for ourselves a kind of workspace that we had never had before, one in which we made decisions in ways aligned with what we valued, and asked questions in ways that matched our epistemologies (our theories of knowledge and knowing). In an essay that our group wrote about the experience of creating our collective, we wrote, "Everyone is responsible for making our space a participatory space. We don't erase ourselves from our work, our whole selves are involved because lots of kinds of skills and thinking are needed, not just one" (Tuck et al., 2008). We also wrote,

> We have come to our project by attending to our felt senses, by listening to our hunches, by being unafraid to ask each other to say more at the point where our felt senses may be just about to break apart, to care about words and ideas, to try things on, to say what feels like small things out loud and listen to the echoes. In this way, we engage collectively in reconstructing our own realities. We engage together in/toward self-determination and re-cognition. We are constantly switching between inhabiting this current world and the world we want to inhabit, struggling to clarify our vision, like shaking a TV antenna to get a clear picture.

> …We realize that reforming the school system and challenging various forms of oppression are linked struggles, so our approach to social justice focuses on challenging the status quo through PAR, and at the same time modeling the kinds of interactions we want to have.

> Many times throughout this work, each of us has said that we have been waiting our whole lives be a part of a space like this. We have wondered aloud what amazing difference it would have made for our schools to be sites of collective inquiry and meaning making, as CREDD has become for us. Our schooling has marked us, but this experience as CREDD has marked us too.

In my work with youth researchers in participatory action research projects, I have been profoundly changed by the experience of struggle and possibility that is inherent in figuring out how to create within a working space that which has been otherwise systematically denied to us. The power of successfully creating a productive collective space that meets one's own needs while engaging in meaning making has altered my experience of the world, and is now at the foundation of how I believe societal change happens. Once a person has engaged in deep participation, her bones will remember it, and will expect it, and set about creating it in other situations.

I have spent a lot of time trying to figure out how change happens, and so far, this is the truest thing I can say: An experience of deep participation, in the classroom, in an after-school setting, in a research collective, in Zuccotti Park, makes an indelible mark upon the human spirit, and can go viral.

Sarah Quinter, a youth researcher in CREDD, came to our collective having been part of numerous youth and art organizations in New York City, and continues to work to create spaces that will incubate and inspire social change. She was among the first several hundred protesters to Occupy Wall Street. Though many pundits have dismissed the Occupy movements for not having a coherent "message," what they are missing is that messages do not cultivate change. Many who have spent time in Zuccotti Park have come away with profound experiences of deep participation, in the General Assembly meetings, in conversations with strangers about the vernacular of the movement, even in Facebook comments regarding the legitimacy of the claims of the 99%; it is these bone-deep moments of participation that protesters will carry into their future collaborations that will serve to spark social change. For example, many Indigenous social critics have pushed back against the language of occupation at the heart of the protests, citing that North America is Indigenous land that is already occupied by settlers, many of whom count themselves among the 99%. This exchange has initiated many crucial conversations which, with mixed results, pressed for recognition of structures of settler colonialism that undergird economic and societal inequity.

I told Sarah that I was writing this letter, and asked her if she had any words for you. This is what she had to say:

> This movement does not fit obediently into the dominant discourse of demands and concessions. We are working to create new social realities, and it is critical that the language used is in a constant state of evolution, incorporating perspectives from the margins and unheard histories. Being part of this deeply participatory process is like learning to speak a new language that is collectively invented as the need to describe fresh possibilities arises. It is a language that listens.

> On October 30th, 2011 Angela Davis told the occupiers of Zuccotti Park "You are re-inventing our political universe. You have renewed our collective passion. You reminded us that it is still possible to build vibrant communities of resistance." It is by becoming radically imaginative and fearlessly open that we construct pathways to spaces which are truly liberatory.

Dear readers, we don't need to let the enormity of change needed (and the enormity of the need for change) paralyze us. Change can be as small as shifting a baby from one hip to the other. This is not to say that change is incremental, but that steps which provide new vantage points can uncover new or forgotten paths. It is not so much the size of the steps, but the possibilities they bring into view. In Sarah's words, "Experiences of genuine participation change us for good. The steps we take together leave ever-expanding passageways into other ways of living. Push on, readers, and let us know what you can see from there."

Txin sismi{taan, in loving support,
Eve Tuck

REFERENCE

Tuck, E., Allen, J., Bacha, M., Morales, A., Quinter, S., Thompson, J. & Tuck, M. (2008). PAR praxes for now and future change: The collective of researchers on educational disappointment and desire. In J. Cammarota and M. Fine (Eds.), *Revolutionizing education: Youth participatory action research in motion* (pp. 49–83). New York: Routledge.

AFFILIATION

Eve Tuck
Department of Educational Studies
The State University of New York at New Paltz

SANDY GRANDE

4. DEAR COMRADES

For some, the intimation embedded in my salutation – that we are brothers and sisters in struggle – may seem hyperbolic. But, in the wake of No Child Left Behind (NCLB), Race to the Top and other neoliberal "reform" efforts, make no mistake; we are at war. Thus, I would feel remiss, as a mentor, not to prepare you for life on the front lines. Hopefully by now, you understand that there is no such thing as neutral knowledge and that teaching is a political act. What I hope to apprise you of here, is how this understanding plays out in the "real existing world" of the teacher: the public intellectual.

As you ready yourself to enter the arena you should understand the following: (1) the foundational ideas of contemporary democracy are in a state of deep, protracted crisis; (2) the "crisis" stems from the suturing of "democracy" to the imperatives of (unfettered) capitalism initiated under and through settler colonialism; (3) the resulting privatization, commodification, and militarization of the public sphere is not possible or sustainable without the takeover of public education. Therefore we – teachers-as-public-intellectuals – can be silent no longer. The time is now to stand up and be counted, to exercise your public voice, to work with and stand alongside our youth and reclaim the public sphere as a space of hope and possibility.

Like any good pedagogue, particularly those who call their students to action, I feel the need to model – to walk the talk. Thus, what follows, is the text of an actual "open letter" I wrote to members of the Connecticut State Department of Education[1] in response to a recent "request" for 10 years of data documenting enrollments and completions in my teacher certification program. We were given less than a week to provide the data. In order to provide appropriate context, the original request is pasted here below. It was sent on a Monday two weeks before the final exam period at my school. I offer this letter and my response as a means of concretizing the work of critical educators but also as public statement of my own convictions to "be the change I want to see in the world," to walk with firm footsteps in struggle, to have your back.

Dear All:

The legislature has asked the Board of Regents to learn about the demand for and enrollment in teacher preparation programs in Connecticut (apparently some national reports indicate that student demand for teacher preparation programs is declining). They have asked to see ten years of data about the

T. M. Kress and R. Lake (Eds.), We Saved the Best for You: Letters of Hope, Imagination and Wisdom for 21st Century Educators, 15–20.
© 2013 Sense Publishers. All rights reserved.

number of applicants to teacher preparation programs and the number of enrollees.

The Board of Regents is coordinating the response from the public institutions and have prepared the attached template to do this. They have asked me to coordinate the responses of the private colleges, using the same template. If 10 years of data are not available, they asked us to provide as many years as possible for which data quality is deemed reliable. Feel free to include a narrative in your response to explain any drastic changes (e.g. the addition or termination of large programs).

If you could get us this data by the end of the day Friday, we would very much appreciate it. Let me know if you have questions or concerns.

Thank you!

My response:

Dear (name omitted),

Our college is in the process of compiling the data requested by the legislature and will be sending it along shortly. That being said, I want to also take the opportunity to share some thoughts about the nature of this query and would appreciate it if you would pass them along to the Board of Regents and the Commissioner.

First, I would like to register my concern that such queries for data always seem to come with short notice (and in this instance in our busiest time at the end of the semester) which is particularly hard on small programs. Second, I want to underscore that this time pressure limits the opportunity for Dean's and Chair's to develop full narratives to accompany data, which is crucial since "data" never speaks for itself. Applications and enrollments (in any college program) are always tied to a variety of factors including but not limited to, the broader socio-political and economic climate, federal and state educational policies and available human and material resources at the university, college and departmental levels. Finally, I respectfully ask the legislature to share the "national reports" it references, which indicate a decline in student demand for teacher education. It seems that we have a right to know what materials they are using to inform their thinking and decision-making. My hope is that they are reading actual educational research (see attached) and not simply "reports" generated by corporate think-tanks invested in the failure of public education (i.e. The National Council on Teacher Quality).

Currently, Connecticut College offers a robust and academically rigorous teacher education program with both applications and enrollments on the rise. That being said, the ostensible "growth" or "decline" in our program is neither historically linear nor ever simply an effect of "student demand." If we had data that went back to the College's founding in 1911, the ebbs and flows would undoubtedly mirror the same fluctuations in the economy, the socio-political context (i.e. opportunities for women), as well as institutional commitment and available resources. Therefore, it is crucially important to take into account the educational landscape in which such data emerges.

It is interesting and significant that we have been asked to produce ten years of data since it has been exactly ten years since the implementation of the No Child Left Behind Act. The Bush policy – which made no attempt to address resource inequities among rich and poor school districts at the same time it provided unprecedented funding for voucher "demonstration programs" and charter schools – has come to be viewed as the first in a series of policy decisions designed to make public education "fail" in order to clear the way for privatized alternatives (e.g. Ball, 2008; Burch, 2006; Cochran-Smith, 2005; Compton, 2008; Giroux, 1999; Hass, 2005; Hill, 2005; Huberman, 2003; Hursh, 2007; Kantor & Lowe, 2008; Kaplan, 2002; Karp, 2003; Klein, 2007; Kohn, 2005; Kovacs, 2008; Lahan 2011; Leyva, 2009; Meier, 2004; Metcalf, 2002; Ravitch 2010; Ross & Gibson, 2007; Saltman, 2005, 2006, 2007; Tamatea, 2008; Weil, 2009). While such efforts were initially aimed at k-12 schools, the logic is now being extended to higher education.

Over the past ten years, potential teacher candidates have become increasingly aware of the myriad ways in which public schools, teachers, and the "public" in general has been under siege by neoliberal policy agendas. They understand that under neoliberalism, government and corporate actors have worked hand in hand to: (1) deregulate "the market" in order to maximize profit; (2) cut public expenditure for social services (i.e. education and health care); (3) privatize state-owned enterprises, goods and services; and, (4) eliminate the concept of "the public good" or "community" and replacing it with the myth of meritocracy and its central trope of "individual responsibility" (Martinez & Garcia, 1996).

As a result of such neoliberal policies, over 300,000 educator jobs have been lost since 2008, 37 states are providing less funding per student to local school districts in the new school year than they provided last year; 30 states are providing less than they did four years ago; 17 states have cut per-student funding by more than 10 percent from pre-recession levels; four states (South Carolina, Arizona, California, and Hawaii) have reduced per student funding to K-12 schools by more than 20 percent (Center on Budget and Policy Priorities, 2011).

Under the watch of a U.S. Secretary of Education with no formal training in education and who never attended a day of public school, we have witnessed a "slow death of the American teacher" (Tye, Tye & Tye, 2010). As the subjects of public attack and hyper surveillance, the "profession" has been deskilled and the teachers, dispirited.

Within this context of the past ten years, I am amazed, no humbled, that any young person (particularly those who attend a school as competitive as ours) would even consider, let alone commit, to a career in public education. Each and every day teacher candidates must consciously make the choice to fight for the soul of American teachers and to resist the coffers of predatory recruitment by private entities such as Teach for America (recently TFA offered one of our candidates of color a starting salary of $40,000, moving expenses, first and last months rent, and a tuition free Master's degree). Further, it is a credit to every beginning teacher who chooses to work for 14% less in salary than any other profession requiring comparable preparation (New York Times, April 30, 2011). Indeed, Eggers and Calegari report that the average teachers salary is equivalent to that of toll-takers and bartenders (New York Times, April, 2011). As a program, we therefore cherish each and every student we have (no matter the rate of enrollment) as a symbol of victory – for public schools, for the teaching profession, for the future of a critical citizenry, and for democracy.

Thus, should the data for any teacher education program in the state show a decline in "student demand" over the past ten years I hope the legislature considers the full-context. Rather than (mis)use the data to serve up yet another pro-privatization policy, I urge them to use this moment to take a stand: to reinvest in public education for the good of our students, our schools, and our communities.

Sincerely,
Sandy Grande

NOTE

[1] The text of the letter is slightly altered for syntactical reasons only; the substance of its content remains the same.

REFERENCES

Ball, S. J. (2008). New philanthropy, new networks and new governance in education. *Political Studies, 56*(4), 747–65.
Burch, P. (2006). The new educational privatization: Educational contracting and high stakes accountability. *Teachers College Record, 108*(12), 2582–2610. Retrieved from www.tcrecord.org
Cochran-Smith, M. (2005, March/April). No Child Left Behind: 3 years and counting. *Journal of Teacher Education, 56*(2), 99–103.
Compton, M., & Weinter, L. (2008). *The global assault on teaching, teachers, and their unions: Stories of resistance.* New York: Palgrave Macmillan.
Eggers, D., & Clements-Calegari, N. (2011, April 30). The high cost of low teacher salaries. *New York Times.* Retrieved from www.nytimes.com/2011/05/01/opinion/01eggers.html
Giroux, H. (1999, Fall). Vocationalizing higher education: Schooling and the politics of corporate culture. *College Literature, 26*(3), 147–161.
Hill, D. (2005). Globalisation and its educational discontents: Neoliberalism and its impact on education workers' rights, pay and conditions. *International Studies of the Sociology of Education, 15*(3), 257–288.

Huberman, J. (2003). *The Bush-haters handbook: A guide to the most appalling presidency of the past 100 years*. New York: Nation Books.

Hursh, D. (2007). Assessing No Child Left Behind and the rise of neoliberal education policies. *American Educational Research Journal, 44*(3), 493–518.

Kantor, H., & Lowe, R. (2006). From New Deal to no deal: No Child Left Behind and the devolution of responsibility for equal opportunity. *Harvard Education Review*, 76(4), 474–502.

Kaplan, D. (2002). Education is not a commodity fighting the privatization of higher education worldwide. Retrieved from http://www.ieps.org.uk/PDFs/kaplan2003b.pdf

Karp, S. (2003, November 7). The No Child Left Behind hoax. *Rethinking Schools*. Retrieved from www.rethinkingschools.org/special_reports/bushplan/hoax.shtml

Klein, A. (2007, February 12). Bush budget would boost NCLB efforts. *Education Week, 1*(25).

Kohn, A. (2005, Summer). Test today, privatize tomorrow: Using accountability to 'reform' public schools to death. *Professional Development Perspectives: A Publication of the Canadian Teachers' Federation Professional and Developmental Services, 5*(2), 1, 6–11, 13–18.

Kovacs, P., & Christie, H. (2008, December). The Gates Foundation and the future of U.S. public education: A call for scholars to counter misinformation campaigns. *Journal for Critical Education Policy Studies, 6*(2).

Leyva, R. "No Child Left Behind: A Neoliberal repacking of social darwinism." *Journal for Critical Education Policy Studies*. 7.1 (2009). Print.

Martinez, E., & Garcia, A. (1996). What is neoliberalism? A brief definition for activists." *Corp Watch*. Retrieved from www.corpwatch.org/article.php?id=376

Meier, D., & Wood, G. (2004). *Many children left behind: How the No Child Left Behind Act is damaging our children and our schools*. Boston: Beacon Press.

Metcalf, S. (2002, January 28). Reading between the lines. *The Nation*, 18–22.

Oliff, P., & Leachman, M. (2011, October 7). New school year brings steep cuts in state funding for schools. *Center on Budget and Policy Priorities*. Retrieved from http://www.cbpp.org/cms/?fa=view&id=3569

Ravitch, D. (2010). *The death and life of the great American school system: How testing and choice are undermining education*. New York: Basic Books.

Ross, E.W., & Gibson, R. (2007). *Neoliberalism and education reform*. Creskill, New Jersey: Hampton Press.

Saltman, K. (2007). *Capitalizing on disaster: Taking and breaking public schools*. Herndon, VA: Paradigm Publishers.

Saltman, K. (2005). *The Edison schools: Corporate schooling and the assault on public educators*. New York: Routledge.

Saltman, K. (2006). The right-wing attack on critical and public education in the United States: From neoliberalism to neoconservatism." *Cultural Politics, 2*(3), 339–358.

Tamatea, L. (2008). George Bush's No Child Left Behind education policy: War, ambivalence, and mimicry." *Review of Education, Pedagogy, and Cultural Studies, 30*(2), 115–139.

Tye, D., Tye, K., & Tye, B. (2010). The slow death of the American teacher. *Scholarly Partnerships Edu, 5*(1). Retrieved from opus.ipfw.edu/spe/vol5/iss1/4

Weil, D. (2009, December 27). Neoliberalism and charter schools. *Dissident Voice: A Radical Newsletter in the Struggle for Peace and Social Justice, 27*(12). Retrieved from dissidentvoice.org/2009/12/neo-liberalism-and-charter-schools/

AFFILIATION

Sandy Grande
Department of Education
Connecticut College

GREG MCCLURE

5. FINDING HOPE AND GIVING THANKS IN "DARK TIMES"

Paying Dues to the Students Who Teach Us

Dear Colleague,

Welcome to the team! Now get to work, for there is much to do! Indicators from across the sociopolitical landscape suggest that we are teaching in dark times. A few details to consider as you prepare those initial lesson plans: Thirteen years after police riddled Amadou Diallo with 19 bullets, the recent murders of Oscar Grant and Trayvon Martin[1] remind us that it is still very much a crime to be a young Black male in America. Graduation rates (Rumberger, 2011), academic achievement (Aud & Hannes, 2011), and social health data (LaVeist & Isaac, 2012) confirm that students of color continue to be disproportionately marginalized from the necessary resources and opportunities to carry out safe and healthy lives. Meanwhile, legislation in states across the nation is framing our national discourse on diverse ways of thinking and being in increasingly restrictive and discriminatory ways: Alabama now requires schools to track the immigration status of students and their families; Arizona has criminalized the teaching of Mexican-American Studies; North Carolina aims to alter its state constitution to claim authority on what counts as marriage, love, and family. Dark times indeed.

As critical educators committed to addressing injustices of race, class, gender, sexual orientation and other forms of oppression, we find ourselves with plenty of work in these times. Our stated daily commitment is to challenge oppressive acts and structures, and to upend the comfortable commonsense of schooling and the inequitable power relationships we find there. As this work places us in constant conflict with the status quo, how do we continue to nurture positive, healthy selves and engage in democratic and critical pedagogies that inspire imagination, creativity, and praxis in our classrooms? I offer two pieces of advice that have proven helpful to me: 1. We must feel that we are in partnership in this endeavor; our critical work cannot be sustained if we feel isolated; and 2. Despite the persistence of "Dark Times," we must remain hopeful for more positive futures. Most importantly, I submit that we can achieve both of these by developing meaningful relationships with our students that subvert the traditional teacher/student hierarchy. Recognizing our *students as teachers* and *ourselves as learners* helps create conditions for a

T. M. Kress and R. Lake (Eds.), We Saved the Best for You: Letters of Hope, Imagination and Wisdom for 21st Century Educators, 21–24.
© *2013 Sense Publishers. All rights reserved.*

learning community that can collaboratively name the world in order to change it (Freire, 1970). Indeed, these are lessons that I learned from a former student.

Of all the students that have influenced my teaching, none have challenged me as consistently as Reynaldo, an emergent bilingual student[2] in my English as a Second Language (ESL) class during my first three years as a teacher. Before teaching in public schools I worked as a human rights observer in Guatemala and a community organizer among migrant farm workers in the US. I had witnessed firsthand how oppressive political and economic structures resulted in poverty and social marginalization for certain groups in society. As a result, I brought a commitment to issues of equity and social justice to my role as a high school ESL teacher. However, for most of those first few years of teaching I failed to develop the ideological and political clarity (Bartolomé, 1996) necessary to see the connections between language, culture, identity, and teaching. While I advocated on behalf of students like Reynaldo and their families *outside* the classroom, *inside* I proceeded to teach the functions and forms of the English language isolated from the sociocultural and political realities of my students.

English, not Reynaldo, was the starting point for my instruction. While most of my students groaned at my decontextualized language instruction, Reynaldo took a different approach. He consistently tried to connect my classroom instruction to his own life in meaningful ways. He interjected personal stories and experiences and often invited me to make time and space for learning more about one another in our classroom. Not only did this help make learning relevant for him and his classmates, but it also significantly influenced the dynamics and the culture of our classroom community. As I reflect back on this experience, I am reminded of Freire's (1970) thoughts on curriculum and content. He asserted that "The starting point for organizing the program content of education or political action must be the present, existential, concrete situation, reflecting the aspirations of the people" (p. 85). Reynaldo's efforts helped me to understand the importance of beginning first with my students and then seeking the connections to our content.

I now recognize that Reynaldo was quite often my co-teacher during my first years. His thoughtful and persistent attempts to insert personal experiences and narratives as relevant compliments to our class content marked a pivotal moment in my development as an educator open to learning with and from my students. He helped me see the beauty of bilingual poetry and code-switching, as well as the drudgery of worksheets and grammar taught in isolation by a novice teacher with little ideological clarity. As I look for support and opportunities to collaborate in these dark times, I find myself turning to the lessons I learned from Reynaldo. I draw on Bakhtin's (1981) theory of language to illuminate how dialogue across time and space can foster collaboration with those who may not be physically present but continue to contribute to our development as teachers. As such, Reynaldo's voice is here in the poem, not only in my reconstructions of his words, but more importantly in his influence on my words. Our utterances, our language, and indeed our teaching and learning processes do not exist in isolation. They emerge to contribute to a dialogue across time and space. This poem is an attempt to pay dues to Reynaldo for what he contributes to my pedagogy, and it continues the teaching and learning dialogue between us.

REYNALDO'S TIE

I still wear it you know,
The tie you gave me on the day of your graduation.
Each time I pull the smooth silk across my neck
I return to China Grove, careening down the hallways
Pushing that rickety media cart, my portable classroom jalopy:
Posters demanding linguistic order, maps of Mexico,
North Carolina; "The World" fluttering behind.

The tie you took from your own neck,
Wrangled out from robes and regalia,
The blue and silver one that laid right on top of your heart.

"Profesor!" siempre me llamabas.
You called me this way, always,
but this time with conviction, confidence, *cariño.*

I used to keep it reserved for special moments:
A wedding, interview, funeral; those
Life moments that really matter.

Matamorros y maquiladoras
Only the first of many borders crossed daily:
Spanish poetry and the 5-paragraph English trainwreck,
Sheets of homonyms, cognates, and irregular verbs
Smelling like stale canned language-sauce alongside
Your bilingual delicacies, your airbrush literacy.

Enseñamos. Aprendemos. ¿Pero siempre juntos, no?
Together weaving knowledge,
Tossing roles end over end
Like some hungry *perro*
Chasing the tail until it is no more.

Cruzando, luchando, the struggle continues.
Was it those life moments? Maybe these? Which?
Like stones that sink or skip across the water
They are all life moments.
Reynaldo, I wear it now quite often in fact.

23

So get to work; there is much to do. Hold fast to that vision and passion that inspired you to teach, to change the world. Name the world of your classroom and your community and collaborate with your students in meaningful ways. When the forecast is dark, and at times it will be, look to your students for a healthy dose of vibrant and critical hope that is the imaginative blueprint for positive social change. Howard Zinn (1994) affirmed that to remain hopeful in dark times is not "foolishly romantic" as some would argue. Instead, hopefulness is grounded in the reality that while oppressive forces may be present, so too are countless human acts of "compassion, sacrifice, courage, and kindness" (p. 208). Your commitment to teach, to develop deeply personal and caring relationships with your students, is the most profound act of compassion and courage you can make.

Thank you for that, and welcome!
Greg McClure

NOTES

[1] The murders of these three unarmed Black males in the USA all received significant media attention. Amadou Diallo was shot and killed by New York City police outside his Brooklyn apartment in 1999. Oscar Grant was shot in the back and killed while he was detained face-down on a subway platform by San Francisco police in 2009. Trayvon Martin was shot and killed by a self-appointed neighborhood watch vigilante as he walked through his father's neighborhood in 2012.

[2] Garcia, Kleifgen, & Falchi, (2008) suggest this term because of its focus on the bilingual potential of students, as opposed to deficit-oriented terms such as "limited English proficient."

REFERENCES

Aud, S., & Hannes, G. (Eds.) (2011). The condition of education 2011 in brief (NCES 2011-034). U.S. Department of Education, National Center for Education Statistics. Washington, DC: U.S. Government Printing Office.

Bakhtin, M. M. (1981). Discourse in the novel. (C. Emerson & M Holquist, Trans.), In M. Holquist (Ed.), *The dialogic imagination: Four essays by M. M. Bakhtin* (pp. 259–422). Austin, TX: University of Texas Press.

Bartolomé, L. (1996). Beyond the methods fetish: Toward a humanizing pedagogy. In P. Leistyna, A. Woodrum, & S. A, Sherblom (Eds.), *Breaking free: The transformative power of critical pedagogy* (pp. 229–252). Cambridge, MA: Harvard Educational Review.

Freire, P. (1970). *Pedagogy of the oppressed.* New York: Continuum.

LaVeist, T. A., & Isaac, L. A. (Eds.) (2012). Race, ethnicity, and health. San Francisco, CA: Jossey-Bass.

Rumberger, R. W. (2011). *Dropping out: Why students drop out of high school and what can be done about it.* Cambridge, MA: Harvard University Press.

Zinn, H. (2004). *You can't be neutral on a moving train.* Boston, MA: Beacon Press.

AFFILIATION

Greg McClure
Department of Curriculum and Instruction
Appalachian State University

CARL LEGGO

6. SPELLING HOPE

A Poet-Teacher's Testimony

Dear Future Educator:

I have been in school since I was four years old. Now, at the age of fifty-seven, I look back on a long life spent in classrooms as a learner, a school teacher, and a professor of education, and I am filled with amazement that I have grown old! Some days I think I am still in elementary school. Other days, I live vividly the first chapter of my teaching life when I taught forty-eight learners in grade seven. I was twenty-two years old, and I was filled with fear that I didn't know enough to be a teacher. As a boy growing up in Corner Brook, Newfoundland in the 1950s and 1960s, I sometimes asked my teachers who were their teachers. When they explained that they were taught to be teachers by professors, I always wondered who taught the professors. My vision of education was hierarchical, like a multi-layered fountain that pours and flows down from one level to another to another. I was probably in my thirties before I began to understand how education always occurs in communities of teachers and learners who teach and learn from one another, who search and research together.

As a beginning teacher, I wavered between feeling powerless and powerful. On the one hand, I assumed that I was in control in the classroom; I was the primary decision-maker. But, on the other hand, I typically expected educational experts to tell me what I should do. I depended on the stipulations of school administrators, the publications of professors, and the professional development workshops of school district consultants to guide, convince, and inspire me in my teaching. Now that I have been a professor for a long time, I realize that as a beginning teacher I was recapitulating the kind of schooling that I had grown up with, an experience of schooling that assumes that I needed a lot of filling up, and programming, and realignment, and re-energizing, much like a trolley car in a roller coaster. And, now that I've been a professor for a long time, I also know that professors don't really know very much. They might profess a lot, but they know the searching is always in process, returning to the beginning of the search again and again in order to know the quests and the questions in other lively ways.

The educator who has influenced me the most is Paulo Freire, a tireless questioner, full of curiosity. I read him during my teacher education program, and again during years of graduate studies, and eagerly again and again for the past couple decades. Freire (1997) teaches me to live with courage and heart: "As I speak with such hope about the possibility of changing the world, I do not intend to sound like a lyrical,

T. M. Kress and R. Lake (Eds.), *We Saved the Best for You: Letters of Hope, Imagination and Wisdom for 21st Century Educators*, 25–28.
© 2013 Sense Publishers. All rights reserved.

naïve educator" (p. 58). Like Freire, I have always wanted to change the world, even when my commitment led to romantic rejection!

MY PROBLEM

After climbing Valley Road
one late spring evening
(summer anywhere else in Canada)
I sat with Cassandra
(seduced by my sixteen-year-old
imagination I had written
her the heroine
of my romantic stories)
on the back steps of her parents' house
looking for God hiding among the stars
and explaining why if I were American,
not Canadian, I would refuse
to fight in the Vietnam War,
and Cassandra said, I don't
want to go out with you anymore,
your problem is you want
to change the world.
I'm glad she told me.
I didn't even know
I had a problem.

Even though Cassandra rejected me at sixteen, I have never lost my conviction about education as inextricably connected to advocacy, activism, and social transformation. But I have learned to temper my enthusiasm with a more realistic assessment of what I can accomplish. Like Jean Vanier (1998), I now know that "we do not have to be saviours of the world! We are simply human beings, enfolded in weakness and in hope, called together to change our world one heart at a time" (p. 163). So, I live in the world as a poet and educator, and like the poet Margaret Avison (2002), I am learning how

Part of a celebration
is to discover
patience? and how
painful hope can be? (p. 9)

Teachers and learners (from infancy to eldership) need to cultivate their inner lives. As teachers and learners we need to attend to and listen to our spirits, our hearts, our imaginations, our emotions, our bodies, our minds. Teachers and learners live such demanding and challenging lives that it is very difficult to maintain the time and location for nurturing the inner life. Teachers and learners literally burn out.

We need a healthy inner life if we are going to help others develop healthy inner lives. Teachers and learners need to attend to the spells, the magic, the alchemy that is always at the heart of language.

SPELLING

in school I learned to spell words with precise correctness
but I seldom learned the sensuous spell of language

in school I learned the rules and stipulations of grammar
but I seldom learned the glamour, the alchemy of prepositions

in school I learned the conventions of syntax
but I seldom learned the lyrical resonances of connections

in school I learned to chant the teacher's dictums
but I seldom learned the enchantment of poetry

in school I learned facts, fat fatuous facts full of lies,
but I seldom learned the restorative joy of fiction and fantasy

in school I learned to color inside the prescribed lines
but I seldom learned about wild places beyond, elsewhere

in school I learned the denotative definitions of words
but I seldom learned the magic of capacious connotation

in school I learned to be good, an anaesthetic obedience
but I seldom learned to ask with aesthetic wonder, what is good

in school I learned to be neat tidy clean even pristine
but I seldom learned to enjoy the body's erotic energies

in school I learned to grow my brain-mind-head like a cabbage
but I seldom heard my heart beat or the hearts of anyone else

in school I learned to fear the arts like wild lions, lacking logic,
but I still caught glimpses of dandelions in the cracks of sidewalks

and so I dance with lines, straight and slant, curvaceous and cursive
and I dance with dandy lions, too, no longer fearing their ferociousness

In order to sustain hope and a healthy inner life, I seek to pursue daily a keen sense of wonder, delight, joy, creativity, attentiveness, and love. Above all, I seek to live with humour, humility, humanity, and heart. My practice is integrally connected to the pursuit of poetry. As Richard Miller (2005) recommends, in writing we can "foster a kind of critical optimism that is able to transform idle feelings of hope into viable plans for sustainable action" (p. 27). A while ago at a gathering of poets and educators, we generated a long list of possibilities for sustaining our lives in the midst of the relentlessly hectic demands that compose our lives as teachers and learners. Out of that long list, I shaped a poem full of advice and wisdom and humor and hope.

THE TEACHER'S CREDO: AN ABECEDARIAN

(for Dr. Seuss)

Awake aesthetically and ethically
Bounce joyfully, even Tiggerifically
Climb up on a table, crawl under the chairs
Dance wild wiggliness and sensuality
Embody our sensate scholarship
Fall in love, fall, love, buoyant with hope
Give generously and generatively
Hope without hindering, without end
Imagine possibilities and impossibilities
Join in joyful light-filled conversations
Know one another in kinship and kindness
Learn from listening, laughter, light longing
Meet ourselves as if for the first time
Notice how beautiful people are
Open our arms to hold the whole big world
Push our boundaries into places of bliss
Question everything, expecting epiphanies
Render the familiar unfamiliar
Start always from the heart
Touch the earth gently with tender thoughts
Unsettle our orthodoxies, embrace our unsettling
Visualize the stories behind the masks
Widen the crack so light can get in
Xerox only our best words to share with the world
Yearn for one another in lovely loneliness
Zip with zest and zeal in the places beyond the alphabet

REFERENCES

Avison, M. (2002). *Concrete and wild carrot*. London, ON: Brick Books.
Freire, P. (1997). *Pedagogy of the heart*.(D. Macedo & A. Oliveira, Trans.). New York, NY: Continuum.
Miller, R. E. (2005). *Writing at the end of the world*. Pittsburgh, PA: University of Pittsburgh Press.
Vanier, J. (1998). *Becoming human*. Toronto, ON: House of Anansi Press.

AFFILIATION

Carl Leggo
Department of Language and Literacy Education
University of British Columbia

CHRISTOPHER DARIUS STONEBANKS

7. BROWN PRIDE IN A COLLEGE CLASSROOM

Dear diverse Brown family,

To those of you who have, are or are thinking about entering the field of education, let me share my experience in the hopes that it will possibly validate your own. I have been the confusing color of Brown all my life. Not that it is confusing for those of us who are Brown; it just seems to be a difficult shade of skin tone for others to wrap their heads around. We encompass so many people and world views, yet our identity and voices are either absent or left to the definitions of others. My primary and secondary school teachers in the seventies and eighties used to say, "In my class, it doesn't matter if you are Black, White, Red, Yellow, or *Purple* ... we are *all* equal." Purple always seemed to be thrown in there at the end to really punctuate the point and to demonstrate the openness of the Baby Boomer generation. It's as if the teachers were saying that they were so inclusive, they wouldn't even bat an eye at a purple-skinned twelve-year-old taking a seat in their classes on the first day of school.

"Johnny, is Purple you say? Oh, I never noticed. I really just noticed what fine penmanship he has and how well he speaks...I don't see colour, you know. I am beyond that."

It was curious, though, that Brown was always absent since it played such a large part of our lives at school in hallways, gym classes, lunchrooms and courtyards. But who could blame that generation of teachers, parents and students? *All in the Family*, *Maude*, *Happy Days*, or *The Facts of Life* never had "a very special episode" on Paki Bashing. Paki, WOG, ay-rab, sand-nigger, eye-ranian, or just plain "shit" – there were no teachable moments, interventions, after school specials, or curricula that included us. My Middle-Eastern, West Asian, Iranian heritage was absent. My skin, hair, nose, lips, and dark circles under the eyes were unusual—my teachers constantly asked if I was getting enough sleep. Racial profiling existed before 9/11 and the racial/ethnic net was cast wide for Brown people on the playground.

"Hey, Stonebanks, what do you call someone in your family who is white and lying in a ditch? A Paki with the shit kicked out of him!"

Hell, we received less recognition than the Purple kid in school and less support for racist encounters – and that Purple kid didn't even exist. When educational spaces of inclusion are extended to the imaginary student before they are extended to you, questioning one's place, worth, or existence in this Western world becomes a daily occurrence.

T. M. Kress and R. Lake (Eds.), We Saved the Best for You: Letters of Hope, Imagination and Wisdom for 21st Century Educators, 29–32.
© 2013 Sense Publishers. All rights reserved.

When I would try and hide my Iranian body behind my one paternal grandfather's British heritage and namesake (and damn it, he was even dark for a Brit!), I was extended the common question: "What are you *really?*" The attempt to connect with the very group that denied my people's acceptance left a bitter taste in both party's mouths. After a while, I lived in a "no man's land," unwelcome and dehumanized. I experienced the daily racism of schooling while being misunderstood and ignored by those from the trenches of teaching and from the ivory towers of multiculturalism that "informed" the teachers. In these academic circles I came to realize far too often that those of privilege guarded acceptance into the "visible minority club" in a perverse manner. Their ways countered the more lofty intentions of solidarity and humanization by a vulgar capitalist mindset of seeing and using visible minorities as personal advancement and economic gain. As the late great Joey Ramone once said, "If you're not in it, you're out of it," and *we* were out…until, of course, there was a use for us.

In a sea of homogeneity in White, Christian, middle-class Canadian suburbia, shame went hand in hand with our Brown experience. It was my single primary motivation to try in some way to change an educational institution that only attempted to understand the experiences of diversity when it was catching up to transformations already in progress in the larger society. Even as I entered the field of education, if Edward Said's work on the Other (1978) was being referred to in university, it was never utilized to illuminate the peoples who were his original focus. In multicultural classes and discussions, the Other became a concept that gave meaning to many groups' experiences, but was rarely applied to the historical work of creating a sense of self in relation to 'the Orient.' Apple's (2004) recognition that the very stories we have repeated within our curriculum, that "[o]ur side is good; their side is bad [and that '[w]e' are peace loving and want an end to strife; 'they' are warlike and aim to dominate" (p. 80) impact the Other beyond the dirty looks in public spaces. Be it formal or informal, it is a pedagogy of dehumanization that plays a role in recent military action from Iraq to Afghanistan, and even what seems to be the inevitable war on Iran. At the peak of hostile language/action between Iran and the USA, and at the peak of 'our man Sadam('s)' war on Iran, I simply shut down. Living history combined with the daily physical and verbal abuse became too much and for two weeks I refused to go to school. Despite many teachers' beliefs that school is some sort of haven, it was the exact opposite for me.

I am sure that none of what I have written so far reads in any way like a "letter of hope," but like a film that begins with the main character's voiceover, we can either assume that I 'made it' in education or that I am an academic ghost. Perhaps a tad too dramatic, but in truth, in the world of schooling and academia I feel like both. I know that I am not alone in this experience. But this is about "hope" and something obviously did occur for me to be a contributor to this book. Something that sparked a personal sense of purpose, a brief connectedness to schooling, a safe space that both challenged and validated; something, or more accurately, *someone* who was able to humanize a student who had been flooded with images and narratives and marked by a dominant culture's possession of facts that reinforced the Other. His name was Professor Leghari, a CEGEP (Collège d'Enseignement Général et Professionnel, a college system in Quebec, Canada designed to act as a buffer between secondary school and university) teacher whose description amongst other college students was that of a teacher who was either from India or Pakistan, who assigned too much reading, was difficult to understand, and marked too hard. My description of Professor Leghari, the humanities teacher who taught political science, was that he was everything I wanted to be as a pedagogue; I admired his confidence, knowledge and repose. He taught courses that had titles like "India, China and Canada: Conflict and Contrast" and used books like *Red Star over China*, by Edgar Snow (1938) and course packs that actually included critical academic articles about the Green Revolution in India, colonialism in the East, the cycle of debt related to foreign aid and other subjects that had been omitted from my education. No one tried to "get in" to Leghari's classes; they were filled to the maximum because they were the last ones to fill up. Early avoidance of the "really hard" class meant that two or three registrar secretaries had no other option than to put a massive amount of reluctant students into the last available class. Leghari had to live the comparison to the Gandhi "little brown man in a loin cloth" description as one of the few academics of South-Asian descent at our college. When a mass of students wearing our college's football team jackets spoke often and loudly of how the readings were too difficult and boring to read, he opened the next class by stating that he had a solution for anyone who had a problem with his course content. When the football players went to the front of the class eager for his solution, each towering over Professor Leghari by at least a foot, he handed them course withdrawal sheets and showed the bewildered lot to the door with a polite disposition.

From the first class when he carried out attendance, read out my name and looked at my face and asked the question about where I was from (and not in a Bissoondath (1994) critique of the "what are you *really*" manner), he challenged my connection to the class readings. In his lessons on lost histories of The East, he broke the current "don't ask a student to be an expert on their culture" mantra and would be terribly disappointed when I didn't know the answer about my West Asian history. When I had an answer, he would beam like a proud relative. When my peers would argue or disbelieve his lectures or readings that suddenly depicted recent histories and current events in a more nuanced manner than they had ever faced, I was finally allowed to speak about the experiences of pre-revolutionary Iran, share examples like the multitude of American soldiers that could be seen in the streets of Tehran, and openly ask questions like, why were the soliders there? He pushed students to rethink their country's charity in a global context and brought some to tears. He dared to show Attenborough's three hour film *Gandhi* (1982) to an age group and generation renowned for their short attention span, and made me openly weep at scenes of dehumanization that hit too close to home. It was the first time I was prepared for class, ready to participate, and eager to please. It was also the first time I felt comfortable, the first time I wanted to be Brown in school, and he fostered that sense of belonging.

I've heard it said and read that "Brown is the new Black" (Bayoumi, 2008) referring to the myriad of peoples that are connected to Browness in the West – from the recent racial profiling laws in U.S. states like Arizona, to the "random" security checks that occur in airports across countries like Canada and the United States. Referring to Brown as the new Black is not meant to appropriate, disrespect, or push aside someone at an imaginary visible minority table with assigned seating. Unfortunately, space is not limited in such settings; it is expansive. Calling Brown the new Black is an attempt to create a connection with lived experiences that have barely scratched the surface of awareness. It's time for us to share our stories, find our own language, capture what binds us, and celebrate the wonderful differences within that make us a whole hue – from shades of wheat to shades of sepia. It's time for us to define *ourselves*, before those of privilege inevitably categorize, include, exclude and *tell us* who we are. Brown is not the new Black and it's not even the new Purple; Brown is Brown and it has a history and an ongoing experience that demands its own voice. Indirectly or not, Professor Leghari taught me that in spite of the inevitable consequences of fighting for an educational space to simply "be," the opposite was much worse. Despite my repeated attempts to locate the good professor, I have received no response as to his whereabouts. I owe him my deepest thanks and I hope this letter finds its way to him, simply to say, "Thank you, Professor."

Christopher Darius Stonebanks

REFERENCES

Apple, M. (2004*). Ideology and curriculum.* New York: Routledge Falmer.
Bayoumi, M. (2009*). How does it feel to be a problem: Being young and Arab in America.* New York: Penguin Press.
Bissoondath, N. (1994). *Selling illusions.* Toronto: Penguin Books.
Said, E. (1978).*Orientalism.* New York: Random House.

AFFILIATION

Christopher Darius Stonebanks
School of Education
Bishop's University

WILLIAM M. REYNOLDS

8. THE STUBBORN PERSISTENCE OF HOPE

I can understand pessimism, but I don't believe in it. It's not simply a matter of faith, but of historical evidence. Not overwhelming evidence, just enough to give hope, because for hope we don't need certainty, only possibility. Which (despite all those confident statements that "history shows…" and history proves…") is all history can offer us (Zinn, 1997, p. 656).

This experience of hope distinguishes a pedagogic life from a non-pedagogic one. It also makes clear that we can only hope for children we truly love, not in a romantic sense, but in the sense of pedagogic love. What hope gives us is the simple avowal, "I will not give up on you. I know you can make a life for yourself." Thus hope refers to that which gives us patience, tolerance, and belief in the possibilities of our children (van Manen, 1985, p. 43).

If you lose hope, somehow you lose the vitality that keeps life moving, you lose that courage to be, and that quality that helps you to go on in spite of all. And so today I still have a dream (King, 2010, p. 79).

Dear future teachers,

It is relatively easy at this historical conjuncture to slip into a fatalistic and pessimistic attitude toward education and our global–corporate-military-industrial -prison complex. But, we cannot give up. As a popular t-shirt says, "There are no White Flags" in education. We must be persistent, steadfast and stubborn in our hope for possibilities. In a world where children survive under zero tolerance policies, overprescribed pharmaceutical drugs, vacuous curriculum, fast food, state mandated high stakes tests, and crumbling and decrepit school buildings it is difficult to see beyond the nightmare that is now. It is difficult to maintain hope when all the solutions provided for schooling are couched in terms of accountability and assessment/ measurement that is, in the fascist orientation of the business mentality of schooling, "when all that matters is the bottom-line" (Pinar, 2004, pp. 163–164). It is easy to lose hope when the solutions and reports of the last thirty years, from A *Nation at Risk* (1983) to *Race to the Top* (2010) have been repetitive and intimately connected to military and business agendas. It is difficult to determine whether education has become a question of national defense or items on a profit margin sheet. It is most likely both. Recognition of the political complexities in education is the first step

T. M. Kress and R. Lake (Eds.), We Saved the Best for You: Letters of Hope, Imagination and Wisdom for 21st Century Educators, 33–36.
© *2013 Sense Publishers. All rights reserved.*

in becoming critical. It is also the initial step in recognizing the obstacles to more democratic education, a critical pedagogy and an outlook with hope.

There is no shortage of criticism of the having of hope. Critics and scholars grin sarcastically at any thought or glimmer of hope. It is frequently condemned as ridiculously naïve and hopelessly utopic or as the introduction indicates the "last thing out of Pandora's box." But, those who wish to engage in critical pedagogy and those entrusted with the education of our youth cannot afford to be hopeless.

> Hope is alive, but it must be practical and not a naïve hope. A practical hope doesn't simply celebrate rainbows, unicorns, nutbread and niceness, but rigorously understands "what is" in relation to "what could be" – a traditional critical notion. (Kincheloe, 2008, p. x)

Practical hope rings with possibilities and can assist in restoring educators from the dim recesses of disillusionment. That disillusionment can end in immobility and surrender. Practical hope also moves educators to more activist positions despite the risks of visibility and vulnerability (Reynolds, 2012). The discourse of practical hope and critical pedagogy in this historical moment of free-market fundamentalism, micro-fascism and right-wing mega church religion (Reynolds & Webber, 2009) must orient itself to the struggles of everydayness in the face of such overwhelming obstacles. "This means recalibrating the discourse so that it 'speaks' to the immediate problems of workers and others who struggle under the daily grind of time edicts, low salaries, disrespectful work environments, etc" (McLaren, 2007, p. 75).

The stubborn persistence of hope operates within a context of radical love. We can only hope for those we love not in a romantic sense, but in the sense that we must as educators entrusted with the welfare of children work as rigorously as we can to make a better world and in doing so provide youth with critical capacities that enable them to ask the difficult questions concerning education and the larger society. That rigorous work demonstrates not only radical love but hope. Radical love dwells in hope and likewise hope dwells with the context of radical love. Radical love and hope are about the project to end human suffering through the critical awareness of the businessification and militarization of education. It is the struggle to fight against what Giroux calls—zombie politics. The zombie world has no place for hope or radical love. Teach kids to buy stuff. It simply is consuming all you can, just like a zombie.

> The figure of the zombie utilizes the iconography of the living dead that signals a society that appears to have stopped questioning itself, that reveals in its collusion with human suffering and is awash in a culture of unbridled materialism and narcissism. (Giroux, 2010, p. 24)

A future generation of teachers will be living and working within an ever growing oppressive schooling system of regulation, examination and accountability with a business and military friendly outlook. This system is a coded configuration. It is education being reconstituted and replaced in a society of control.

So we can see not only factories being replaced by business, but also schools being replaced by continuing education and exams through continuous assessment. Originally different but analogous sites, such as families, schools, armies and factories, converge into a transmutable or transformable coded configuration of a single business (Deleuze, 1995, p. 174).

Even within this control society and its zombie politics (see Giroux, 2010) of consumption, critical pedagogues must have a stubborn persistence of hope which allows them to tactically resist authoritarianism of business and the state in education. Hope resides in the creativity and imagination of pedagogical, cultural workers who daily create "line of flight" (Deleuze, 1995, p.182) pedagogical resistance. This means that pre-service teacher education must no longer solely involve itself in lesson plans, bulletin boards, and bowing to the dictates of state-mandated prescriptions for success on market-driven testing and textbooks. Teacher education both for pre-service teachers and graduate education for practicing teachers must confront these obstacles to creativity, hope and radical love. Teachers must see these phenomena as obstacles to freedom that must be overcome and not simply as regulations to follow. Intrusions need to be resisted.

I know that one of the last vestiges of my modernist mind is always living within the metanarrative of hope. But, in this age of nightmare schooling with its consumer/business/bottom-line mentality in which are placed the "values of a billionaire – sponsored market driven educational movement that wants to transform schooling into a for profit investment rather than a public good" (Giroux, 2012, p. 2), I refuse to become fatalistic without hope. It is as I have tried to demonstrate a different type of hope, a practical hope for the 21st century. Not that we will win in the end and arrive in a perfect utopian paradise, but that there are moments of hope (Reynolds 2003), moments when lines of flight allow us to move through cracks in the spaces, moments that allow for hopeful flight. These moments of tactical flight within education can merge with larger global political movements and critical pedagogy to reveal our outrage at the present. Hope animates action.

> We therefore maintain our call for a rebellion – peaceful and resolute –against the instruments of mass media that offer our young people a worldview defined by the temptations of consumption, a disdain for the weak, and a contempt for culture, historical amnesia, and the relentless competition of all against all. To the men and women who will make the twenty –first century we say with affection: To create is to resist. To resist is to create (Hessel, 2010, p. 29).

As Hessel (2010) explains, indifference is the worst attitude that we can have as we dwell in the 21st century. Hope in the 21st century can be creative lines of flight that speak to the immediate educational, societal, economic, political, class, race, gender, and sexual preference issues we face. There is hope in the struggle to create a more humane world and in the attempt to alleviate human suffering.

William M. Reynolds

REFERENCES

Deleuze, G. (1995). *Negotiations 1972–1990.* New York: Columbia University Press.

Freire, P. (1999). *The pedagogy of hope: Reliving pedagogy of the oppressed.* New York: Continuum.

Giroux, H. A. (2012). *Education and the crisis of public values: Challenging the assault on teachers students, and public education.* New York: Peter Lang.

Giroux, H. A. (2010). *Zombie politics and culture in the age of casino capitalism.* New York: Peter Lang.

Hessel, S. (2011).*Time for outrage.* New York: Hachette Book Group.

Kincheloe, J. (2008). *Critical pedagogy* (2nd ed.). New York: Peter Lang.

King, M. L. (2010). *The trumpet of conscience.* Boston, MA: Beacon Press.

Pinar, W. F. (2004). *What is curriculum theory?* Mahwah, NJ: Lawrence Erlbaum.

Reynolds, W. M. (2012, in press). I won't back down: Counter -narratives of visibility and vulnerability in a bleak house, In E. Daniels & B. Portfilio (Eds.), *Dangerous Counter stories in the corporate academy: Narrating for understanding, solidarity, resistance, and community in the age of neoliberalism.* Charlotte, NC: Information Age Publishing.

Reynolds, W. M. (2003). *Curriculum: A river runs thought it.* New York: Peter Lang.

Reynolds, W., & Webber, J. A. (2009). *The civic gospel: A political cartography of Christianity.* Boston: Sense Publishers

Van Manen, M. (1985). Hope means commitment. *The History and Social Science Teacher, 20*(3–4), 42–44.

Zinn, H. (1997). *The Zinn reader: Writings on disobedience and democracy.* Westminster, MD: Seven Stories Press.

AFFILIATION

William M. Reynolds
Department of Curriculum, Foundations and Reading
Georgia Southern University

ROSALINA DIAZ

9. FINDING YOUR PASSION, FEEDING YOUR SOUL

Dear Future Educator,

I'd like to begin this letter with some brutal honesty. Public Education in the United States has come upon very difficult and trying times. Teachers have become scapegoats for a slew of societal ills, from the failing economy to our nation's political and societal fall from grace in the international arena. Standards and assessment have become the educational buzzwords of the 21st century as they were in the early 20th century during the social efficiency movement, when intelligence tests were used as weapons of social control that effectively annihilated the dreams and aspirations of thousands upon thousands of American school children, particularly newly arrived immigrants. This time, however, the attack is more widely dispersed and it is not just students, but schools, teachers and even the teaching profession that have come under the microscope and been dissected, in order to be "assessed." In this process many have been found inadequate, failing, or sub-standard. Many loving, caring teachers have lost their jobs as a result; many welcoming community schools have been forced to close their doors. More and more frequently I am finding it difficult as a teacher educator to encourage idealistic young people like yourselves to pursue a field that currently promises little to no creative fulfillment, inadequate spiritual, emotional or financial compensation, and dehumanizing and degrading conditions and treatment.

Every year, I teach a course called "Introduction to the World of the Learner." It is the introductory course for the education department at the college where I am presently employed. Every fall I am confronted with twenty to thirty eager faces in my classroom—clueless as to the realities of their chosen occupation, but desirous to impart knowledge, change lives, and in so doing improve the world. I teach them about the great power and responsibility they hold in their hands. I tell them that teaching reading, writing, and arithmetic is but a miniscule part of what they will actually be doing as educators—a "front" for the much greater enterprise of nurturing the human mind and the cultivation and development of future leaders, thinkers, activists and change agents. I teach them to love their students, to be compassionate, to teach tolerance and acceptance for all humanity. In response they look at me perplexedly and ask, "How?" How can they be expected to achieve any of these lofty ideals when daily they are handed scripted lesson plans, asked to teach out of racist and biased textbooks and are bombarded with the pressures of teaching

T. M. Kress and R. Lake (Eds.), We Saved the Best for You: Letters of Hope, Imagination and Wisdom for 21st Century Educators, 37–40.
© 2013 Sense Publishers. All rights reserved.

test prep skills for the never ending stream of standardized exams that plague their existence as educators? I insist that it can be done – that it must be done – that it is our job to teach truth regardless of the constraints placed upon us as educators in the American public school system. But then, after the class has been dismissed, I often feel hopeless, drained, and sad. Am I in fact deluding myself and lying to my students? Am I simply playing the role of the Greek King Sisyphus destined to roll the proverbial boulder up the hill only to watch it roll back down time and time again? Recently I have days when I truly believe that our public school system is done for – that charter schools and privatization gurus will rule the day and our country will take a huge step backward and in the process destroy the single most successful example of true democracy in America. I am so tired of fighting against what seems like the inevitable that it barely even registers as a disappointment.

So what can I say to you that can instill hope, optimism and light during this educational "dark age?" I became a teacher over twenty years ago for various reasons-to be honest, most were of a practical nature. I was a young mother and needed a job that would provide a stable income with health benefits and summers and holidays off to be with my child. Many of you may have initially been attracted to the teaching profession for similar reasons. My first teaching job was as an ESL instructor for adult immigrants, and later for at risk-teens at a neighborhood community school. I chose to teach these particular groups because I cared about their circumstances. Perhaps it was partly because I saw in them my own parents, who had also come to this country as immigrants many years earlier. Regardless of the reason, I found that teaching them fed my soul in some inexplicable way. I discovered a sense of self worth that I had never experienced before.

I loved literature, so I decided to teach English literature; I loved acting and theater, so I became a drama teacher; I loved human diversity and the richness of world cultures, so I became a social studies teacher; I loved learning about the wonders of our natural world, so I became a science teacher. I pursued all knowledge that was available to me and was passionate about it all. There is perhaps no other profession in the world that would have encouraged and satisfied my quest for knowledge in so many diverse areas. If all the schools in the world were to disappear tomorrow, I would still teach because teaching is what I do and a teacher is who I am. I have a deep yearning for knowledge and for sharing that knowledge with others. For me there is no greater satisfaction than seeing that spark of understanding in a person's eyes and knowing that I have helped put it there, or knowing that I have improved the quality of another human being's life by exposing them to new possibilities and experiences. Knowledge has the ability to transform, reshape, and alter all that we know. Its potential is limitless. And as educators it is this gift, the gift of transformation, that we bring to all those whose hearts and minds we touch.

So let the politicians, economists, bureaucrats and billionaires rage their ugly battles regarding education they cannot win and don't despair. Public education will survive in this country, and in the world, because it is only through education that we have tasted the profundity of true freedom the freedom to know, understand dream, achieve and transform the freedom to recognize and overthrow all forms of oppression and control. And we will not be turned back ever again. Let the storm rage on it will blow over as it has in the past-but the flame of knowledge ignited in the human mind over 35,000 years ago at the dawn of civilization cannot be extinguished. Because when all is said and done, education is not a building or a curriculum or a lesson plan. It is life itself. By becoming a teacher, you have chosen to become a conduit of knowledge and truth in a world often marred by deception, manipulation and greed. It is a "calling" that will both challenge and fulfill you in ways you cannot begin to imagine. I cannot conceive of a greater purpose in the entire world.

Rosalina

AFFILIATION

Rosalina Diaz
Department of Education
Medgar Evers College

GILLIAN U. BAYNE

10. LETTER OF HOPE

The Wangari Way

Esteemed Educators,

I open this letter to you with a quote from Dr. Wangari Maathai's 2004 Nobel Lecture:

> In the course of history, there comes a time when humanity is called to shift to
> a new level of consciousness, to reach a higher moral ground. A time when we
> have to shed our fear and give hope to each other. That time is now (Maathai,
> 2004).

Dr. Wangari Maathai, the first African woman and the first environmentalist to win
a Nobel Peace Prize lived a rich and purposeful life – one full of challenges, hopes,
dreams and inspiration. One aspect of her work involved founding the Green Belt
Movement, a foundation that set out to reforest Dr. Maathai's native Kenya and
other African nations. The nexus of her personal and professional missions were
closely and carefully tied to upholding the dignity of human life while protecting,
respecting and sustaining our oftentimes very fragile living environment. Imbued
within her way of being were the tenets, philosophies, and theoretical frameworks
inherent to those that underscore courage, compassion and love for a collective
concerned community. I take inspiration from Dr. Maathai's life, and through this
inspiration, I write this letter of hope to you, while simultaneously presenting you
with a challenge.

One could argue that Dr. Maathai led her life based upon a number of dares, which
when examined collectively can serve as examples of how educators can harness the
potential to have incredible impacts on the ways that humanity evolves, beginning
with interactions and conversations that we have with ourselves on a visceral level,
with colleagues, students, parents and the community. She dared, for example, to
share her voice, to listen carefully to others, to press onward with her goals despite
facing political, intellectual, and gender biases. By writing this letter, I urge you to
consider that such a collection of dares can be fashioned into a springboard that can
serve as a tool to teach with and learn from others. As you begin your profession as an
educator, as you celebrate the triumphs and embark upon the challenges, in the spirit
of Dr. Maathai, take on a dare that is fitting for the occasion. I share here in this letter
with you some of her essence and present to you, dear educators, 7 considerations

*T. M. Kress and R. Lake (Eds.), We Saved the Best for You: Letters of Hope, Imagination and Wisdom
for 21st Century Educators, 41–44.*
© *2013 Sense Publishers. All rights reserved.*

that are meant to challenge your understanding of hope and, perhaps, provide you with some new ideas toward enacting hope – The Wangari Way.

1. Dare to radically listen and observe – Strive to understand the individual and collective capital that students bring with them to their respective learning environments. Hold yourself and others accountable for words said and actions taken while respecting varied perspectives. Pay attention to each student's needs as well as your own, taking careful measure to ensure balance and equity. Build a foundation for mutual understanding, compassion and dialogue.

2. Dare to be courageous – In the face of inequity, poverty, deficit perspectives, political and social upheaval, develop the strength and tenacity to take a stance – to question, to oppose when it is called for, to seek value in the contrary and to create a sense of solidarity around difference – to stand up for what is just and good – as a practice of freedom.

3. Dare to be open to a changing ontology – Become a reflective practitioner by being mindful of the unfolding of social life and by being present in each experience with others. Reflect upon how skillfully both learning and being in a classroom with others are being attended to. Critically analyze and consider the degree to which intelligent actions are being enacted as you formally and informally research your own emic constructions over time.

4. Dare to nurture and love - "Nothing is impossible when we work in solidarity with love, respect and justice as our guiding light…Love is the basis of an education that seeks justice, equality and genius" (Kincheloe, 2008, p.3). Nurturing and loving sometimes requires herculean efforts, especially when we consider how deep we may need to probe our own possibilities for transformation from within. It is through sincere efforts and the harnessing of our creative powers that we can maximally realize our full potential as educators and can help our students to do the same.

5. Dare to take initiative – Determine that encouragement and inspiration begin with self. Determination is a fundamental element to personal and professional growth and can serve as a source of strength. If we see the present (issue/challenge/situation) clearly through encouraging the sharing of multiple and oftentimes varied perspectives and understandings, we can collectively envision the future that we want and need, and then take appropriate actions to have them materialize.

6. Dare to create and deepen value in learning interactions – The philosophy and practice of humanism and respect for life are means for bringing about change. We ought not to take lightly the value of upholding the dignity of human life, or the value added to life by being with and working alongside others. Aligning oneself to those in need of and/or of wanting a mentor can add value to the human experience while awakening new talents and insights of both educator and student.

7. Dare to provide and seek support – Find those who will provide support and sustenance throughout your journey. Know that your efforts and hard work are

positive causes being made toward effecting change within each student, class, school, community, and within society at large. Whether it is apparent immediately or not, we are changing the face of humanity and of the world.

In the spirit of Dr. Maathai, dare to be a trailblazer. Dare to stand and serve, as does a healthy mighty oak tree. It is not a dry or burnt tree, but a living tree – a wise tree that feeds, provides shelter and generates the essential breath of life. By toiling and working as children of the earth and by planting the seeds of our future joyously through hard work and perseverance, we can create a firm foundation of hope and inspiration with far-reaching roots. Thriving from attentive care and nurturing, roots are sure to support the trunks of strong bodies and minds. The connecting leaves of courage and the fruits of our labor provide the sustenance and vitality needed for our work as a community of educators ahead.

Dare to shift to a new level of consciousness. Dare to reach a higher moral ground.

Peace and Hope,

Gillian

REFERENCES

Gettleman, J. (2011, September 26).Wangari Maathai, Nobel Peace Prize Laureate, Dies at 71. *The New York Times.* Retieved December 17, 2011 fromhttp://www.nytimes.com/2011/09/27/world/africa/wangari- maathai-nobel-peace-prize-laureate-dies-at-71.html?pagewanted=all
Kincheloe, J. L. (2005). *Critical Pedagogy Primer.* New York: Peter Lang.
Maathai, W. (2004, December 10). Wangari Maathai- Nobel Lecture. Nobelprize.org. Retricved December 18, 2011 fromhttp://www.nobelprize.org/nobel_prizes/peace/laureates/2004/maathai-lecture-text.html
Tobin, K. (2009). Tuning into others' voices: radical listening, learning from difference, and escaping oppression. *Cultural Studies of Science Education, 4*(3), pp. 505–511.

AFFILIATION

Gillian U. Bayne
Department of Education
Lehman College

PART II

LETTERS OF IMAGINATION

CHRISTINA SIRY

11. IMAGINING EDUCATIONAL SPACES OF POSSIBILITY, HOPE, AND JOY

Dear Comrades-in-Arms,

As I write this letter to you, I think about the impetus behind a collection such as this, and find inspiration in the editors' use of hope and imagination. These words represent powerful notions and I use them to structure my letter, with the wish that you might find inspiration to imagine the possibilities in educational spaces that are filled with hope and joy.

HOPING FOR DIFFERENCE

Hope: to Cherish a Desire with Anticipation.[1]

My wish, and indeed, the desire that I cherish with anticipation, is that we as educators find possibilities to work towards classrooms that push against present dehumanizing forces of standardization and accountability, in order to create new ways of framing what schooling can be. In more than two decades as a science educator, I have witnessed the power of classrooms where students are active learners defining educational paths collectively, rather than being passively subjected to mandates that reduce learning solely to things that can immediately be measured. The strong current emphasis on accountability is not a new phenomenon, though it is certainly increasing at an alarming speed. My research and teaching is with elementary students and teachers, and I am shocked at pressures put upon teachers to prepare rather than to teach, and consequentially on children to perform rather than to learn. In this climate, the act of learning is reduced to something measurable in bite-size chunks. As children become subjected to test-taking at younger and younger ages, teachers are pushed to focus on discreet skills far removed from the complex acts of communicating, thinking, and learning.

When I see children in Kindergarten being already schooled that there are single "right-answers" to questions, and no alternatives to knowledge production other than the facts to regurgitate, I am reminded of my own son's experiences in Kindergarten. One day he handed me a worksheet with various drawings of items, and instructions to write the beginning letter of the word on the line next to the picture. My son's sheet had many of his letters crossed out in red pen. For example,

T. M. Kress and R. Lake (Eds.), We Saved the Best for You: Letters of Hope, Imagination and Wisdom for 21st Century Educators, 47–50.
© 2013 Sense Publishers. All rights reserved.

two letters (of many) that were marked wrong were the "U" he had written next to a drawing of a stringed instrument and the "B" he had written next to a drawing of a car. When I asked him why he chose "U" for what (to me) looked like a guitar, he looked at me with surprise, and said: Because that's a ukulele. Look here (pointing at the neck of the instrument) – it is too short to be a guitar. On further discussion about this worksheet, I learned, among other things, that: Cars with rounded tops are usually Beetles. Do you see how round it is on top? Most cars aren't that round. The teacher was expecting children to write "G" for guitar, and "C" for car, and my 5-year old son did not do this. With this teacher's expectation, his responses were wrong. However, in a conversation of less than 5 minutes, it was clear he simply had different perspectives of what these images represented. At that time, I wondered how many students had similarly identified the images with other words than those the teacher intended. Now, however, as I have been in countless other Kindergarten classes and seen similar patterns, I wonder, what would happen if teachers had supports to engage in dialogue with children around the work that they produce rather than solely evaluating it?

In a system that only looks for "G" for guitar, there is no room to know that my son lived in a home with many instruments, and that he himself played the ukulele. Yet, it is such differences in perspectives, experiences, and thinking, that makes contact with one another interesting. The difference that I hope for, indeed, the ideal that I cherish with anticipation, is that schooling be structured to highlight, recognize, and embrace difference in all its complexity. While we might all recognize that in the institution called "school" there is embedded the idea of "evaluation", I ask you to consider, what would happen if we consistently were positioned to use students' work as a beginning to a process of dialogue around ideas, rather than the ending point of checking for specific facts? What would classrooms be like if worksheets, notebooks, even exams, were starting points for conversations about knowledges, rather than solely the ending point for grading? I have written previously that in having a space for dialogue, children can reveal diversities of perspectives (Siry & Lang, 2010), and this can be used as a strength for teaching and learning. If there were structures in place to support teachers in consistently dialoguing with their students, could classroom practices be transformed?

IMAGINING NEW WAYS

Imagination: the Act or Power of Forming a Mental Image of Something not Present to the Senses or Never before Wholly Perceived in Reality.

From my work with young children, to my own children's education, to my experiences as a teacher educator being "told" what to emphasize, I have witnessed coercive educational contexts in which participants (teachers as well as students) are told what to do and how to do it. As complex content areas are reduced to measurable bits and isolated facts, teachers are evaluated on how well they prepare students for standardized exams, and students' futures are determined in large part by their performance on these exams. Such teacher-as-technician (Sleeter, 2008) climates create indifference and apathy, and give the false impression that there is nothing we can do to change oppressive and ridged structures. Quite the contrary, I have found in over 20 years of working with children and teachers that if we lay these notions out and deconstruct them, we become positioned to reconstruct something more equitable, just, and very much possible.

In specifically deconstructing notions of knowledge / evaluation / performance, and roles of teacher / student, we can become positioned to reconstruct institutional roles and structures that better recognize the inseparable relationship "between subject and object, individual and environment, self and society, outsider and community, living consciousness and phenomenal world" (Greene, 1988, p.8). I have seen the power of classroom communities structured to not only recognize this relationship, but also to welcome it, and go so far as to insist upon it (Siry & Zawatski, 2010). I know that it is possible. I take comfort in this knowledge, and it inspires my imagination, as I consider how to reconstruct schooling to insist on the necessity of recognizing the inseparability of student from community, individual from collective. There are a multiplicity of knowledges, experiences, and perspectives in any classroom at any given time. The experiences of our students cannot be empirically defined, and thus cannot be measured.

The hope that I have for the future provides support as I look at "what is", but much more importantly it supports me as I look at "what could be". What are the possibilities in a given context for working towards classrooms of joy, hope, and imagination? In approaching this question, I find inspiration in Maxine Greene's call that we "look at things as though they could be otherwise" (1995, p. 19). This is the real meaning of hope and imagination for me. Certainly it is important to ask "Why?" Why are things as they are? But more important is the value of asking "Why not?" Why can't children expect to be taught in classrooms that nurture community, ideas, collaboration, and inquiry? Why can't disciplines be recognized to be multifaceted, complex? Why not? What structures prevent this? What can we do to push back against these structures?

Highlighting differences can move us towards educational spaces that are filled with hope; as we find value in differences in opinions, different experiences, different approaches for being held accountable, different notions of teaching and learning… With this recognition of the value of differences, we can also find the joy in teaching and learning. Hope inspires me to imagine new ways of being within (and against) institutional structures. In imagining, I conceptualize new possibilities and I encourage you as a reader and a teacher to reexamine, reconsider, and reimagine what could be possible. In finding hope and drawing on our imaginations, we can use our own agency to work to change structures so teachers and students can accomplish contextually relevant learning and produce knowledges together. My hope is that in deconstructing and reconstructing the assumptions of schooling, children are not only provided with the opportunity to be given "voice" but that their voices are heard, acknowledged, and acted upon.

Christina Siry

NOTE

[1] The Merriam Webster Dictionary: http://www.merriam-webster.com/dictionary/

REFERENCES

Greene, M. 1995. Releasing the imagination: *Essays on education, the arts, and social change.* San Francisco, CA: Jossey-Bass.
Greene, M. (1988). *The dialectic of freedom.* New York, NY: Teachers College Press.
Siry, C., & Lang, D. (2010). Creating participatory discourse for teaching and research in early childhood science. *Journal of Science Teacher Education, 21*(2), 149–160.
Siry, C., & Zawatski, E. (2011). "Working with" as a methodological stance: Collaborating with students in teaching, writing, and research. *The International Journal of Qualitative Studies in Education, 24*(3), 343–361.
Sleeter, C. (2008). Equity, democracy, and neoliberal assaults on teacher education. *Teaching and Teacher Education, 24*(8), 1947–1957.

AFFILIATION

Christina Siry
Educational Sciences
University of Luxembourg

ROBERT LAKE

12. IMAGINATION, PLAY AND BECOMING THE TEXT

A child's greatest achievements are possible in play. In play a child always behaves beyond his average age, above his daily behavior; in play it is as though he were a head taller than himself (Vygotsky, 1978, p. 102).

Dear Teacher,

I have been working with pre-service teachers for a number of years now and one thing that still amazes me is how so many of you pretended to be teachers at an incredibly young age, with friends or family members or if no one else was around, many dolls might have been taught quite a few things as well. I am sure that there are days when you feel like your dolls listened much better than your real students. It would be really interesting to know what the imaginary students might have said in dialogue with their imaginary teachers. Maybe you pretended to be quite a few different grown up characters when you were young. I remember even as a teenager pretending to be Frodo Baggins and Woody Guthrie. Also as a teen, my friend Danny and I listened to Ray Charles' records in a completely dark room to try to connect with the inner source of his musical verve. Music is itself an emotional language and we longed to absorb by some kind of invisible osmosis the wellsprings of the soul genius of Ray Charles.

Many years later I read the work of another genius, Lev Vygotsky. He was a revolutionary thinker in the field of social and historical processes of learning. I was excited to learn that as a teenager, Vygotsky and his friends would pretend that they were historic figures (Vygotsky 1978, p. 102). Two Vygotsky scholar/practitioners named Joan Wink and Le Ann Putney add to this idea by writing that "children at play are in a zone of proximal development. In play, children are acting out real-life situations in which they develop rules that move them beyond their current level" (2002, p. 113). As an 18 year old pretending to be Woody Guthrie, I sought to take on the "rules" of his thought, especially his criticism of post war corporate America's influence on the recording industry and his disdain for commercialism in general. The adaption of this genre influenced my speech and gestures too, even though I had never seen Woody Guthrie or heard him speak. I had only read his autobiography and of course heard some of his music. These texts of his life carried an imagined language identity.

T. M. Kress and R. Lake (Eds.), We Saved the Best for You: Letters of Hope, Imagination and Wisdom for 21st Century Educators, 51–56.
© *2013 Sense Publishers. All rights reserved.*

LANGUAGE IDENTITY

Linguists often speak of the power of the language ego. This phenomenon involves the ability to take on the identity of a speaker of any language or dialect. This not only includes target vocabulary and syntax of a language. It also includes gestures and the learner's perceptions of the attitude of the language. In the film *Ray* for example, Jamie Foxx took on the language identity of Ray Charles and went much deeper with it than Danny and I ever did. Fox won an Oscar for this outstanding portrayal of the "text" of Ray Charles' life. To prepare for his role in the movie, he actually went to a school for the blind, in order to learn how to read Braille and to immerse himself in the culture of blindness (Benjamin & Hakford, 2004). By taking on the identity of the language there comes an unpredictable point when communication becomes part of the subconscious. Anyone who has studied a foreign language intensely is aware that when you begin to think or dream in that language, you are on your way to fluency. By far, the best method of language learning comes by taking on the identity of the language in the context of authentic communication. Indeed literacy involves imaginative connections to text, speech inflections, gesturing, and the ability to "read" a person's intent.

READING FROM THE INSIDE OUT

In the present context of literacy education, the great debate between phonics vs. whole language instruction seems to never end. The National Reading Panel endorses a strong emphasis on phonics, or "bottom-up" processing. Others continue to emphasize the role of context in "top-down" processing. Gallas' view of inside-out learning presents a view that is outside this dichotomy. In actuality, both these models are implicit in what she calls an "inside-out" approach to reading. This model describes three aspects of language learning. The first is the identity stage, the second is the discourse acquisition stage, and the third stage involves a concept that she calls "authoring". In order to understand how this approach might work, it might help you if I take the time to briefly describe the features and function of each "stage" and how they all connect to Vygotsky's work. I do not personally like the word "stage" but use it here for accuracy of citations.

IDENTITY FORMATION

In the identity stage, the learner takes on the prescribed role of the text. This was my experience with reading Woody Guthrie's life story, I was "reading" the text from the "inside out." Gallas quotes from Lave and Wenger in this connection. They write that, "Learning involves the construction of identities" (2003, p. 70). This theory came alive for her as she took her students on a field trip to a science museum. As four of her students stood next to a display of dinosaur bones, they began to pretend they were scientists. They adopted what they perceived to be the speech and appropriate tone of scientists in their role play. She further supported this position from her own childhood experience. She remembered learning about using measurements for cooking when she was a child with a toy oven. If only math was taught that way in schools today! She sums up the identity stage by saying that "first the child takes on the role of a scientist; second, the student takes on the point of view of the object or text under study" (2003, p. 74). Of course this is not limited to the field of science, cooking or music. It could just as easily be applied to role playing a figure from history like Vygotsky did with his friends, or being a mathematician or chef or a kayak builder.

DISCOURSE ACQUISTION

The next stage that Gallas presents is discourse acquisition. This stage takes identity several steps further. What is involved here is the appropriation of the identity through a "tool kit...of a discourse" a term she borrowed from the prominent Vygotsky scholar, James Wertsch (1991). This consists of appropriating the language, tools, text, and forms of inquiry that are discipline specific and using them to master an identity. She succinctly sums up this stage in saying that "the tools and texts of a subject gain their vitality when they are brought into *productive* [italics, hers] contact with a student's experience" (Gallas, 2003, pp. 86–87). This involves mental, emotional and somatic productivity. Of course in my case, this would involve singing and playing one of Guthrie's songs on the guitar. Vygotsky drew much on this topic from one of the most prominent directors in the history of theatrical drama, Konstantin Stanislavsky. In fact his work is still used today in drama education. The system that Stanislavsky developed "was based on the emotive subtext each actor was supposed to convey by linguistic and paralinguistic means. This work "left a lasting impression on Vygotsky, who used Stanislavsky's notes for the actors to demonstrate the role of emotive subtext in the decoding of verbal messages" (Kozulin, 1990, p. 28). Dear teachers just imagine for a moment the ways that we could use this kind of play to have our students read content from the inside out through the power of imagination and exploratory drama.

This was the experience of Tonya Perry. In a wonderfully well written narrative style, she discusses her experience of using exploratory drama to break wide open *The Diary of Anne Frank* to a high school class. This came about after she witnessed the enormous disconnect in her students' ability to recall facts about the text and the students' ability to actually grasp the meaning of it. Instead of just moving on to the next required book in her mandated curriculum, she decided to try having the students focus on the lines in the text that referred to the periods of silence in the attic that Anne Frank's family had to practice.

> Instead of reading the play the next day, I asked the students to enter the room without talking. As they sat, I told them they were all hiding from the Nazi forces like Anne Frank. Immediately, without any additional description, I showed them video clips of what we would face if anyone discovered our

whereabouts. We quietly watched images of soldiers looking for the Jewish people in their homes and taking them to ghettos. As time progressed, we watched trains fill with people heading to concentration camps. Images of families separating and deplorable living conditions occurred more frequently. Students silently transitioned to the large taped square in the middle of the floor. I asked them to sit quietly for five minutes without talking and think about what we would face if we or someone else talked, placing our lives in grave danger. (Perry, 2005, p. 122)

This exercise proved to be effective in increasing comprehension by taking vicarious meaning making to a much higher level. Perry summed up the value of this exercise by pointing out that "authentic drama assignments capture the students' ability to understand complex concepts and use them in multiple contexts" (ibid.). What struck me the most about this classroom experience is that the students read the text with great phonetic facility, but still lacked the context that was needed to really feel, see, touch, and understand the story, to transcend walls between 21st century students in Alabama and the scene inside an attic in Nazi-occupied Amsterdam in 1942! Of course there is no method to fully convey the sheer terror that this family experienced. At the same time, through use of discourse and in this case the accompanying rules of silence along with the emotional subtext of fear, the students were enabled to look through the cracked door into the lives of others through identifying with the text and reading it with their bodies.

AUTHORING

The final phase of this process Gallas calls "authoring" by a public act of presenting it in another form, for a real audience. This can accomplished through a musical performance, or dance, writing, solving an equation, drawing or painting, storytelling, drama, or repairing a car. This stage requires a demonstration of text in a way that can be validated by others through the recreation of meaning. She succinctly states this through her observation that *"literacy is a process of merging who we believe we are with what we show we can do"* (Gallas, 2003, p. 100). One small comment on this quote: I would change the word "literacy" in the above quote to "meaning"! Wouldn't it be amazing if we did more assessments this way instead of relying on the regurgitation of facts on multiple guess tests? Teachers of all age levels, turn the imagination of your students loose to show what they can do through the many millions of diverse and unique ways of expressing authored meaning! As Tonya Perry and a growing host of other teachers are discovering, we can lead a revolution right in the middle of the current deep crisis of mis-education through play, imagination and reading from the inside out. I will close with a quote from one of the most important writers about imagination and education.

Imagination may be responsible for the very texture of our experience. Once we do away with habitual separations of the subjective from the objective, the inside from the outside, appearances from reality, we might be able to give imagination its proper importance and grasp what it means to place imagination at the core of understanding. (Greene, 1995, p. 141)

Regardless of how dark things look, how limited our resources are or how rigid and confining the present system of education might be, through play we CAN take our students to the core of understanding! Imagine!

All my best to each of you,
Robert Lake

REFERENCES

Benjamin, S. (Producer), & Hakford, T. (Director). (2004). *Ray* [Motion picture]. USA:Universal Studios.
Gallas, K. (2003). *Imagination and literacy: A teacher's search for the heart of learning*. New York, NY: Teachers College Press.
Greene, M. (1995*). Releasing the imagination*. San Francisco: Jossey-Bass.
Kozulin, A. (1990). *Vygotsky's psychology: A biography of ideas*. Cambridge, MA: Harvard University Press.
Perry, T. B. (2005). Taking time: Beyond memorization: Using drama to promote thinking. *English Journal. 95*(5), 120–123.
Stout, H. (2011, January 5). Effort to restore children's play gains momentum. *The New York Times*. Retrieved December 31, 2011 from:http://www.nytimes.com/2011/01/06/garden/06play.html?pagewanted=all
Vygotsky, L. S. (1978). *Mind in society: The development of higher mental processes,*eds. & trans. M. Cole, V. John-Steiner, S. Scribner, & E. Souberman. Cambridge, MA: Harvard University Press. (Original works published 1930, 1933, and 1935).
Wertsch, J. V. (1991). *Voices of the Mind: a sociocultural approach to mediated action*. Cambridge MA: Harvard University Press.
Wink, J., & Putney, L. (2002). *A vision of Vygotsky*. Boston, MA:Allyn & Bacon.

AFFILIATION

Robert Lake
Department of Curriculum, Foundations and Reading
Georgia Southern University

MIKE ROSE

13. PORTRAIT OF THINKING

A Novice Cabinetmaker

Dear 21st Century Educators,

Judgments about intelligence carry great weight in our society, and we have a tendency to make sweeping assessments of people's intelligence based on the kind of work they do. Unfortunately you have inherited a system of education that views conceptual and symbolic "learning" of facts while sitting down for most of the school day, in an unnatural position for our species, as the most important education. Along with this value system is the view that work with your hands in specific skills such as auto repair, plumbing or being a waitress should all be relegated to the "loser track".

As I've been arguing for some time in much of my written work—we tend to think too narrowly about intelligence, and that narrow thinking has affected the way we judge each other, organize work, and define ability and achievement in school. We miss so much. As an attempt to show you what I mean, I offer you this portrait of intelligence at work in a cabinet making class.

Felipe, a student in a high school wood construction class, is the head of a team assigned to build a cabinet for his school's main office. At this point in his education Felipe has built one small, structurally simple cabinet, and this current, second, cabinet has a number of features the earlier project didn't. His storehouse of knowledge about cabinets, his "cabinet sense", is just developing, and the limits of his knowledge reveal themselves at various points throughout assembly. Like this one.

Felipe is trying to record final figures for all the components of the cabinet—he and his co-workers are eager to begin assembly. He is working with Gloria and Jesus, and he is sketching with them one more three-dimensional representation of the cabinet, using several lists and a sketch he and the others had produced during planning.

When I approach the team, Felipe is looking back and forth from lists to the sketch and talking to his peers. He seems puzzled. He asks Gloria to get the first sketch they made of the cabinet. She retrieves it from her backpack and unfolds it. They study it for a moment. He says something to Jesus, then takes a tape and measures—as if to confirm—the length of the cabinet. Sixty-eight inches.

Felipe continues this way, double-checking, trying to verify, looking up occasionally to snag the teacher, Mr. Devries, who, however, is helping a group across the room.

T. M. Kress and R. Lake (Eds.), We Saved the Best for You: Letters of Hope, Imagination and Wisdom for 21st Century Educators, 57–60.
© 2013 Sense Publishers. All rights reserved.

The source of this vexation is a discrepancy that emerged as Felipe, Jesus, and Gloria were listing final numbers: The length of the sheet of plywood for the bottom of the cabinet—this is found on the list of materials—is sixty-eight inches. But the length of the top panel—listed on another sheet—is sixty-seven inches. This makes no sense. As Felipe explains it, exhibiting a nice shift from numbers to their structural meaning, the top can't be shorter than the bottom, or the cabinet will look like this: and here he makes an abbreviated triangle in the air with his hands. What's going on?

Finally, Mr. Devries is free, Felipe goes to get him, and they confer. The sketch Felipe has is inadequate, is not detailed enough to reveal that the top panel rests inside notches cut into the top of the side panels. These are called rabbet cuts. Felipe's discomfort resolves quickly into understanding. The bottom panel extends to the very ends of the side panels, but the top will be shorter by a half inch on each side, the dimensions of the rabbet cuts. Thus the mystery of the sixty-eight inch bottom and the sixty-seven-inch top.

The depictions of the cabinet in Felipe's plans do not provide enough information—through graphics or numbers—to enable him to figure out the discrepancy in measurement between top and bottom. Yet he must rely on these lists and sketches, for he does not yet know enough about cabinets to enable him to solve the problem readily...or not to assume that the discrepancy is a problem in the first place.

Fast forward now to the next cabinet Felipe builds, a few months after the completion of the one we just witnessed. This time there is no confusion about the length of the top and the bottom panels; that earlier episode taught Felipe a lot. And there is evidence of his emerging "cabinet sense." This new cabinet requires a plastic laminate over its surface. Felipe is laying the cabinet's face frame over a long sheet of plastic and tracing the outline of the frame onto it. This will give him the covering for the frame but leave two fairly large door-sized squares of the plastic. Felipe stops, takes a step back, looks the cabinet over, and then reaches for his list of measurements and a tape measure. I ask him what he's doing.

We're short on laminate, he explains, and here you'll have these two excess pieces of it cut away from the frame. We'll need to use them. But, he realizes, they won't cover the doors themselves, because the doors will be larger than the opening; they'll attach onto and over the face frame. So, he's trying to think ahead and picture where the as yet uncut surplus might go. What other, smaller pieces of the cabinet could be covered. That's what he's about to check. When I describe this event to the teacher, Mr. Devries, he smiles and says, "That's how a cabinet-maker thinks."

* * *

Several times during the construction of the wall cabinet with the puzzling sixty-seven inch top, Felipe would comment on the mathematics involved in cabinet assembly. And I asked him about it myself. His comments were a bit contradictory, and the contradiction resonated with something that was intriguing me as well. At times he would note that the math is "simple," "just numbers," "only fractions."

At other times, though, even within the same few sentences, his face registering perplexity, he would observe that "a lot of math is involved" and that "it's difficult."

Felipe has taken algebra and is currently enrolled in college math; he knows what more advanced mathematics looks like. On the face of it, the math involved in cabinet assembly is pretty simple: reading a ruler; adding and subtracting (and, less frequently, multiplying and dividing) whole numbers, mixed numbers, and fractions; working with the basic properties of squares and rectangles. Yet, he says, "there's so many pieces you need to take into consideration, otherwise, you'll mess up somewhere."

Felipe's puzzlement, I think, is located in the intersection of traditional mathematics, learned most often in school, and the mathematics developed in the carpenter's shop.

Traditional mathematics is in evidence throughout Mr. Devries' workshop: from the calculations students do to determine cost per board foot to measurements scribbled on scraps of paper spread across the room. Considered from the perspective of school math—that is, if lifted from context and presented as problems in a textbook—the operations here would be, as Felipe observes, fairly rudimentary, grade-school arithmetic.

But as these measures and calculations play out in assembly—particularly an assembly that is unfamiliar—things get more complex, and thus Felipe and his crew move slowly and with some uncertainty. With an incomplete sense of a cabinet's structure, Felipe must keep a number of variables in mind, arrayed in three-dimensional space, with each variable having consequences for the other. The top of the cabinet will be shorter in length by the sum of the two rabbet cuts in the side panels—but what about the width of the top? Will it rest in a cut in the back panel, and if so, what are the implications for the measurements of the back panel? Will the top extend into or onto the face frame? What does that mean for the face frame? And so on. In neurologist Frank Wilson's phrasing, this young carpenter is developing the ability to "spatialize" mathematics—and as Felipe notes, that means taking "so many pieces…into consideration." Mr. Devries tells me that he has students taking calculus who have a hard time with such tasks.

There is a small but growing research literature on mathematics in the workplace—from the tailor's shop to the design studio—and a few of these studies focus on carpentry. Listening to Felipe puzzle over the nature of the mathematics of assembly led me to look more closely at the math in Mr. Devries' shop, and what I saw matched earlier studies, some of which were conducted in other cultures, such as in South Africa, suggesting some cognitive commonality to the way carpenters do the work they do.

One of the findings of this research is that a wide range of mathematical concepts and operations are embodied in carpentry's artifacts and routines, and in ways suited to the properties of materials and the demands of production. The carpenter's math is tangible and efficient.

Take, for example, measurement. The ruler and framing square provide measurements, but so do objects created in the shop: one piece of wood, precisely cut, can function as the measure for another. Tools are also used as measuring devices. A sixteen-inch claw hammer laid sideways on a wall provides a quick measure for the location of studs in a wall frame. And carpenters use their hands and fingers to measure and compare. ("I use my forefinger and thumb for calipers," reports master woodworker Sam Maloof.) They develop an eye for length and dimension and for relations and correspondences.

Working in the shop, the young carpenter learns a range of other mathematical concepts: symmetry, proportion, congruence, the properties of angles. Planing straight the edge of a board, cutting angles on the miter box, laying out the pieces of a cabinet's face frame to check for an even fit—through these activities, Mr. Devries' students see mathematical ideas manifested, and feel them, too, gaining a sense of trueness and error. Fractions were never more real to Felipe than during the episode with that cabinet top.

Once revealed, the complexity and efficiency of the intellectual work of the cabinetmaker illuminates just how rudimentary standardized and decontextualized classroom mathematics actually are. When mathematics are decontextualized, education standards may classify algebra as a more advanced level of mathematics than addition, subtraction, multiplication, division and fractions (i.e., "basic" math). When taken out of context, it would appear that algebraic equation solving involves more cognitive facility than "basic" math. When contextualized, however, algebraic problem solving not only has almost no use value in the craft of cabinetmaking, but it is tremendously rudimentary. Classroom algebra involves only linear abstract problem solving; whereas, cabinetmaking requires not only linear problem solving, but also a synthesis and application of many types of knowledge including geometry and physics and "basic" math. It also requires cognitive flexibility, estimation, prediction, improvisation, and an understanding of functional and aesthetic characteristics of cabinetry.

Finally, because you are the educators of the next generation, I leave you with a challenge to imagine a different type of education:

What would learning look like if we recognized intelligence in context, rather than simply in the brain or in the book? Is it even possible or desirable to rewrite educational "standards" to capture the highly complex intellectual activity of the cabinetmaker? And if so, what would these standards look like? How would this alter the content and pedagogy of our own classrooms?

The answers to these questions, like the intellectual activity of cabinetry, are themselves contextual in nature. When learning is contextualized, knowledge becomes exponentially more complex, and the possibilities are endless.

Mike Rose

AFFILIATION

Mike Rose
Education Department
University of California Los Angeles

KEVIN SMITH

14. THE TAU'OLUNGA

A Pacific Metaphor for a Caring, Critical Pedagogy

Dear Teachers,

On October 5, 2011, I sat in Queen Salote Memorial Hall in Nuku'alofa, Tonga watching the festivities marking UNESCO's World Teacher Day. The hall was filled with teachers, administrators, choirs, dancers, and dignitaries. October is a warm month in Tonga, but my Kakala was cool against my skin and I could smell the sweet fragrance of its flowers as they were draped around my neck. The program consisted of speeches and performances, but for me the most poignant event was the Tau'olunga[1]. A young woman was escorted to the stage. Her oiled skin gleamed in the sunlight cascading through the tall windows in the hall. She wore a Tapa dress and stood silently before the dignitaries smiling, her knees slightly bent as she waited for the music to begin.

The music played, the men sang, and she began to dance. She smiled as she performed the Haka – the specific gestures that comprise the dance. Her eyes followed each gesture as she attempted to emphasize the meaning of the movements and message of her performance. Occasionally, she would turn her head and body to the side in a fluid movement called Kalo. At other times, in tempo with the beat, she would quickly dip just her head to the side in a gesture called Teki. The audience smiled and called out as they clapped their hands in response to the dancer's performance, and soon many approached the stage and pressed money against her oiled skin. The Fakapale is an expression of appreciation to the dancer, and tells her that not only is she performing well, but that she has touched the audience culturally, socially, and emotionally – an experience called Mafana. Eventually, the Tulafale would begin and the cries from the audience would increase as women would join the soloist, dancing in similar movements behind her. Eventually, men would also dance behind the soloist with exaggerated movements that emphasized the beauty of her performance.

I was deeply touched by this experience. Not only because the dance was aesthetically beautiful, but because the collaboration between dancer and audience was equally beautiful. The dance was not simply a representation of a cultural artifact; instead, much like school, it operated more significantly as a method of reaffirming, redefining, and communicating social relations. Again, much like school, it was

T. M. Kress and R. Lake (Eds.), We Saved the Best for You: Letters of Hope, Imagination and Wisdom for 21st Century Educators, 61–64.
© *2013 Sense Publishers. All rights reserved.*

a process of producing and reproducing culture. For me, it was also a metaphor for teaching, but not just any kind of teaching. The emphasis on participation and collaboration, on feelings of community and mutuality, made this a particularly poignant metaphor for a certain type of teaching – a caring, critical pedagogy that I believe engages an active and hopeful disposition in students and teachers in ways that reveal possibilities for a better world.

I taught in the Cincinnati area for nearly six years, and during this time my belief in schools as not only sites of instruction and reproduction, but also of resistance and transformation was regularly enforced and invigorated. These latter descriptors were especially important as I understood them to be key components for developing and delivering a critically-informed sense of hope for students and teachers alike.

I was fortunate to have read Paulo Freire's *Pedagogy of the Oppressed* (2006) before my first job as a teacher. It had a profound effect on how I worked with my students and piqued my interest in understanding what a critical pedagogy is and why it is important. I was not always successful in incorporating a critical pedagogy in my classes, but I knew it was important to try. The results were sporadic and unpredictable, but there were moments when we felt that what we were doing was greater than "just school." My students weren't just learning curriculum objectives, we were learning to think. Prior to moving to Tonga, I was able to design and teach a middle school technology course that allowed us to tackle a diversity of topics rising from the lived experiences of my students. Racism, gay rights, poverty, and more – topics that typically were discussed "in the fringes" of the classroom – were our main objectives because these were the issues the students were facing in their lives. They wanted to talk about them, to express their voices, and to understand the nature of the issues and problems they were facing. Until that class, the students had found the institution of school unable to help them examine their lives or to live a life worth living (to paraphrase Socrates); school was too concerned with high-stakes test scores and KUDER results.

My basis for a caring, critical pedagogy is influenced by the work of Paulo Freire and Nel Noddings. Freire is perhaps best-known for his book *Pedagogy of the Oppressed* and his denunciation of what he called the "banking model of education." For Freire, this model of education is a system in which teachers authoritatively deposit content into students' minds. Teaching then is "a gift bestowed by those who consider themselves knowledgeable upon those whom they consider to know nothing" (Freire, 2006, p. 72). In this scenario, the teacher exists as the ultimate knowledge-authority and students are reduced to unthinking objects robbed of the opportunity to not only question and reflect upon the content they've received and the circumstances in which they received it. Freire refuted this type of education by demanding that teachers and students embrace a critical approach to learning – a dialogical process of problematizing the reality of the lives of students and teachers and posing questions that seek to unveil the social, cultural, economic, and political contradictions present in their lives (Freire, 1985). Freire emphasized that there is never "teaching without learning" (Freire, 1998, p. 31) – that teachers must recognize that which is known by the student and honor students' curiosity as they work to understand what is being taught. In doing so, Freire also emphasized that teachers must demonstrate humility, tolerance, and "impatient patience" in crafting a critical approach to learning (Freire, 1998, p. 80), and it is with these relational elements of a critical pedagogy that I find the work of Noddings and Freire to be most complementary.

Acknowledging the real experiences of students, the knowledge they possess, and their right to see an unfair world as subject to change, is a demonstration of the recognition of the humanity and distinctive worth of that student. Such a demonstration exists as a type of caring. Noddings, who is well known for her work involving the ethics of caring, provides an important distinction between caring in terms of virtue and relational terms (Noddings, 1995). It is my belief that a teacher must constantly strive to maintain an attitude of relational caring with students in order for a hopeful and critical pedagogy to be enacted. One important feature of relational caring is that the "carer" is attentive and receptive to the needs of the "cared-for" to such a degree that the carer's personal motivations are placed into a heightened correspondence with those of the "cared-for" (Noddings, 2003). This correspondence then contributes to a reciprocal relationship in which the cared-for recognizes the caring attitude of the carer.

So what does all this mean in regard to teaching? The Tau'olunga is a dance of specific movements interpreted through a performer and members of the audience, and it is a practice that recognizes the historical significance of social and cultural elements while acknowledging the potential of such practices in the future. A notable performance is built upon the performer's active, real-time reflection on her performance, the audience's knowledge, and their shared reaction and participation in the elements of the dance. It is an experience that illustrates the importance of relational care, and the collaboration of the audience and the dancer create new opportunities for epistemological, ontological, cultural, and social forms of meaning-making. Schools should operate in much the same way. But what about the critical element? There is no component in my metaphor of the Tau'olunga that compares to a critical perspective. However, similar to how the Tau'olunga engages both audience and dancer in an active representation of the social ties shared by those involved, a critical pedagogy should engage both the teacher and students in active investigations of the elements of their lives. Freire wasn't describing a teaching method when he wrote *Pedagogy of the Oppressed*. He was specifically addressing the necessity for teachers and students to critically engage with the real circumstance of their lives in the hope of transforming an unjust society into a society that no longer has the capacity to reproduce oppression. "Hope" is the operative word here, and it is fueled by caring, by shared-resistance, by solidarity, and by the joint actions of teachers and students in the struggle to achieve common goals. It is my hope that you and your students will engage in the metaphor of the Tau'olunga as you engage in a critical, caring approach to learning and teaching.

Kevin Smith

NOTE

[1] I would like to thank Malu Kava, a well-known and respected *Punake*, for sharing his knowledge of the Tau'olunga with me in preparation for this letter.

REFERENCES

Freire, P. (1985). *The politics of education: Culture, power, and liberation* (D. Macedo, Trans.). South Hadley, MA: Bergin & Garvey.

Freire, P. (1998). *Teachers as cultural workers: Letters to those who dare teach.* Boulder, CO: Westview Press.

Freire, P. (2006). *Pedagogy of the oppressed: The thirtieth anniversary edition.* New York, NY: The Continuum International Publishing Group Inc.

Noddings, N. (1995). Care and moral education. In W. Kohli (Ed.), *Critical conversations in philosophy of education* (pp. 137–148). New York, NY: Routledge.

Noddings, N. (2003). *Caring: A feminine approach to ethics and moral education* (2nd ed.). Berkeley, CA: University of California Press.

AFFILIATION

Kevin Smith
Fellow in Curriculum
Institute of Education, Tonga

PATRICIA PAUGH

15. STAYING OPEN TO SURPRISE…A NECESSARY RESPONSIBILITY

"Let your students surprise you," I tell my preservice student teachers as we begin a new semester in EDC G 689, the teacher research class connected to their student teaching. "In order to build a classroom that is truly intellectual everyone learns something new, including the teacher." Hearing that the final criteria for passing the course is to collect and analyze evidence in their practicum classrooms (and discover the unexpected) is a bit disconcerting for my students who, like you, are preparing to teach. Being "surprised" is not necessarily part of the discourse that prospective teachers are socialized into, especially those entering public schools in this "Race to the Top" era. The criterion of surprise is (initially) a relief for some of my students who quietly smirk, "This class will be easy…thank goodness." However, as the smirkers discover, surprise is a radical idea in school culture. To understand the unknown requires taking up an "inquiry stance" (Cochran-Smith & Lytle, 2009) toward students and selves where both are challenged to think differently and work together to build a mutually respectful classroom community.

The reality of opening up to the unexpected is actually quite difficult for those of us immersed in the day-to-day practices of institutional schooling. Dominant cultures in schools push us toward certainty. In the large urban school district adjoining our university, the dominant drive toward certainty reflects a national quest to standardize curriculum and along with that, standardize children. It seems to be "common sense" that achievement gaps will disappear if every school in a district, state, or the nation is "on the same page" in a leveled curriculum. Putting students in boxes based on clean and neat measurement tools (a.k.a high stakes testing) is the default solution to the grand inequities that exist in public education. Numbers and charts are clear and easy tools to easily measure large groups of students. In this age of data mining, school administrators and policy makers want the news to be clean and neatly displayed.

At the start of my twenty year career as an elementary teacher I wanted such certainty. During those first years, it was a challenge to teach diverse learners in a town where factories that had sustained families for generations were rapidly closing, and new families were beginning to arrive, navigating unfamiliar terrain in a new country and with a new language. Most of the children in my classes were constantly ready to surprise me, as I shared little background experience with any of them. However, the last thing I wanted was surprise. Each day found me clinging

T. M. Kress and R. Lake (Eds.), We Saved the Best for You: Letters of Hope, Imagination and Wisdom for 21st Century Educators, 65–68.
© 2013 Sense Publishers. All rights reserved.

to my plan book, my reading series manual with daily lesson plans, and desperately seeking a classroom management strategy that would keep us all happy and learning, but most importantly keep the teacher (me) within her comfort zone.

Flash forward ten years. I'm a first grade teacher with some experience under my belt. I'm committed to making sure that my classroom provides space to acknowledge different talents and perspectives that each child offers to the community. I'm proud to be fighting deficit ideas about children who do not fit the norm. I resist the system that sorts kids into "levels" and separates them from their peers into remedial programs designed to "fix" their supposed "problems" but instead steers them into narrow, often "dumbed down" educational programs. It's a typical morning in this setting. I'm attempting to get everyone's attention for a reading lesson. Melly, the resistant girl, is driving me crazy once again. "It's not polite to interrupt the teacher," I tell her for the fourth time. Outside in the hallway the clicking of heels tells me my principal Karen is heading to her office. I am eager to meet her there later to grab a cup of coffee after dismissing the class for recess. As Melly and her peers head out the door I fill up my mug. "Melly needs to learn respect," I sigh, beginning the tale of my morning ordeal. "Would you be telling me this story if Melly was a boy?" Karen asks. I am surprised. Despite my feminist and liberationist intentions, I realize that I am putting Melly in a box that sends a message: it's okay for boys to test limits but it's not okay for girls. I need to reevaluate whether I'm conflating respect with compliance. When is speaking out of turn disrespectful and when does it show courage and voice? Am I shutting girls down too soon? Who else might be unwittingly silenced in this community? Am I missing the chance to explore this question with Melly and my students? Can I trust first graders to help me figure this out?

Toni Morrison's book "The Big Box" is a children's book I share with classes now that I'm a university professor. Toni's son, Slade, inspired this book when his teacher told him "you can't handle your freedom." The theme of the book challenges the goal of conformity as a classroom norm. Morrison introduces us to three child characters who do not conform to what adults expect of them. The first, Patty, reminds me of Melly. Patty "made the grown ups nervous" when she talked in the library, sang in class, ran in the hallway, and wouldn't play with dolls. For this reason the grownups "had a meeting one day to try to find a cure" deciding that she needed to abide by the rules because "she just could not handle her freedom" (Morrison, 1999). Of course students need to recognize issues important to the health and safety of the community; the problem is that as students are socialized into school, the pressures for certainty push adults to ignore who students are and how they are making meaning of the world. Conformity rather than intellectual independence becomes the priority for school success.

For me, becoming a teacher researcher was a vehicle for welcoming surprise and learning from it. Teacher researchers teach with an inquiry stance. That means that as educators we learn to question the problems that arise in practice, such as, "What is actually going on when a young girl continually interrupts classroom lessons?" And then we systematically collect evidence across multiple perspectives to better understand the meanings children are making and reshape instruction to both respect and challenge them. I've been lucky as a university professor to work with several research partners, experienced teacher researchers, to investigate questions about student learning in their urban elementary classrooms. One is Mary B. Moran, a third grade teacher in a large urban school district. Mary could be called a "warm demander." Warm demanders are teachers who "communicate both warmth and a non-negotiable demand for student effort and mutual respect" (Bondy & Ross, 2008, p. 54). Mary allows herself to struggle with surprise – and learn from it. She is a teacher who trusts students with freedom but who does not abdicate her responsibility to guide and instruct.

For Mary, an inquiry stance means always paying close attention to what students care about. She then systematically considers how that information links to the curriculum. Her stance celebrates and builds on children's resources rather than pushing them to fit into a standardized or prescriptive curriculum. Mary gets to know her students through instruction that begins with meaningful activity. She argues that rather than starting with "skills first," learning should be purposeful, a "natural extension to go and do something and learn through it." One surprise for Mary was the shift in engagement she found in a student, Joseph, a boy who had been transferred out of a previous school due to behavior problems. In fact, Joseph spent a great deal of time in the principal's office at Mary's school as the year began. However, he slowly found himself interested as Mary and his classmates engaged in one of her third grade community focused projects: creating a raised bed garden on the pavement at their school. So engaged was Joseph that he one day announced a new identity. "Call me Farmer Joe not Joseph," he announced.

While Joseph's reconnection with classroom activities was a positive surprise, Mary was not satisfied. She looked for ways for Joseph to grow not just socially but academically. What was going on with his language and literacy development? Indicative of Joseph's new identity was increased classroom participation. For example, he took on the high level of engagement indicative of all Mary's students, asking questions during a reading lesson where the students examined seed packets before planting. "Why are they called heads of lettuce?" Joseph asked. Mary built on this curiosity, linking it to vocabulary development, writing for different purposes, and examining content-specific language. These were outgrowths of starting with meaning and then building literacy skill in Mary's classroom.

While it is not easy to shift from delivering a scripted program mandated at your school to developing academic learning that respects the meaning making potential of your students, it can be done. The point is that such a stance leads to rigorous academic learning while preserving an ethic of care not always apparent when standardized practices tend to ignore the personal, social, and cultural dimensions of what it means to be human. The ongoing challenge is to remain surprised for as long as you teach…it's a necessary responsibility.

Patricia Paugh

REFERENCES

Bondy, E., & Ross, D. (2008). The teacher as warm demander. *Educational Leadership. 66*(1), 54–58.
Cochran-Smith, M., & Lytle, S. (2009). *Inquiry as stance: Practitioner research for the next generation.* New York: Teachers College Press.
Morrison, T. (1999). *The big box.* New York: Hyperion
Winter, Ariel. (2010). We too were children, Mr. Barrie: Toni Morrison: The Big Box, http://wetoowerechildren.blogspot.com/search/label/Toni%20Morrison

AFFILIATION

Patricia Paugh
Department of Curriculum and Instruction
The University of Massachusetts Boston

JENNIFER D. ADAMS

16. TEACHERS AS DJ'S

Making Music in Unlikely Spaces

Hang the D.J., hang the D.J., hang the D.J., because the music that they
constantly play says nothing to me about my life – *Panic*, The Smiths

Dear Future Educator,

When you enter the teaching profession, you will hear a lot of music played by different
D.J.s of policy, many of them playing tunes that are discordant to our students' ears.

Often this noise of standards and accountability, passed off as music, says nothing
about the lives of students, especially those who have been historically at the margins
of the dominant culture. Many scholars have written about schools as "contested
cultural sites" (Kincheloe, Steinberg & Tippins, 1999) where certain cultures are
legitimatized and reinforced while other cultures are viewed as deficient: "[U]nder
the guise of transmitting a common culture, schools dignify and reinforce a dominant
culture replete with particular ways of knowing and experiencing" (Kincheloe et al.
1999, p. 6). In other words, the D.J. of schools does not play music that is familiar
to the lives of many students; in fact the music that is played is akin to nails being
dragged across a blackboard—uncomfortable and often damaging.

Emancipate yourselves from mental slavery; none but ourselves can free our
minds. – *Redemption Song*, Bob Marley

The words of Jamaican artist and philosopher Bob Marley resonate with
oppression that comes with the often culturally narrow and confining standardized
education. Even Diane Ravitch, once an ardent supporter of standards, testing, and
"accountability" changed her tune, noting that after ten years of the No Child Left
Behind act, "there has been very little change in the gaps between the children of the
rich and children of the poor, between black children and white children, between
Hispanic children and white children" (2011, p. 3). The children who were left behind
remain left behind and the mental slavery of current educational assessment and
standards persists—the music does not move them to higher achievement. However,
you as an educator have the ability to change the music in your classroom to one that
is melodic, familiar, and liberating to your students. Music that encourages students
to sway to their own rhythms while learning the tunes of other cultures that they will
encounter and need to navigate as they find their places in society.

*T. M. Kress and R. Lake (Eds.), We Saved the Best for You: Letters of Hope, Imagination and Wisdom
for 21st Century Educators, 69–74.*
© *2013 Sense Publishers. All rights reserved.*

This emancipation comes when educators use their creativity and professional agency to make changes in their classrooms that will improve the quality of education that our children receive. The standards exist and there will most likely always be some degree of standards to guide instruction, but you need not be constrained by the words written in policy. Rather, expand what is given to you to include content and experiences that are meaningful to the lives of our students. You can play music that celebrates who students are while being reflective of knowledge as it exists and as it is enacted in the real world and connects students to the places they inhabit.

CLASSROOMS THAT CELEBRATE WHO STUDENTS ARE

Our students, no matter the skin they are in, enter the classroom with a wealth of experiences and rhythms that reflect who they are. They carry in their bodies the wisdom of their elders and ancestors and knowledges they gain from their lived experiences in their homes and communities. They also bear facts and concepts that they learn on their own through informal means such as the television and Internet. This is a reflection of their personal interests, the things that inspire a sense of wonder and curiosity in them, and this is also a part of who they are. This is the "the brilliance that students bring with them 'in their blood'" as Lisa Delpit (1995, p. 45) mentions, and it is this brilliance that changes the rhythm of the classroom to one that is more meaningful and relevant.

Teachers can draw on these rhythms and make them central to the classroom culture. Teachers, especially those working in classrooms with broad cultural diversity, have multiple opportunities to learn about and "appreciate the wonders of the cultures represented before them" (Delpit 1995, p. 45). These are opportunities not only to create meaningful learning experiences for students, but also to increase our collective cultural knowledge about how different people learn, to experience the world and the different things that people value or hold sacred. Rather than viewing communities as deficient or lacking, especially those marginalized by race, culture or language, we can use a lens such as that of "community cultural wealth" through which to view the social, linguistic, familial, resistance and other forms of capital (Yosso, 2005) as sources of legitimate and valuable knowledge, both in and out of the classroom. This offers powerful anchoring points on which to build lessons and experiences that blur the borders that artificially separate the classroom from the community (Adams, 2010).

CURRICULA THAT REFLECT KNOWLEDGE IN ACTION

Current standardized curriculum is based on what Santos (2009) calls orthopedic thinking, "the constraint and impoverishment caused by reducing the existential problems to analytical and conceptual markers that are strange to them" (p. 110). This resonates with what dance scholar Yvonne Daniels notes: "[T]he intellectual, compartmentalized-only model of knowledge has deficiencies, which appear in narrow and inflexible perspectives. We can find their consequences ultimately in disruptive social behaviors and debilitating states of self-worth" (2005, p. 57). If we reflect on how we build and enact knowledge on a daily basis, all of the *subjects* are truly integrated. When we shop for groceries, we enact math, social studies, science and other disciplines at once as we meal-plan, budget and actually purchase items. This is very unlike school in which these subjects are presented in artificial silos as if there were no relationships between them. This is neither reflective of how people *live* these subjects, nor responsive to the social, political, and economic realities that students experience, nor in keeping with the decisions that they and their families make on a daily basis. This is like listening to only one musical instrument at a time and never hearing them played together in a band or orchestra.

In addition, schooling often values one way of knowing over another. The very real parallel with music is considering European classical music "high culture" while considering all others folk, primitive, plebian, and so on—all adjectives that subjugate, for example, Miles Davis to Mozart. In other words, knowledge that comes from the community in which it is enacted is neither valued nor recognized in schools: "If we are to free our students' minds and emancipate ourselves we must understand these processes, these organizations and their effects" (Kincheloe et al., 1999, p. 7).

Recognizing this consciousness construction (Kincheloe et al., 1999) is the first step. It requires reading the works of critical pedagogues and actively reflecting on the societal structures one encounters both in and out of schools. It also requires teachers to engage in self-reflection and on-going practitioner research to learn about themselves as teachers, their students and how to engage student learning in ways that a) make them aware of this consciousness construction, b) legitimate their embodied ways of knowing and c) value difference, as "the power of difference expands each person's conceptual horizon and socio-psychological and cultural understanding" (Kincheloe et al. 1999, p. xxi). We want to have classrooms in which students not only move to their own rhythms, but also learn to hear and appreciate other rhythms, perhaps becoming fluent in a second or even third form of music!

LESSONS THAT CONNECT STUDENTS TO PLACE

Students learn to sway to rhythms in the places that they inhabit and experience on a daily basis. These are the communities in which they live, the places where they socialize, and the places that they create within spaces of schools and communities that reflect their emerging identities as members of particular cultural groups (ethnic, youth, interest-related, and so on). Places and experiences with places are mediated by culture, schooling and personal experiences—"places produce and teach particular ways of thinking about and being in the world" (Gruenewald, 2003b, p. 10). We need to consider place in education so that teaching and learning has a direct influence on the well-being of the places that people inhabit in an ecological, social, and economical sense (Gruenewald, 2003).

We should not think about school in opposition to the community or vice versa. But rather schools should provide students and teachers the space to reflect on their relationship with places, including the social, historical, and political forces that produce places. Also, schools should provide the tools to redefine places in ways that improve the quality of life of communities. In addition, we should reimagine the borders between school and the community as porous, allowing a free-flow of culture between the two.

We can also begin to see the places where we teach as resource-rich. While teaching in the urban setting is often portrayed as being oppressive and laden with violence and failing schools, there is the positive flip-side: access to rich lived experiences with diverse cultures and places, access to a rich range of cultural resources (museums, zoos, parks, and so on, many of them offering free and or reduced admissions for school groups), and the ability to obtain a certain common sense or "street smarts" that can only come from being raised and educated in such an environment.

Teaching and learning is a creative profession. It is one that encourages life-long learning and expansive thinking and provides ample opportunities to positively influence the lives of children and our communities. While we are often questioning ourselves about the lives and identities of our students, no matter what skin we are in, it is important to turn the lens of cultural inquiry onto ourselves and ask critical questions, including: Who am I in relation to my students? What might my culture represent to them? What are the things that my culture values and/or holds sacred that may be similar to and/or different from that of my students? How do I reconcile the differences so that I maintain an equitable learning environment for my students and myself?

In other words, we must ask: How can I be a D.J. that keeps the music in my classroom interesting, meaningful and relevant? How can I encourage my students to be proud of their own music while being open to hearing the music of many others?

Jennifer Adams

REFERENCES

Adams, J. (2010). On hundred ways to use a coconut. In D. Tippins. M. Mueller, M. van Eijick, & J. Adams (Eds.), *Cultural studies and environmentalism: The confluence of eco-justice, indigenous knowledge systems and sense of place* (pp. 331-335). Netherlands: Springer Press.

Daniel, Y. (2005). *Dancing wisdom: Embodied knowledge in Haitian Vodou, Cuban Yoruba, and Bahian Candomblé.* Chicago, IL: University of Illinois Press.

Delpit, L. (1995). I just want to be myself: Discovering what students bring to school "in their blood." In W. Ayers (Ed.), *To become a teacher: Making a difference in children's lives.* (pp. 34-48). New York: Teachers College Press.

Gruenewald, D. (2003). The Best of both worlds: A critical pedagogy of place. *Educational Researcher, 32*(3), 3–12.

Grunewald, D. (2003). Foundations of place: A multidisciplinary framework for place-conscious education. *American Educational Research Journal, 40*(3): 619–654.

Kincheloe, J., Steinberg, S. & Tippins, D. (1999). *The stigma of genius: Einstein, consciousness and education.* New York: Peter Lang.

Ravich, D. (2011). Whose children have been left behind? National Opportunity to Learn Summit. Conference address given on December, 9, 2011.Washington D.C.

Santos, B.S. (2009). A Non-occidentalist west?: Learned ignorance and ecology of knowledge. *Theory Culture Society, 26*(7–8), 103–125.

Yosso, T. (2005). Whose culture has capital? A critical race theory discussion of community cultural wealth. *Race Ethnicity and Education, 8*(1), 69–91.

AFFILIATION

Jennifer D. Adams
School of Education
Brooklyn College

JULIE MAUDLIN

17. TOWARD A NEW AUDACITY OF IMAGINATION

To the educators of the 21st century:

As I consider what insight I might impart to your generation I am left to question, as you may well wonder, whether my words have any relevance for this new era. The nation in which my ideas emerged was different from the one you now inhabit, and the vast and enduring changes spanning my lifetime from 1859 to 1952 are unmatched by the profound scientific and technological advances of your information age. Not only am I unfamiliar with the particular circumstances of your daily lives, I myself have claimed that ideas and philosophies are meaningful only when "applied to some particular society existing at a definite time and place" (LW 8, 44)[1]. Therefore, it is you who bears the responsibility to invent the ideas that will inform this moment in public education. Furthermore, I have warned of the need to avoid trapping one's self with outdated theories or plastering on general ideas to existing practices to "provide a new vocabulary for old practices and a new means for justifying them" (p. 44). And yet, when I consider how little has changed in the way of American public education, both its ideals and its methods, I am struck by the similarities between the institutional context in which you are situated and the one I sought to reform.

Let us "begin with the situation in which education now finds itself, with the predicament of the schools affecting students and teachers alike" (LW 9, 128). Those of you reading this letter know well the features that define the current crisis. They are, to a large extent, the same elements I acknowledged in the midst of the Great Depression, primarily "reduced appropriations at the time when the schools have increased responsibilities put upon them by increased number of pupils and other factors due to the economic collapse" (LW 9, 129). Furthermore, these elements include now, as then, "reduced school years, enlarged classes, failure to build and equip to keep up with increase in population and obsolescence of old equipment; the closing of kindergartens; elimination of manual training, art work, music, physical training, domestic arts" (p. 129). It is clear that once again, "the public schools are under attack," and, just as in my time:

> The foundation heads of the attack everywhere are large taxpayers and the institutions which represent the wealthier and privileged elements in the community. Those who make the least use of public schools, who are the least dependent upon them because of superior economic status, who give their

T. M. Kress and R. Lake (Eds.), We Saved the Best for You: Letters of Hope, Imagination and Wisdom for 21st Century Educators, 75–80.
© *2013 Sense Publishers. All rights reserved.*

children at home by means of private teachers the same things which they denounce as extravagances when supplied in less measure to the children of the masses in schools, these are the ones most active in the attack upon the schools. (LW 9, p. 129–130)

This situation reveals the extent to which the general state of society and the condition of schools are related. The causes of your society's problems, of your nation's inability to meet its own economic needs, do not lie solely within the schools. I say now, as before, "Whatever will remove or mitigate the forces which brought about the collapse of industry, the terrible insecurity of millions of our people, the breakdown in government due to the decrease in revenues, will have the same beneficial effect on education" (p. 130). In order to address the inadequacies of our schools, we must look closely at the shortcomings of our society.

In light of the close connection between the economic arrangements that persist in your society and the crisis in education, consider the nature of learning in schools today. It is my understanding that, generally speaking, a preoccupation with measurement has initiated the mandated use of content tests, which reduce the curriculum to a series of discrete facts to be mastered over the course of one's education. As a result, you continue to teach subjects as information not in connection with things that are done, need to be done, and how to do them. And yet, the curriculum was already overburdened with knowledge in my time, when I argued at length that students in public schools ought to be learning to "understand the social forces that are at work, the directions and the cross-directions in which they are moving, the consequences that they are producing, the consequences that they might produce if they were understood and managed with intelligence" (LW 11, p. 183). Note my use of the word "understanding" as opposed to "knowledge." Your curriculum emphasizes not the contextualized understanding of which I wrote, but information, "knowledge about things, and there is no guarantee in any amount of 'knowledge about things' that understanding – the spring of intelligent action – will follow from it" (p. 183).

Herein lies a problem of your day and generation – that, concerning public education, our society has long recognized a need for change, and yet we have failed to develop among ourselves the kind of understanding that is rooted in action. But progress requires intelligent action; it is not inevitable. It is up to us "as individuals to bring it about. Change is going to occur anyway, and the problem is the control of change in a given direction" (LW 14, p. 113). If you expect to see any substantial progress in American public education, you cannot continue to repackage old practices under the guise of accountability. You must seek a shift toward understanding that moves the heart and mind to action. This is the challenge of democracy. Democracy "signifies something to be done" through "the constant meeting and solving of problems" rather than signifying "something already given, something ready-made" (LW 7, p. 350). It is not the government machine, but you as individuals who bear the responsibility to act through intelligent action based on your understanding of the time and place in which you are situated.

The institution of public education, as it stands today, is not only failing to impart agency, but lacks the capacity to strive toward the democratic ideal, "that each individual shall have the opportunity for release, expression, fulfillment, of his distinctive capacities, and that the outcome shall further the establishment of a fund of shared values" (LW 7, p. 350). Perhaps you question whether embracing the vast diversity of humanity can contribute to a sense of solidarity, but it is my belief that there is no intrinsic incongruity "between individual human beings integrated in themselves and a community life marked by diversity of voluntary groups representing different interests" (LW 14, p. 40). The discord that arises from difference is not fixed; it "is always changing its constituents so that the problems it sets have forever to be solved anew in construction of new forms of social relationships" (p. 41). It is the process of ongoing reconstruction – the constant meeting and solving of problems – that keeps democracy alive, and it is the responsibility of schools to encourage it.

The variability of human capacities and relationships lies at the heart of the social forces we should be equipped to understand, and therein lies the challenge for schools in a democracy. As I have written at length:

> Just as democracy in order to live must move and move forward, so schools in a democracy cannot stand still, cannot be satisfied and complacent with what has been accomplished, but must be willing to undertake whatever reorganization of studies, of methods of teaching, of administration, including that larger organization which concerns the relation of pupils and teachers to each other, and to the life of the community. Failing in this, the schools cannot give democracy the intelligent direction of its forces which it needs to continue in existence. (LW 11, p. 183)

If you wish to keep democracy alive in your society, the schools in your society must reflect such an intention. However, by privileging a passive knowledge of things, schools in their current state are more likely working against that aim.

This contradiction begs the question of whether the continuation of democracy, in fact, remains a primary concern. If so, of what purpose is a system that prizes knowledge over the capacity of a person to act in their world? That is not to say that the desire to evaluate the extent to which education is meeting its intended goals is itself incompatible with democracy. The contradiction lies between the aims of public education and that which is being measured. If the goal of schools is to produce citizens capable of understanding the social forces at work in your society, then it would stand to reason that you would seek to measure the extent to which your educational institutions are doing just that. This kind of measurement, however, requires not only a willingness to continually reorganize the institution to meet the needs of a changing society, but also necessitates a longitudinal commitment to observation and analysis that does not result in the simplistic data your policymakers have come to expect.

Yet, the circumstances of your time have not convinced me that my faith in democracy was mistaken. On the contrary, I suspect that you, in particular, still cherish the democratic ideal, but feel powerless to advance it. After all, you yourselves have had little, if any, part in the decisions that have reduced you to technicians of discrete knowledge. Perhaps these circumstances have led you to grow weary "of the responsibilities, the duties, the burden that the acceptance of political liberty involves" (LW 13, 294). But the responsibility for the mandates that have exhausted you does not rest solely in the hands of bureaucracy. This is an egregious fallacy, one that we must acknowledge. "There is no greater sign of the paralysis of the imagination which custom and involvement in immediate detail can induce than the belief, sedulously propagated by some who pride themselves on superior taste, that the machine is itself the source of our troubles" (LW 5, p. 87). The failings of the institution of education cannot be blamed for the shortcomings of our nation, or vice versa, and neither can be considered in isolation of the social forces at work in your society. "We are part of the causes which bring them about in what we have done and have refrained from doing" (LW 9, p. 131). You must recognize your own responsibility, and find courage in the "belief that the specific conditions which exist at one moment, be they comparatively bad or comparatively good, in any event may be bettered" (MW 12: p. 181–82). It is this melioristic spirit that brings hope that reform is possible through human effort.

Change, as I have already noted, will happen whether or not you, collectively or as individuals, take part. Transforming the inevitable into meaningful reform not only compels us to "fasten attention upon our own problems" (LW 14, p. 75) through intelligent action, but requires a leap of faith toward what might be accomplished. "All endeavor for the better is moved by faith in what is possible, not by adherence to the actual" (LW 9, p. 17). We must possess the ability to imagine what might be, and to act to upon it. As James Campbell (1995) has so aptly noted, "It is this faith that makes it possible for us to act in the face of uncertainty, to live in an evolving world bereft of guarantees. In this kind of world we need an experimental philosophy, one which can guide us as we move onward into the unknown" (p. 261–262). Yet, such uncertainty discomforts us. We remain wary of action without guarantee. But faith in the possible demands that we renounce "the traditional notion that action is inherently inferior to knowledge" and embrace the belief that "security attained by active control is to be more prized than certainty in theory" (LW 4, p. 29–30).

Consider the nature of scientific discovery. "It is not too much to say that science, through its applications in invention and technologies, is the greatest force in modern society for producing social changes and shaping human relations. It is no exaggeration to say that it has revolutionized the conditions" of our daily lives (LW 11, p. 186). And yet, these changes could not have occurred in the absence of faith in what was possible. "Every great advance in science has issued from a new audacity of imagination. What are now working conceptions, employed as a matter of course because they have withstood the tests of experiment and have emerged triumphant, were once speculative hypotheses" (LW 4, p. 247). The world as you now know it has been transformed by these hypotheses, which are as imperative for innovation not only in science, but in education, and in life:

They open new points of view; they liberate us from the bondage of habit which is always closing in on us, restricting our vision both of what is and of what the actual may become. They direct operations that reveal new truths and new possibilities. They enable us to escape from the pressure of immediate circumstance and provincial boundaries. Knowledge falters when imagination clips its wings or fears to use them. (LW 4, p. 247)

By imagining and experimenting with possibility, individuals can produce positive change and shift the direction of public education toward the democratic ideal. For the realm of imagination lies beyond the literary: "As it is used in connection with the psychology of the learner and there treated as fundamental, it signifies an expansion of existing experience by means of appropriation of meanings and values not physically or sensibly present" (LW 11, p. 210).

This is not to say that progress can be achieved through random acts of experimentation. "Experimental method is not just messing around nor doing a little of this and a little of that in the hope that things will improve" (LW 11, p. 292–93). Rather, "hypotheses are fruitful when they are suggested by actual need, are bulwarked by knowledge already attained, and are tested by the consequences of the operations they evoke goes without saying. Otherwise imagination is dissipated into fantasies and rises vaporously into the clouds" (LW 4, p. 248). In order to produce intelligent action, imagination must be coupled with reflection and situated within particular circumstances. And, producing the conditions in which students can move beyond adherence to habit and bygone tradition to imagine new possibilities requires not simply knowledge of the actual, but understanding.

Creating such conditions requires you as educators to develop a deeper understanding of the responsibility you bear in bringing about change, or in your failure to do so. You must understand that the work of reform is never finished. While democracy can be undermined and contradicted by your own actions, it cannot be fully attained because it is contingent; it must continually be reexamined in the context of your particular circumstances. It is something we must work toward, it is "an ideal in the only intelligible sense of an ideal: namely, the tendency and movement of some thing which exists carried to its final limit, viewed as completed, perfected" (LW 2, p. 328). With each new age, as scientific and technological advancements reshape social relations and human realities, we must reconsider the purposes of our institutions. "Any present always offers itself as a transition, a passage, or becoming" (LW 5, p. 363). Consider this not a Sisyphean task but an opportunity to renew and reimagine our commitments. We are always beginning in this particular moment, keeping our eyes on the long-term future of humankind.

Once we have recognized the infinite nature of our responsibilities, we begin to act on that understanding by taking ownership for the circumstances of the present. We must accept social problems as "something of our own; that they, and not simply the consequences, are ours; that we are part of the causes which bring them about in what we have done and have refrained from doing, and that we have a necessary share in finding their solution" (LW 9, p. 131). This share is not a burden of blame, but a springboard for action, an opportunity to declare your agency and assert yourselves "more directly about educational affairs and about the organization and conduct of the schools" in your own communities (p. 134). You must strive for "a greater amount of teacher responsibility in administration, and outside in relation to the public and the community" (p. 134), in order to stake your rightful claim in educational reform. "The present dictation of policies for the schools by bankers and other outside pecuniary groups is more than harmful to the cause of education. It is also a pathetic and tragic commentary on the lack of possession of social power by the teaching profession" (p. 134). It is your responsibility and your right, as educators, to claim that social power with your own activities and functions.

Your profession will not be transformed "on paper nor by means of plans on paper however perfect in theoretical principle. The problem is more than one of adjusting certain impersonal functions, like production and consumption" (p. 134). Reform results from action; it must be done by people. It is up to you to reflect on the conditions of your time, to consider what is known and what is needed, and to act on your faith in what might be. The work starts at home. A new audacity of imagination begins with you.

Julie Maudlin

NOTE

[1]   In this essay, I will be quoting passages from Dewey's writings from the Critical Edition of his works edited by Jo Ann Boydston, abbreviated as follows: MW = *TheMiddle Works, 1899–1924*, fifteen volumes; LW = *The Later Works, 1925–1953*, seventeen volumes.

REFERENCES

Campbell, J. (1995). Understanding John Dewey: *Nature and cooperative intelligence*. Chicago: Open Court Publishing.
Dewey, J. *The middle works of John Dewey*, 1899–1924. Edited by Jo Ann Boydston. 15 vols. Carbondale: Southern Illinois University Press, 1976–1983.
Dewey, J. *The later works of John Dewey*, 1925–1953. Edited by Jo Ann Boydston. 17 vols. Carbondale, Southern Illinois University Press, 1981–1990.

AFFILIATION

Julie Maudlin
Department of Teaching and Learning
Georgia Southern University

RICK AYERS

18. LETTER TO A YOUNG TEACHER

Reframing Teaching in No-Respect Times

So my nephew Malik, a fabulous Renaissance man, a six-year sixth grade math, science, and Spanish teacher, and basketball and baseball coach, was given a pink slip. Again. It's a March ritual around here. School districts are dealing with slashed budgets and are not certain of enrollment. In response they send out a flurry of layoff notices. I'm pretty sure Malik will be hired back. He's got some time in, he's a beloved teacher, and he is extremely successful teaching students in his working class and low-resourced middle school. But the whole thing is infuriating. I texted him to say I hoped he was doing OK. He texted back to tell me that he would never advise a friend to go into this profession. I was so sad to think about this response, the kind of feeling that so many teachers get at this time of year.

I tried to send him back some words of encouragement. I'm a teacher educator, after all, and it's my calling to encourage people to become teachers and help them to be successful. I wrote him something about the fact that the pink slip is an insult, only that, and he would certainly still have a job. But as I thought about it, I realized the slip was one insult piled on top of the many others that are being offered to teachers. While there is a small problem of some bad and ineffective teachers hanging on to their jobs (as there is with bad, ineffective, lazy lawyers, doctors, nurses, architects, bankers, cops, financial analysts, cooks, firefighters and farmers) there is a huge bleeding gash in the system – the 40 percent of new teachers, mostly excellent teachers, who quit in the first three years. They are discouraged, demoralized, scorned, and ridiculed by the media, politicians, and their bosses.

But I want you all to hang in there. So here is my attempt to pull together my thoughts. It is my "letter to a young teacher."

Dear Malik,

We are, sadly, living in the year of hating teachers. Whether it's Wisconsin Governor Scott Walker rewarding of the super-rich while complaining about the high compensation of teachers, or Obama's education secretary Arne Duncan applauding the mass firing of teachers and endorsing the teacher-bashing rhetoric of the Right, we're having it hard these days. After decades of "devolution" of federal funding and escalating military budgets, state governments are de-funding education. Policy

T. M. Kress and R. Lake (Eds.), We Saved the Best for You: Letters of Hope, Imagination and Wisdom for 21st Century Educators, 81–84.
© 2013 Sense Publishers. All rights reserved.

wonks fantasize about making schools in the U.S. that look like those in Singapore – with compliant students who study desperately to make the grade – and the President talks about education designed to compete with China and India – as if that were the purpose of education in a democracy. The national discussion of education, driven by right-wing media and think tanks, suggests that teacher education, teachers, teacher unions, and just about everything else about schools is worth trashing. Professor William Watkins may be right – these people may really have in mind closing down public education altogether.

On the teacher profession side we find plenty of despair. Teaching, like the other caring professions, has been regarded as women's work and therefore worthy of less respect and pay. And now teachers are being forced more and more into mindless scripted curricula, which amount to low-intelligence test-prep exercises. Teacher education programs are cutting back their offerings and fewer people, particularly with math and science degrees, are willing to go into teaching. Getting that March pink slip is just another turn in the barrage of insults teachers suffer.

As I was thinking about this, and how to respond to you, something dawned on me. I think we pretty much should stop waiting for respect. It's not going to come, not for a long, long time. We know we are creative, growing professionals who are engaged in one of the world's most demanding jobs and we know we should be honored for our work with children and adolescents. But perhaps we should simply stop thinking along the lines of that framework of professionals who should be respected.

Here are a few other ways we might frame our job:

First, the miracles. We teachers fight for success in the classroom every day and many days we fail – like health professionals, it's part of the job and we try to learn from the losses. But sometimes we work our magic and it comes out right. That's when we want to leap up and give a fellow teacher or a student a high five. Yes, we get both emotions, 20 times a day. We have the honor of being with these students more than any other adults – laughing and crying, seeing transformations before our eyes. And we usually find ourselves in a wonderful community of teachers – intense, funny, brilliant, and deeply ethical colleagues who help us through.

I remember when I first went into teaching. I had been a restaurant cook for 10 years and I knew the slog of production: bring in raw materials, work on them, push product out the door, charge money, get a little pay. Mostly it was hard, physical work. I remember how amazed I was when I first started teaching: I could get paid for reading, writing, talking, and listening? What a delight. And it was the most intellectually and ethically challenging job I could imagine – on the level of course content (we are always scavenging, studying, borrowing, innovating, learning more) and even more so on the level of human interaction (constantly studying the kids, doing close observation, trying to figure out how to be successful at inspiring, encouraging and challenging them). We get joy, real joy and satisfaction, from our students. Yes, that's the secret delight of this profession, working with inspiring colleagues, knowing these kids and being with them through the small and large changes in their lives, knowing their families and the heroic struggles of the communities they come from. We have the coolest job ever – we are privileged to be working with young people every day.

Secondly, as that T-shirt says, "Be an activist, be a teacher." We might head off to work with more joy and positive feeling if we think of ourselves as organizers. Teaching, after all, is not only community service, it is a project of social change. We don't go to work to blithely reproduce the inequities that exist in our society. We want students to learn, not just the ropes of the game and the gatekeepers, but their own power, their own capacity. We want them to have the creativity and imagination to know that another world is possible; we want them to have the skills to make it so. If you were organizing Mississippi sharecroppers in the '60s or Flint auto workers in the '30s, you would not be waiting for someone in power to say you're great. You would expect to be insulted and vilified. You do the work because you know it's right. We teachers do this job because we are change agents. A lot of people jaw about social change and activism but teachers do the work every day. Like an organizer, you are fighting for broader goals, ones tied to the doors you open for this student, the progress you make on that project.

We go back to work again and again for those goals, not for the ones defined by those who are selling off the public domain and the promise of equality, justice and the common future, the policy wonks who seem to be in charge today. My hero and heroine teachers are not the savior types you see in the movies. They are people like Septima Clark teaching in rural South Carolina, Paulo Freire organizing in the mountains of Brazil, Father Lorenzo Milani transforming peasant kids in Tuscany, Sylvia Ashton-Warner empowering Maori children in New Zealand, and so many others. They got no respect. They changed the world. Like organizers, we learn the hard lessons of social change – it never comes when we are patronizing and hand out charity; it only succeeds when we respect the people we teach and act in solidarity with them. And, like organizers, we are energized by the knowledge that we just might win together, by the knowledge that we do win small victories every day.

Thirdly... there is no thirdly. Just those two. The joy of working with kids. The commitment to organizing and social justice. The pay is bad but, really, not that bad. One can have a decent, if modest, living doing this. And we may be scorned by idiots but we are revered by parents, communities, and students. All in all, not such a bad gig. Of course I'm pretty sure you're going to stick with it, Malik. And I hope you encourage other friends to join our ranks. We need them!

Affectionately,
Tio Rick

AFFILIATION

Rick Ayers
School of Education
University of San Francisco

WILLIAM H. SCHUBERT

19. LOOK DEEPLY WITHIN AND SHARE

Dear Teacher of the 21st Century:

It is a pleasure to write to you, for you have committed already to a most noble calling. I feel as if I am sending a message to the future. It is a pleasure as well, insofar as I have just retired from 44 years of teaching – first in elementary and junior high schools for eight years and then in higher education for 36 years – urban, rural, college town, and suburban. It would seem that I would have something to draw from my experience that is worth saying, and my first compulsion upon being invited to contribute to this volume was to do just that. I doubtless will include a bit of professing; however, doing too much would counter what I want to profess.

There is a wise Zen saying: "The brilliant gem is in your hand." This aphorism doubtless has both Buddhist and Hindu roots. The Judeo-Christian counterpart could be translated as "The kingdom of God is within you." By "kingdom of God" I mean wisdom. The Confucian variation recently taught to me by Ming Fang He (In Press) holds that only through self-cultivation can one move successively to cultivate (educate) family, community, nation, and humanity. Insofar as the call of teaching is a call to cultivate humanity, this continuously expanding process must reveal the wisdom in everyone who desires to teach. To be told how to teach is an oxymoron. We are taught as we learn and grow. Of course, as John Dewey would say, we never fully grow – rather we are always in the making, always becoming. Maxine Greene's oft noted position, "I am not yet," says it another way.

My point to you is this: You have within you the wherewithal to teach, and that wherewithal embodies hope, wisdom, and imagination. You want to teach because behind the grotesque world of greed and power machinations, you see a spark of light within each person. You want to ignite that spark into a fire of compassion and a quest to know, even though we must realize with Socrates that we can know nothing in fullness. Nonetheless, we can reach increasingly higher levels of not knowing. I urge you to strive for this.

After I taught in several different elementary school settings, I decided to pursue doctoral study to become a teacher educator and curriculum theorist. So, I asked myself what I could offer other teachers based on my experience. I pondered considerably and finally concluded that imagination and philosophy were my two best tools. I do not use the term "tools" in the traditional mechanistic sense; rather, I consider these two dimensions of my life to be my best resources – except

T. M. Kress and R. Lake (Eds.), We Saved the Best for You: Letters of Hope, Imagination and Wisdom for 21st Century Educators, 85–88.
© 2013 Sense Publishers. All rights reserved.

perhaps for love which must infuse both if education is to serve justice (Schubert, 2009b). Moreover, they are augmented and honed by what I have long considered my personal "in-service" study. Usually, teachers have several "in-service" (the old term; I am old) or professional development activities (I don't care for the term "professional" since it conjures elements of fakery). Too often such events are "how-to" dog and pony shows that do little to influence the deep structure of one's capacity to teach. My real in-service derived from studying philosophy and literature, visiting art galleries, attending concerts, participating in political causes, and engaging in myriad conversations with respected friends and relatives from diverse walks of life. Such studies augmented my philosophical and imaginative capacity to engage with children and create journeys into the deeper caverns of what is worthwhile.

Let me say it again: never expect to find ultimate answers about what is worthwhile. Matters of what is worth needing, knowing, experiencing, doing, being, becoming, overcoming, sharing, contributing, and just plain wondering about are never finalized; nevertheless, one of the supreme joys of life is to explore their vicissitudes, as elsewhere I have elaborated the question of worth as the central curricular question (Schubert, 2009a). As we increasingly realize that the greatest thinkers in every field frequently express the inconclusivity of knowledge, it becomes difficult to tolerate the unwarranted certainty of educational policy makers who specify knowledge as discrete bits of information to be consumed by students in schools. The objective tests they make you use to provide the facade of achievement are based upon multiple layers of subjective decision about what should be tested and how it should be asked. Don't be afraid to ask: What knowledge? Whose knowledge? Who benefits from its acquisition? How do you know that the test tests something of worth?

As you ask such heretical questions you must be prudent about deciding where to ask them and with whom. Sometimes you must ignore the pundits and give what they want so that you can continue meaningful dialogue with students. The younger students, particularly, usually will understand more readily than the policy makers and implementers. The latter are too often debilitated from bowing down so that they can no longer give a straight answer. In the midst of battering you will receive from such sources, try not to lose heart. Know that children know the power of pretending, and they see through the disingenuous pretending of others. When they follow their curiosity, go with them. Do not see their pursuits as needing correction. Try to have faith that their interests symbolize the deepest and most profound of human interests (birth, death, love, tradition, justice, goodness, beauty, integrity, courage, and more). Learn to relate to their modes of expression and to empathize with and respond to the oppression that befalls them and the concomitant hurt that can feed their despair. When you do this, I urge you to try to overcome stereotypes of the teacher by suspending commitment to cover topics irrelevant to students' lives and by extinguishing the propensity to focus on deficits, to belittle, and to correct. Instead, uncover, discover, and recover the curriculum together with students, and build on their capacities and strengths with encouragement and a willingness to learn with them. Doing so, you will move into the rare realm that Martin Heidegger calls the most difficult task for teachers – "to let learn" (Heidegger, 1968). If you come this far, be prepared to learn a great deal from your students.

Enough preaching; let's return to the brilliant gem that is in your hand – how to teach with hope, wisdom, and imagination. Look inside. Reconstruct your own experience. Let me suggest some ways to find that gem.

1. Reflect on a teacher who deeply reached you. You might select one from your own pre-school, elementary, middle school, high school, undergraduate, or graduate experience. Or you might select one from as many of these as you like. Tell a story about how they reached you and what it meant to be reached in the way you are considering it. Analyze the story for messages about what good teaching is. What enabled the teacher to reach you? What environment, methods, modes of relationship? Could you reach students in similar ways?

2. Reflect similarly on teachers outside of regular school settings, and ask the same sub-questions. Such teachers might be parents, other family members, employers, coaches, teachers of the arts (acting, music, art, dance), ministers or other church leaders, leaders of clubs and organizations. How did they reach you and add meaning and worth to your life? This, too, is part of the brilliant gem of knowledge about teaching that you hold within.

3. Ponder a book, play, poem, song, film, or other work of art that moved you greatly or even perhaps modified the principles by which you live. How was the author or artist a teacher, and how was the work a curriculum? This raises important questions about the need to know students. How does an author or artist reach you without even knowing you? We too seldom consider such authors and works as teachers and curricula, though they surely are – perhaps more powerfully so than those who pose directly as teachers. How might you use works of art, literature, film, and music as central pedagogical dimensions of your work as a teacher? How might you emulate ways in which artists and authors have reached you as you reach students?

4. Imagine a quality that you wish everyone in the world could have. Might it be kindness, empathy, honesty, curiosity, peacefulness, imagination, courage, or one of a multitude of other characteristics? What could you do to help others (e.g., students) embody that quality in their lives? What experiences would you design for them? What resources (books, video, art, science, other) would you share with them? In what kind of environment, with what kind of relationships, with what kind of persons? How would you know if they embodied the quality and how could you understand the consequences of their living it?

These are merely a sample of ways (see Schubert, 1986) to probe your own resources about what it means to be a wise, hopeful, and imaginative teacher. I encourage you to explore them more fully, and to share with others who do the same. The crescendo that could be reached from such study and reflection is the essence of what I have called teacher lore (Schubert & Ayers, 2000). It can be the mainstay of your continuously evolving project of self-cultivation as a teacher. Onward!

Sincerely,
William H. Schubert

REFERENCES

Dewey, J. (1916). *Democracy and education*. New York: Macmillan.

Greene, M. (1999). *Exclusions and awakenings: The life of Maxine Greene* [documentary]. USA: Hancock Productions. (Available from: Hancock Productions, 505 West End Avenue, New York, NY 10024).

He, M. F. (In Press). East~West epistemological convergence of humanism in language, identity, and education: Confucius – Makiguchi – Dewey. *Journal of Language, Identity and Education*.

Schubert, W. H. (1986). *Curriculum: Perspective, paradigm, and possibility*. New York: Macmillan. (special reference to the Recommendations for Reflection sections at the end of each chapter)

Schubert, W. H. (2009a). What is worthwhile: From knowing and needing to being and sharing? *Journal of Curriculum and Pedagogy, 6*(2), 21–39.

Schubert, W. H. (2009b). *Love, justice, and education: John Dewey and the utopians*. Greenwich, CT: Information Age Publishing.

Schubert, W. H. and Ayers, W. (Eds.). (1999). *Teacher lore: Learning from our own experience*. Troy, NY: Educators International Press. (Classics in Education reprint of the 1992 edition by Longman).

AFFILIATION

William Schubert
Professor Emerita
College of Education
University of Illinois at Chicago

PART III

LETTERS OF WISDOM

SONIA NIETO

20. THE WAY IT WAS, THE WAY IT IS

Challenging Romanticized Notions of the Life of Teaching

Dear Teacher,

It wasn't always like this, you know.

There was a time when becoming a teacher was more hopeful, more noble, and more rewarding than it is now. There was a time when teachers were respected as professionals, when they were not forced to slavishly follow the senseless mandates of politicians and policymakers who knew nothing about education. There was a time when teachers had some autonomy in what, when, and how they taught. There was a time when Kindergarten was for playing and exploring, and when school was less stressful for both teachers and students – at least, for some of them.

Now, mind you, I am not one of those people whose memories have clouded over with time, who remember only the idealized classrooms of their childhood, who fondly recall their caring and engaging teachers, and who felt completely at home in school. No, I'm not one of those because I did not have those idealized experiences.

First of all, school as play was never an option for me because I didn't attend kindergarten. The strain of going up and down the five flights of stairs of our tenement building to take my sister to first grade, while packing me and my three-year old brother up for the three-block walk, and later in the day take me to school for a half day along with my brother, and later still, at 3 pm to pick up my sister with my brother and me in tow – this all would have been too much for my mother. So I missed Kindergarten and instead, I stayed home, a 5-year old minding a 3-year old while my mother dropped off and picked up my sister at school.

My sister Lydia, a year older than me, did go to kindergarten, but rather than idyllic memories, all she remembers is that she didn't speak English and she was afraid. There was no grassy playground but only a concrete yard, no beautiful building but only a century-old dilapidated structure. Lydia also didn't participate in making the fun projects the other children made because she didn't know how to ask our mother for a milk carton or popsicle sticks or the other materials the children were asked to bring to school for art projects.

When I got to school a year later for first grade, I didn't have warm, cuddly teachers welcoming me with open arms. Like my sister, I remember not speaking English and being afraid. I skinned my knees many times on that concrete yard when

T. M. Kress and R. Lake (Eds.), We Saved the Best for You: Letters of Hope, Imagination and Wisdom for 21st Century Educators, 91–94.
© 2013 Sense Publishers. All rights reserved.

we went out for recess. As I picked up English that year, I learned to feel ashamed of speaking Spanish and of my Puerto Ricanness. I remember being asked to not speak Spanish, to sit in straight rows with hands folded, to raise my hand to speak, and to be quiet and obedient. In junior high, I learned to be afraid because of the tough neighborhood we lived in: afraid of walking home, afraid of being in the deserted school halls and stairways, afraid of being on the playground, afraid of being the good student I was because other kids would pick on me. In my final year of junior high and later in high school, after we moved to a more middle-class neighborhood, as one of only three Puerto Ricans in a very demanding and competitive school, I remember feeling alienated and alone.

At the same time, and in spite of my feelings of marginalization and fear, I loved school. I loved learning to read, and I loved – of all things – finishing workbooks; I loved some of my teachers, and I loved learning. In elementary school, I loved art projects and I loved spelling tests. I loved that one of my teachers taught me how to jump rope and another helped me to love science. I loved when teachers told my mother what a smart girl I was. In junior high and high school, I loved French and English and history, and I even learned to love geometry. I was, in fact, often riveted by learning.

All of which means that, for me, school was full of contradictions. It was neither the pleasant and fulfilling experience that others recall, nor was it a wholly negative experience. Public education, then and now, was more complicated than we might choose to remember. I don't understand people who wax poetic about "the way it was." The way it was, was certainly worse for some than the way it was for others. I refuse to idealize or romanticize it, as some people do. Perhaps this is because, except for a year in junior high and later in high school, I lived in poor neighborhoods and attended poverty-stricken schools where we did not have the expansive and green playgrounds that we saw in our *Dick and Jane* books, where our bookshelves were sparsely filled, and where there was little or no communication between home and school. I did not know then, although I certainly learned when I was a teacher myself, that some schools had many more resources, as well as teachers who wanted to be there. That was not the case in some of the schools I attended. Even worse, until I went to high school, many of my teachers had low expectations of me and my peers, most of whom were Puerto Rican and African American. The majority of my peers didn't make it through high school, and many did not even make it past junior high. Little surprise, then, that I do not long for "the way things were."

"The way things were" was not always a good thing. When I first went to school in 1950, Black and White students in the South were prohibited from studying in the same school; in the North, although we had no such prohibition, segregation based on race, ethnicity, and social class existed. Nowadays it is illegal to segregate students who live in the same neighborhood, but our public schools are nevertheless more segregated than ever because of White flight and the proliferation of private schools that attract many of the White students who live in urban areas. In spite of the Civil Rights Movement, in spite of *Brown v Board of Education*, and in spite of hard-fought demands for integrated education, multicultural and bilingual education, gender-fair education, equal rights for students with disabilities, and other such reforms, our schools are still remarkably unequal.

When I went to school, most of my teachers knew precious little about me or my community. There was never a mention of people other those who were White and middle-class in the books we read, and everyone seemed to live in the suburbs, something that most of us in urban areas did not even know existed. Teachers did not have to take classes in special education or diversity, and I don't remember any who spoke Spanish, at least until I reached high school. There were no accommodations for language minority students. In fact, the common remedy was to expect parents, many of whom could barely speak English themselves, to speak English at home to their children. There also were no accommodations for students with special needs, such as my brother Freddy, who had autism, or for other children with medical, physical, behavioral, or learning issues. Freddy was, in fact, sent home from kindergarten a few days after he started, with a note that said he was "not normal" and could therefore not be educated in the public schools. The year was 1951 and, as a result, my parents felt there was little that was good or fair about public schools.

So, when people start romanticizing about "the way things were," please take what they say with some skepticism. As you enter the teaching profession, I urge you to take off your rose-tinted glasses and see what really exists now, and what existed in the past. There was tremendous inequality and there were differing expectations for students based on who they were and where they lived. In that sense, things have not changed that much.

It is true that some things are far worse now than they were then. The testing frenzy that currently characterizes our public schools is worse than anything I remember as a student or, later, as a classroom teacher in the 1960s. Yes, we had tests, and in New York City, "teaching to the test" in high school meant preparing students for the subject-matter Regents examinations. But nothing can compare to the current laser focus on high-stakes accountability for both students and teachers. The surveillance of teachers has reached epic proportions, and the so-called "teacher-proof curricula" that I thought had disappeared with the growing professionalization of teachers in the 1980s have come back with a vengeance.

Given the current situation, in some ways, I wonder why people enter the teaching profession nowadays. Teachers spend countless hours preparing for class, grading tests, and doing research to develop creative lessons and units. They spend hundreds of dollars of their own money each year to buy the supplies they need. They get few rewards for pursuing their own professional development. In some schools, "professional days" are a thing of the past, and money to attend conferences vanished long ago. With little status and few monetary rewards, it is little wonder that many potentially exceptional teachers stay away from the profession, and many who do enter the profession leave it in short order.

In spite of this grim scenario (and I know it sounds counter-intuitive to say this), I believe there has never been a better time to be a teacher. I say this because there has never been a better time to make a difference – for our children, for our schools, and for our nation. It is a time to speak truth to power, to challenge the way things are, to take a stand, and make history. It is a time to join forces with other like-minded smart teachers who understand that to make a difference means to work together for change. It is a time to tell the world that the Emperor (the politicians, the test-makers, the vested interests, the privatization promoters) has no clothes. It is the teachers who have the clothes.

I have been privileged to work with extraordinary teachers over my many years as a teacher and, later, as a teacher educator. I am inspired by those who stay in spite of it all, who love their students, who continue to learn even after 30 or 40 years in the classroom, who believe in public education and are zealous in their support of democracy, who fight back, and who find joy in teaching, even when that joy is tempered – and challenged – by the everyday drudgery of schools that are increasingly characterized by scripted curricula, senseless mandates, and low expectations of our most vulnerable students.

Depending on whom you ask, teaching is neither worse nor better than it was in some mythical "before." We are treated to all sorts of media images of teachers, few of which ring true. But teaching is not about being a knight on a white horse, or a missionary. No, teaching is not a romantic endeavor, although it certainly has its moments of magic and transcendence. Nothing compares with the impact of good teachers, and my hope is that you will experience what this means many times over in your teaching career. You will no doubt influence the future of our young people and our society in more ways, and more significant ways, than the politicians, the nay-sayers, and the test-makers. You have a big job to do, but given your energy, your enthusiasm, your fresh ideas, and your devotion to the profession, you may just be able to do it.

I wish you well.
Sonia Nieto

AFFILIATION

Sonia Nieto
Language, Literacy and Culture
School of Education
University of Massachusetts Amherst

REBECCA MARTUSEWICZ

21. THE MOST UNLIKELY PLACES

Eros and Education in the Commons

Dear Educators and Future Students,

In many ways, as I sit down to write this letter, I do so with a sense of heaviness even while I know I want to write to you about the importance of love, relationship, and community. We are facing so many critical problems—ever-widening income gaps between rich and poor; protracted wars; corporate greed; violence in our cities, schools, and neighborhoods; species loss; climate change; and damage to our oceans, water and soil sources. Given the mess we've made of so many of our communities and this planet, how do I begin a letter to you about hope or wisdom? Where do we look, given all these challenges? The answer that I want to offer in this letter to you is not about any of the high-status knowledge that comprise our high-tech consumer lives. It doesn't look to science to fix the myriad problems our hubris has created. It's about recognizing and giving value to those practices all around us where we learn mutual care, connection, respect, and protection of what is needed to live. These are the essential ingredients of happiness, wisdom, and hope.

For my whole professional life, I have been dedicated to teaching for justice. Questions circulating around sexism, racism, and socioeconomic inequalities have dominated my thinking and teaching. A few years ago, maybe ten years now, I went through a rather startling transition that taught me a lot about how narrowly focused my commitments had been. I won't say that this was a transformation, because what I discovered was really already there, knowledge that I had kept neatly packed away for most of my life, certainly my adult life. My discovery started to unfold when I wrote a letter to my mother to thank her for teaching me so much: about how to be in gentle respectful relationship with the animals—dogs, cats, horses, rabbits, birds, woodchucks— by which we were always surrounded; how to appreciate the soil beneath my feet and under my fingernails; how to plant, cultivate, and prepare a whole range of flowers and fruits and vegetables.

As I wrote to her, I began to realize that my deepest, most important learning had come from her and other elders in my life. Not from school, not from my university degrees, but from lessons about how to take care of myself and others, how to connect in deeply meaningful ways with all kinds of creatures and the more than human world pulsing around us. I realized as I wrote that letter that my earliest sense

T. M. Kress and R. Lake (Eds.), We Saved the Best for You: Letters of Hope, Imagination and Wisdom for 21st Century Educators, 95–98.
© 2013 Sense Publishers. All rights reserved.

of justice was connected to a deep love and ethical commitment that I have since come to understand as "eco-erosic love" (Edgerton, 1996). These are the embodied experiences "that draw us closer, that create connection and pleasure, happiness and well being, and thus could move us to protect each other and the life systems we live in" (Martusewicz, 2005).

I grew up in rural northern New York State, within a mile of my grandfather's small dairy farm. We had a huge garden that my mother tended—we worked in it, and ate from it. She canned, made preserves and pickles, and the best fresh rhubarb pie! My mother taught my siblings and me how to be at ease in the woods, identifying with us all sorts of trees, berries, and wildflowers there and in the nearby meadows. This area of New York—St. Lawrence County—is the poorest and least populated county in the state, composed primarily of small struggling or failing dairy farms on rocky pasture land located between the mighty St. Lawrence River and the rolling foothills of the Adirondacks.

We certainly didn't experience it as poor, however. My sister, brothers, and I ran and played in those fields and rode our horses along the shores and into the waters of the streams near our neighborhood. We learned to work in the garden and muck stalls, and tend fence lines. We were taught a whole array of manners and skills, including how to "mind" adults other than our parents who took responsibility for our safety and our behavior.

But it was my mother who taught me to pay attention to the more than human world. She would never have agreed with this assessment, but my mother held enormous wisdom, old wisdom about being part of a larger community. More than anyone else, she showed me what it means to be in the world ethically, with poise and strength. She taught me that it was important to feel the suffering of animals as well as humans. Who would guess that I would learn the most about responsibility and justice from her as I sat on the back of a horse ("Run your hand over his neck, let him know you're pleased. Watch his ears, he's listening to you") or as I stooped to look as she pointed to the subtle colors of a dogtooth violet ("Look, don't pick!")? She taught me to connect and love in the most important ways.

These lessons learned in meadows and streams, from animals and neighbors, were part of my cultural and environmental "commons," my earliest community. My memories of those years growing up, and the relationships that remain still, comprise a fundamental source for imagining a healthier, happier, saner world. There are diverse commons-based practices all around us and all across the world: values, practices and belief systems that hold immense power to heal us from the damages that our hyper, consumer-oriented industrial systems have caused. They really don't need to be reinvented; you'll notice them when you least expect to if you're ready to see and listen differently (The Ecologist, 1996 ; Martusewicz, Edmundson & Lupinacci, 2011).

This became so clear to me about ten years ago, just as I was learning to embrace my mother's wisdom. I began to read about diverse "commons sense" knowledge from different parts of the world (Appfel-Marglin, 1998; Batalla, 1996;

The Ecologist, 1993), knowledge that does not require money to access, but is about building deeply satisfying relationships and maintaining the skills needed to live well together in specific bioregions. At about this time, I was invited by a friend to join him and a small group of folks in a brownfield cleanup project in his neighborhood on Wabash Street in Detroit. I went there for several May and June Saturdays, filling and pushing wheelbarrows of rubble off a former factory site, working side by side with Charles and his neighbors and listening to their stories about this part of Detroit.

I listened to a woman named Johnny tell me all about what she was growing in her backyard garden, about medicinal qualities of certain plants growing in the nearby ditches, and the plans that this group had for transforming this old lot into raised beds to feed folks on this street. Soon this experience led to other introductions to incredible work being done across this city: artists, farmers, carpenters, poets, teachers, and activists all working in their various spaces to imagine a different Detroit. I looked around and saw that this Detroit was one made of connections among people and with the land, neighbor-to-neighbor, elder-to-child, hand-to-soil.

Don't misunderstand me: Detroit suffers from deep wounds of racism, poverty, and violence; life here is complicated and painful. Driving through the city today one sees the effects of economic abandonment in boarded up storefronts, whole blocks of abandoned houses crumbling into the ground or burned out. Asthma levels are three times the national average, and diabetes, malnutrition and obesity signal critical issues of food insecurity. Most people would probably not think to go looking for answers to the crises we face here.

Yet, as I have worked with and listened to the people in the neighborhoods, non-profits and schools in Detroit, I have begun to recognize again this deeply erotic grassroots understanding and a particular kind of wisdom—old wisdom that recognizes the power of mutuality, generosity, and kindness, and measures wealth in terms of rich soil, sweat equity, seedlings, and seed exchanges. This is embodied wisdom, the kind that settles in one's bones, in one's hands, shoulders, and gut. It's in the sheer pleasure of putting one's mind and muscle into creative collaboration with others and seeing the product of one's loving work grow into healthy, nourishing food, or in a growing friendship with someone from a completely different background. It is, in short, erotic wisdom—the pleasure you can feel deep down when you collaborate to create something that provides beauty, nourishment, and companionship: love in responsibility to others.

When I started coming into the city to learn from these folks, there were around 150 community gardens being supported by the Detroit Garden Resource Program, a division of a non-profit called The Greening of Detroit. Ten years later there are over 2000 community gardens across this city, a handful of multi-acre urban farms, and a well-established food security policy collectively drafted by community members and accepted by the City Council. A network of non-profits, individual activists, and educators worked to develop strong language about the need for public schools to address public health and for community education that addresses the need for locally grown food that can contribute to a strong local economy.

So what is this all about, these stories connecting my childhood and Detroit? What I want you to understand is that the wisdom and hope that you need is in your relationship to the "commons," to those diverse and mostly unconscious, unvalued practices, relationships, beliefs, and traditions that have been passed down over many generations to teach us what we need to live ethically and sustainably together. Pay attention! Wisdom and hope will be found in the most unlikely of places, with the most unheralded people. Listen to the lessons you can learn from the everyday relationships you have with the elders in your life, and allow yourself to connect and learn from the more than human world. There are incredible teachings happening all around you all the time about what is required to go on living with beauty, strength, and happiness. We do not need more science or better technology. We need the wisdom found in those deep, passionate connections and patterns. And so, I leave you with the words of ecofeminist Susan Griffin (1995, p. 151) : "To exist in a state of communion is to be aware of the nature of existence. This is where ecology and social justice come together, with the knowledge that life is held in common."

In solidarity and love,
Rebecca Martusewicz

REFERENCES

Apffel Marglin, F. (Ed.). (1998). *The spirit of regeneration: Andean culture confronting Western notions of development.* London: Zed Books.
Batalla, G.B. (1996). *Mexico profundo: Reclaiming a civilization.* (Philip A. Dennis, Trans.). Austin, TX: University of Texas Press.
Edgerton, S. (1996). *Translating the curriculum: Multiculturalism into cultural studies.* New York, NY: Routledge.
Griffin, S. (1995). *The eros of everyday life: Essays on ecology, gender and society.* New York: Doubleday.
Martusewicz, R. A. (2005). *Eros in the commons:* Educating for eco-ethical consciousness in a poetics of place. *Ethics, Place and Environment: A Journal of Philosophy and Geography, 8*(3), 331–348.
Martusewicz, R. A., Edmundson, J., & Lupinacci, J. (2011). *EcoJustice education: Toward diverse, democratic and sustainable communities.* New York: NY: Routledge.
The Ecologist. (1993). *Whose common future: Reclaiming the commons.* Philadelphia, PA: New Society Publishers.

AFFILIATION

Rebecca Martusewicz
Social Foundations of Education
Eastern Michigan University

JENNIFER L. MILAM

22. OM MANI PADME HUM

Seeking Interdependence, Metta and Peace in the Classroom

Dear Teachers,

I write to you today not from my position as educator, professor, or researcher, but as a mother of a five-year-old who began her journey in/with/through school just a few short months ago. As she began her journey, I began one of my own: I found myself no longer someone else's teacher, nor the caretaker and nurturer of other people's children in schools, nor the preparer of future teachers; instead, I am classroom volunteer, new member of the PTA, and Kindergarten mom. In each of these, I am implicated and inextricably intertwined in my daughter's education and deeply enmeshed in the daily rituals of school. And every day that I drop her at her classroom door, warmly greeted by her first formal school teacher, I am sad--deeply, terribly, horribly sad. Not for the reasons you might think. I am not the type of mother who distrusts others to care for her children, who questions the qualifications of the professional in the classroom, or just cannot bear to give my child over for 7 hours a day; instead, I'm saddened by the lack of heart in school.

In nearly every school I have visited or been invited to enter in the last ten years, something is missing. Sure, the hallways are clean, children's work adorn the hallways, and teachers and children are going about the business of school; but the warmth, the spirit, is just simply not there.

Today, I write to you as mother and fellow teacher, with a plea. A plea for you to hear, to listen, to honor a deep sense of humanity and compassion, of nurturance, of respect for the children who will be entrusted to your care and service. Cherish their ideas and be committed to their growth as people. Realize that your happiness and theirs are interdependent.

A BUDDHIST PATH TOWARD PEACE AND JOY

I recognize the school as a representative space of the larger society in which the very same heart appears to be a distant memory, if ever it existed at all. I recognize the sadness in schools as many things. It is the frustration of teachers for the overburdening of stipulations and standards, increased paperwork, immeasurable demands, and scathing critiques by policy makers, administrators, and communities. It is the challenge of teaching children to read and develop academic habits of mind

T. M. Kress and R. Lake (Eds.), We Saved the Best for You: Letters of Hope, Imagination and Wisdom for 21st Century Educators, 99–102.
© *2013 Sense Publishers. All rights reserved.*

with fewer resources each year, fuller classes, and less time. It is children who come to school each day, many unsure of where they will live next month, eating their only two meals for the day provided by the school, and moving throughout their day with no genuine connection to a peer, a teacher, or a family member because the world is moving too quickly. It is school buildings, schedules, and routines that separate, isolate, and contain. It is each of these and the sum of their whole that leaves each of us sad, unfulfilled, and unloved – suffering.

Buddhism teaches us that our wounds, our hurts, our concerns, our feelings of isolation and loss, are shared – by each of us, by all of us: "Our individual suffering also unites us in a community of suffering...not separate from others. Our wounds are commonly shared" (Roshi, 1999, p. 11). The fundamental realization of Buddhist practice is that enlightenment is "the liberation of intimacy in our relatedness with all beings" (Roshi, 1999, p. 12). This relatedness is a challenge to our Western individualism, our practices that label and differentiate, sort and separate. Buddhist perspective suggests that when we fail to realize the inescapable connectedness of each of us, we allow for terrible hurt, tragedy, violence, and isolation of our fellow beings and ourselves. More simply, when we see others as separate from ourselves it becomes palatable, even acceptable, to treat them as less than we would treat ourselves. Conversely, when we turn inward to seek out peace and compassion we find a spirit and wisdom toward compassionate, nondual action – action that sees no "other" or separateness. This action seeks to comfort, nurture, and liberate from suffering.

You see, I believe that the core of the sadness in our schools is the lack of connectedness among the people who inhabit those spaces from day to day. Teachers see children as belonging to someone else or worse, as someone else's problem; administrators view teachers as workers in a system and a means to an end; and the children see teachers as monitors and their peers as competition for resources, attention, and acceptance. Our schools are simply not places of kindness or compassion. Standards dictate the daily topics, schedules manage the interactions, and policies and procedures have replaced responsive relationships and human connection so crucial to our lives. Teaching is a deeply personal, demandingly intimate journey – when mothers, fathers, or grandparents entrust you with their children, they are saying to you, "I trust you to do the very best with my very best." It is simply not enough to teach children the alphabet, math facts, and how to sit quietly in the library. It is not enough to meet their superficial needs on a daily basis – it is not enough for the child, and it is not enough for you, dear teacher. You must turn inward. You must realize that your happiness and your growth are dependent upon that of others, including your students. Teachers, students, administrators – each and every person that enters a school building or lives in this world – needs connection and relationships; without this radical intimacy and interconnectedness, we are certain to be lost in isolation and suffering.

Buddhism calls us to let go of our attachments to material success, fleeting emotional connections, and individualistic motivations in exchange for a journey toward metta, karuna, upekka and mudita – loving kindness, compassion, equanimity, and sympathetic joy. At first glance, or contemplation one may think that the cultivation of these four states of being and the practices that accompany them seems fairly simple-- these are things that good people do. But Buddhism reminds us that the journey, this life, is much more complex and that no relationship, no interaction, no circumstance is without suffering and therefore is not easily confronted.

CONSIDER FOR A MOMENT EACH OF THE FOLLOWING

What would it mean to respond to the most difficult child in your class with loving kindness? To welcome her to the learning space with open arms, a fresh outlook, and a deep realization that her struggle is also yours, her teacher's? And to do so not because you must coerce her into learning and satisfactory performance on an achievement test, but because her joy and happiness are dependent upon your loving kindness and your joy is intimately tied to hers.

What would it mean to embrace an emotionally and psychologically wounded student with compassion? To recognize that his outbursts, misbehaviors, and failures to comply with your requests are reflections of his inner struggles with sadness, alienation, and hurt? To nurture him in spite of the frustration and disorganization he may cause in your classroom because you know his happiness and ability to heal in this life are intimately linked to your own?

What would it mean to express sympathetic joy and to model a deep sense of appreciation, respect, and admiration for each student's unique gifts, successes, and achievements? To reward unique contributions to the classroom in a different language, to allow children to demonstrate their learning in a way that honors their mode of expression, to encourage children to help one another rather than to put up dividers and discourage conversation? When you model this joy, your children will learn it, too; they will come to see each other as important, worthy of praise and respect.

What would it mean to allow for calm, generative, thoughtful and contemplative learning to grow in your classroom? To open opportunities for collaboration, reflection, and peace rather than force all children to sit in one direction during lunch without talking, to not speak forcefully at/to children, and to refrain from reprimanding students in such a way that they feel shame and sorrow? And in practicing equanimity in your classroom and school, you will find that students are more delighted to be at school, happy to respond to your requests or directions, and considerate and thoughtful in their own contributions to the classroom and school.

You see, dear teacher, while you are busy writing lesson plans, aligning standards to assessments, organizing your classroom, hanging up pre-cut Carson Delosa © figures on interactive bulletin boards, completing paperwork for the latest round of district reports, or complaining about a student in the teacher's lounge, your students are suffering, your school is sad, and you are missing an opportunity to find the real joy in teaching—and in living. In each of your students, as in both of my own children, is a tender, worthy spirit requiring nurture. Your ability to meet this young person with love, compassion, and kindness is directly tied to your ability to see yourself, and your future, as intimately connected to theirs.

I leave you, again, with my plea – seek for yourself kindness, compassion, joy, and equanimity and recognize that you are one with the rest of the universe. When you can see yourself in your students, when you can see your students as part of you, when you work tirelessly to nurture both, our schools may become places of joy. And this is far more important than any teaching method or curriculum standard I know.

Namaste.
Jennifer Milam

REFERENCE

Roshi, J.H. (1999). Foreword. In Chappell, D.W., *Buddhist peacework: Creating cultures of peace.* (pp.11–12) Boston: Wisdom Publications.

AFFILIATION

Jennifer Milam
Department of Curricular & Instructional Studies
University of Akron

JAMES C. JUPP

23. WEST'S SELF-CREATION

Against the Odds, Against the Grain

To those who would dare to teach,

I don't think I really understood it when one of the administrators who hired me (I can't remember his name) in Raymondville, Texas told me: "It takes five years to make an English teacher." For me, it took four – or – after four I finally understood the pleasures of public school teaching. Though even after those four years, I still struggled and had to immerse myself in the community and students' lives to achieve that pleasure. For a new teacher, my advice would be to expect difficulty and practice self-forgiveness for errors you are going to make with your students and community. In order to proceed along the lines of expecting difficulty and practicing self-forgiveness, I'll suggest Cornel West's (1993, 2001) notion of self-creation as a source of hopeful becoming in dark times for education.

To start, I think we need to expect difficulty when working as teachers in public schools. Jonathon Kozol (1967/1985, 1992, 2005) has written at least three books narrating savage historical and social inequalities in schools. As a classroom teacher who spent eighteen years teaching Mexican, Mexican-American, Latino and Latino immigrant, and African-American students in predominantly Title I (lower income) rural and inner-city schools, Kozol's writings reflect, very exactly, my experiences as a teacher. Working with poor students in geographically and historically segregated communities with backgrounds that differed from my white middle class one was at first a challenge, then a professional vocation and identity, and finally a topic of research. As I earned my certification through the University of Texas at Brownsville's alternative certification program, Raymondvillle ISD hired me in the middle of the year on a "temporary teaching credential," and I was unaware – really – of what the demands, difficulties, and pitfalls would be, but upon entering the classroom routine, I immediately felt the exhausting demands of planning, difficulties of student discipline, and struggles of creating authority with students in my new school and community. My experience of becoming a teacher in rural and later inner-city Title I schools is in fact an ever-increasing norm as resentment against public institutions devalues public service, divests from humanistic caring professions, and diminishes teachers' professional authority (Giroux, 2012; Reynolds & Webber, 2009). Bill Ayers, when I saw him speak in 2009, was correct in saying that "public" in public schools increasingly has come to mean the same thing as the

T. M. Kress and R. Lake (Eds.), We Saved the Best for You: Letters of Hope, Imagination and Wisdom for 21st Century Educators, 103–106.
© 2013 Sense Publishers. All rights reserved.

"public" in public housing. That is, public schools, when represented in news and popular media, are understood as noblesse oblige of social "remediation" by (an elite) leadership burdened with "custody" as the elite, middle class, and upwardly mobile working class frequently abandon, and thereby degrade, public schools for other choice "options." Taking up teaching in the present, West (1993) would say (and I agree), represents the "heroic action of ordinary people" (p. 32).

Nonetheless, I also advise the practice of self-forgiveness to new teachers in public schools. I have to practice self-forgiveness and tacitly ask for my ex-students' forgiveness regarding my first year of teaching in Raymondville. After accepting the job, I learned my fifth period had "run-off Mr. Davis" before me as my self-selected mentor José Luis Chavez confided in me. Fifth period, for me, was particularly hard to handle, motivate, routinize, or especially, teach anything let alone "the standards." I struggled through that year, very publically, trying out projects that degenerated, putting on movies to fill time, reading Stephen King stories aloud, working with premade lists of "spelling demons," covering disorganized snatches of grammar, doing whatever "might work" for tomorrow. Very little, in fact, did work that first year. The only glimmer of light, as I recall the experience of my first year, was that I began to develop a unit on South Texas legends from Stories that Must Not Die as my mentor Jose Luis Chavez had mentioned. Very certainly, it was through Dr. Chavez, who saw something in me worth rescuing, that I learned to forgive myself and had hope for who I could learn to become as a teacher. West's understanding of self-creation, what I'm driving in the balance of my letter, reminds me in difficult moments that I have to forgive myself and have hope as a crucial aspect of professional identity. That I can change myself, my students' responses to me, the working conditions, and the communities' responses to myself and teachers' work. Even so, that first year, my students and I counted the days (and then class periods) till the end of the year when we would be free of each other.

I will assure you, though not in any facile way, that things got better (after more difficulty…), and as I mentioned above as a turning point for me, it was in my fourth year that several of my classes expressed sadness at parting in the last week of school – an expression that, given my first year and some experiences in other years, came as quite a surprise. (They didn't want the year to end because I wouldn't be their teacher next year?!?! I was perplexed, aghast, grateful, relieved, and touched at such an expression in several of my students.) Nonetheless, I need to mention, as counterbalance to my assurances, that many, many colleagues – like ghosts walking the halls, staying a year or two, "teaching-for-America" (some) – didn't expect difficulty, couldn't forgive themselves, and didn't engage in the any type of self-creation and they failed at creating a professional identity and left teaching with no or even negative impact. Even worse were the colleagues who failed at self-creation of professional identity but decided that their failure was really the students' and families' fault, and so, their classroom became permanent shrines to bad teaching, dysfunctional relationships, and social-political resentments personalized quite literally between student and teacher. So, in expecting difficulty and practicing self-forgiveness, I'll insist that self-creation, the type that I talk about below, really concerns professional life-and-death for teachers, especially those who wish to have a positive impact on students and communities.

Of course, self-creation as it relates to teachers' professional identity is very personal, even a form of autobiography (Pinar, 2012; Slattery, 2006), as well as social identity. Self-creation is carried out painstakingly in personal and public spaces through developing moral commitments to students, colleagues, and schools – all very specifically. Cornel West's (1993, 2004) notion of self-creation, very much a professional identity resource and source of hope for me, understands professional identity – and other identities, too – are bounded but-not-yet-determined by social history or identity "groups." West's self-creation, drawing not on multiculturalism's "groups" but rather a democratic moral position in Emersonian and cosmopolitan traditions in the US (e.g., Addams, 1902/2002; Dewey, 1902/1990; Du Bois, 1903/1995; Whitman, 1855/1975), refers to and emphasizes that we can – all together –, through heroic and collective effort against-the-odds, change ourselves and make ourselves better and more moral people. We can transform the conditions of our lives and work, and aide others in enabling progressive-democratic change in students and communities – though none of this is easy and, in fact, we might very well fail, tragically fail. This possible tragic failure (un-hope, really), in self-creation, shadows personal and social moral commitments, guides efforts at becoming teachers and improving our craft as teachers, provides a pragmatic ideal to follow in dark times in which defeat seems imminent but-not-yet-determined as final outcome. West (1993) reminds us, despite crass and shallow hope peddlers who "are manipulative, charlatan-like, blinding, obscuring" (p. 5) who promise to fix schools with data or provide us with cocksure solutions to our problems, we must return to and engage hope and the un-hope of possible failure in ways that confront difficulty with faith in ourselves and others. West (1993) explains:

> And yet, we must talk about hope. To talk about hope is to engage in an audacious attempt to galvanize and energize, to inspire and to invigorate world-weary people. ... We must face that skeleton [weariness] as a challenge, not a conclusion. But be honest about it. Weary, and yet keep alive the notion that history is incomplete, that the world is unfinished, that the future is open-ended and that what we think and what we do can make a difference. (p. 5)

This is what is important about self-creation in dark times. It re-establishes personal-community-social-political self-reliance (Emerson, 1844/2000) willing to continue against the odds, against the grain.

My advice then, which was to expect difficulty, practice self-forgiveness, and to suggest West's (1993, 2004) notion of self-creation, is really just trying to put some little-known ideas, under-referred to concepts, and hardly-mentioned resources in teacher education into your hands.

James C. Jupp

REFERENCES

Addams, J. (2002). *Democracy and social ethics*. Urbana, IL: University of Illinois Press. (Originally published in 1902).

Dewey, J. (1990). *The child and the curriculum*. In J. Dewey's *The school and society/The child and curriculum* (pp. 181–208). Chicago, IL: The University of Chicago Press. (Originally published in 1902).

Du Bois, W. E. B. (1995). *The souls of Black folk*. New York, NY: Signet Classics. (Originally published in 1903).

Emerson, R.W. (2000). Self-reliance. In B. Atkinson (Ed.), *The essential writings of Ralph Waldo Emerson* (pp. 132–153). New York, NY: The Modern Library Classics.

Giroux, H. (2012). *Education and the crisis in public values*. New York, NY: Peter Lang.

Kozol, J. (1985). *Death at an early age*. New York, NY: Plume Books. (Originally published in 1967).

Kozol, J. (1992). *Savage inequalities: Children in America's schools*. New York, NY: Harper Perennial.

Kozol, J. (2005). *Shame of the Nation: The restoration of apartheid in schooling in America*. New York, NY: Crown Publishers.

Pinar, W. F. (2012). *What is curriculum theory* (2nd ed.). New York, NY: Routledge.

Slattery, P. (2006). *Curriculum development in the Postmodern Era* (2nd ed.). New York, NY: Routledge.

Webber, J., & Reynolds, W. (2009). *The civic gospel: A political cartography of Christianity*. Rotterdam: Sense Publishers.

West, C. (1993). *Beyond Eurocentrism and multiculturalism v1: Prophetic thought in postmodern times*. Monroe, MA: Common Courage Press.

West, C. (2004). The Deep Democratic Tradition in America. In C. West *Democracy matters: Winning the fight against imperialism* (pp. 63–106). New York, NY: Penguin.

Whitman, W. (1975). Song of myself. In F. Murphy (Ed.) *Walt Whitman: The complete poems* (pp. 63–124). New York, NY: Penguin Education. (Originally published in 1855).

AFFILIATION

James C. Jupp
Department of Teaching & Learning
Georgia Southern University

CLYDE COREIL

24. LANGUAGE, CREATION, AND MLK

Dear Teacher,

There are two aspects of writing I would like to mention before making brief remarks about "Monarch Waiting": the developmental and the highly personal. By the former, I refer to organization, balance, pace, timing, point of view, alliteration, internal and end rhyme, level of formality, occasion, length, timing, sincerity, mockery, dialogue, the sound of words, variety, length of line, use of breaks in the text, the numbering of such breaks, and other such features, all of which should, of course, interact. And who am I to suggest such a list? A shadowy, insubstantial persona. But I do have an assortment of nuts and bolts in my bag. I majored in English literature, worked as a reporter and an editor, and hold a master's in playwriting, and a doctorate in linguistics. This gives me a diverse and oddly stocked storehouse that I can rummage into for, let us say, technique. But by no means do I mean to make light of these features. After all, the face of a beautiful woman is composed of structured muscles, bones, teeth, nostrils, proportion and the like. And yet one is often breathless as she strides across the dance-floor.

The "highly personal" includes gut-feel, dark gutters, intuition, high-mindedness, speculation, and willingness to fix a flat on a red clay road in pouring rain. I have not mentioned language yet because that would involve genuflection, commitment, the mystic, and luck. The ability to put words together is truly one of the most powerful of our abilities as human beings. And it is not an ability of our conscious minds: its source is to be found in the area of Jung's collective unconscious. We can pervert this to tell – with satanic gesticulation – the Big Lie. We can promote the evil ambitions of tyrants who tell us to hate our fellows and to call them "vermin" and "subhuman." But we can also study the twisting mists and myths of the nether world and string shards of meaning into phrases as did Raphael Lemkin who, in 1944, coined the word "genocide." He combined the Greek prefix "genos-" or community and the suffix for murder, "-cide."

We can now call on language to refer to the monstrous crime of "genocide" and to fashion a yet larger and more precise definition of what was hitherto unnamable. Once we have named and conceived of an action or a deed, we can proceed to classify it as deserving of humble admiration or terminal condemnation. And it is not only the deed itself that has earned the name, it is a profoundly deep part of ourselves that has come together and been baptized. Dr. King knew that and found in it the basis for his support of a phrase made popular by Thoreau. "Civil Disobedience" approaches the status of an oxymoron until we see that it can indeed be an effective means of beginning to deal with generations of malevolence.

T. M. Kress and R. Lake (Eds.), We Saved the Best for You: Letters of Hope, Imagination and Wisdom for 21st Century Educators, 107–112.
© *2013 Sense Publishers. All rights reserved.*

Language indeed allows us to see the rancid mist as through a glass darkly, to name that specific evil, and to set out on a march to defeat it. Not the march of the Northern Self-Righteous Yankee to kill the Slave-Owner Southerner – but the long journey of self-discovery, informed by the insight and energy to externalize and cognitively condemn what is probably the greatest of social evils: the attempt to enslave the human will, the willingness to make ourselves the hellish counter of what we know we should become.

For me, this is what Martin Luther King represents: the wisdom and willpower to lift us from ourselves through a sharpness of conscience that knows no equal. This is nothing less than the courage to proceed without flinching in a terrible fear and trembling, and to have cojones big enough to fashion the part of the self that needs refashioning. It was, however, in the excruciating vision of what he knew was his probably imminent assassination that I sought to find the motivation for this poem. I wanted to capture the confluence of terror and the mad drive to flee which King controlled masterfully, transmuting it to humor and small talk in consideration for those around him.

Dr. Robert Lake, one of the editors of this book, said with excellent and articulate insight that he saw the poem as concerned with "how imagination can bring historical events to life and even transcend time in a way that creates a vivid and palpable vision, as if you were right there on the balcony of the Lorraine Motel in Memphis, as the dreaming monarch was crowned with bullets." Of course, I was flattered at the accuracy and closeness of his reading. I was also struck by the unexpected manner in which he expressed in language his imaginative response. Words were helping us to reach into the primal horror of the murder and come out with an enriched meaning that helps me, at least, construct something positive in a bone-chilling reality. Life frightens and mystifies, yet it also allows us to find the door that will be opened. So, with the clarity of 72 years, I urge you to never lose confidence in the magnificent and necessarily continuing value of language to search for who we are and what we want to become. Dr. King knew that the path was there, and he was profoundly brave enough to take the first and the last steps to a fateful destiny that was his final gift to us.

Language will never fail you because it is the most essential part of you, of us. If vague feelings about something arise in you, language will always be present to magically and mysteriously develop and elaborate those feelings. It will find their name or it will invent a word or a phrase for them. I dare you NOT to carry a pen and paper with which to capture impressions that are as fleeting as hummingbirds. When you see something in the mist, you must set it down. If you don't, the feelings will fade like dreams in the morning sun. If you do note those marvelous mysteries, they will multiply like rabbits in springtime. And it's not only that needed words will come together like magic: your very ability to bring together and articulate thoughts will also increase. I have witnessed this fascinating growth in the linguistic drive to find the exact word or the precise phrase – le mot juste. This expansion via thought spills over into personality. Language is capable of nothing less than enabling us to continually create ourselves in the flashing images of divine neurons that dart around in our brains. This I sincerely believe.

Language allows old men to look at their lives and see what they have done and what they have failed to do. The young have to find the doors they must open. Young teachers have an especially tough row to hoe: they must help their students to see and understand the world that they themselves are fashioning. If there were peaceful valleys in which they could linger, there might be a choice. Unfortunately, that topography is not yours. You must gird your loins for a really tough, really long struggle. You have to realize that as a human being, you must find the single, highest quest that speaks to you and to no other. Ignore this at your peril. That is the ultimate legacy of Dr. King as it was of Socrates.

I wish you peace and good speed.
Clyde Coreil

Monarch Waiting
by
    Clyde Coreil

More like Hamlet
than like Hamlet's father,
he walked among us,
trying to pretend that he
was simply another man
scanning the heavens,
searching for a way
that led around what
he already knew was his.

He did not spend his days
studying different ways
than those that twisted men
harbored like dark voyages,
unseen in the distant angles
of eyes hidden behind the
monstrous pointed masks—

Brave cannot be brave
Without the fallen angels
stoking and fanning and blowing
flickers of the fearful flame
come down and glowing
with their stinking breath –

He knew that,
and he was afraid,
but he knew that
of other ways
there was none.

II

On the stage from which
he could not stray,
he was always in
the play within the play:

The king whose destiny it was
to trace the rounded arcs,
the steps that led where no one
would choose to go, no one
would choose to sleep,
not knowing
when or how or where
the morning might find him
but he would not find the morning –

Always feeling
the flame with every sound,
the cross-hairs
burning in his brain,
until their mark
they finally found.

III

He was a nervous man, trying to see
from jails in Birmingham, steadfast
like his friends
hanged and nailed onto a tree.

Dreading the fear
he knew he had to fear,
the gift that waited in the wings,
waited waiting for the final cue,

The flash flashing,
the unseen awful angels
spinning in the air
a single web, pinning in the hair

110

the pearls and emeralds
of vast eternity
when
time and the sun have run
and spun their place in space
filled with the emptiness
of waiting's when and with
the vaults of flesh and bone
become one
with the silence of the stone
thrown after before, before after—
the split of spilt blood
caught there in a single empty and all
of time running forward and back
and back and forward to black.

IV
When hope and the yearning
for the minute after the last, the last that
his black brow and matted hair
that bore the sweat
and made the vow—

His last words were spoken laughing,
something
anything to keep him from adding
the final exhaled
graceful punctuation

That would mark his flight from
friends, fathers, mothers, children –
who would plant him like a well known song,
instantly and forever green and strong.

Nothing onto nothing
until his cup had runneth over –
and it was done.

AFFILIATION

Clyde Coreil
English as a Second Language Department
New Jersey City University

RIANE EISLER

25. PARTNERSHIP EDUCATION

Nurturing Children's Humanity

Dear Friend and Colleague:

I want to first congratulate you for choosing the profession of teaching, so vital to children's future – and to us all. I also teach – not to children but about children, about society, about our collective future. I have done this for decades, through university undergraduate and graduate courses, as well as through my books, articles, speeches, and most recently, videos and webinars.

One of my books is about K-12 education, and follows in the tradition of earlier progressive thinkers about education such as Johann Pestalozzi, Maria Montessori, John Dewey, Paolo Freire, and Nel Noddings.[1] The book is *Tomorrow's Children: A Blueprint for Partnership Education in the 21st Century*.[2] It is designed to help young people better navigate through our difficult times as well as to help them create a future oriented to what in my study of 30,000 years of cultural evolution I have identified as a *partnership system* rather than a *domination system* of beliefs, institutions, and relations.

Although we may not use the terms "domination" and "partnership," we're all familiar with these two kinds of relations. We know the pain, fear, and tension of relations based on domination and submission, on coercion and accommodation, on jockeying for control, on trying to manipulate and cajole when we are unable to express our real feelings and needs, on the miserable, awkward tug of war for that illusory moment of power rather than powerlessness, on our unfulfilled yearning for caring and mutuality, on the misery that comes from these relations. Most of us also have, at least intermittently, experienced another way of relating, one where we feel safe and seen for who we truly are, where our essential humanity and that of others shines through, perhaps only for a little while. These interactions lift our hearts and spirits, enfolding us in a sense that the world can be right, after all, and that we are valued and valuable.

But the partnership and domination systems not only describe individual relationships. They describe systems of belief and social structures that nurture and support—or, alternately, inhibit and undermine—equitable, democratic, nonviolent, and caring relations. These categories also describe two different approaches to socialization, and hence education.

T. M. Kress and R. Lake (Eds.), We Saved the Best for You: Letters of Hope, Imagination and Wisdom for 21st Century Educators, 113–118.
© *2013 Sense Publishers. All rights reserved.*

My interest in transformative education is rooted in my early life experiences. On November 10, 1938 – later known as Crystal Night because so much glass was shattered in Jewish stores, homes, and synagogues – a gang of Nazis came for my father, shoved him down the stairs, and dragged him off. Miraculously, my mother obtained his release, and my parents and I fled my native Vienna and eventually arrived in Cuba. Had we remained in Europe, we would almost certainly have been killed.

These early childhood experiences led to burning questions. Why is there so much cruelty, destructiveness, and hate in the world? Is this our inevitable lot? Or can we create a more peaceful, just, and caring world?

It was only much later that I began to systematically look for answers to these questions. Eventually, to answer them, I embarked on my own research, which has now been represented in many books and articles, including my writings on transformative education.

THE THREE COMPONENTS OF PARTNERSHIP EDUCATION

As you know, there are three primary elements in education: *process* (how we learn and teach), *structure* (the learning environment); and *content or curriculum* (what we learn and teach). Partnership process is about *how* we learn and teach. It applies the guiding template of the partnership system to educational *methods* and *techniques*. Are young people treated with caring and respect? Do teachers act as primarily lesson-dispensers and controllers, or more as mentors and facilitators? Are young people learning to work together or must they continuously compete with each other? Are they offered the opportunity for self-directed learning? In short, are students and teachers partners in a meaningful adventure of exploration and learning?

Partnership structure is about *where* learning and teaching take place: what kind of *learning environment* we construct. Is the structure of a school, classroom, and/ or home school one of top-down authoritarian rankings, or is it a more democratic one? Do students, teachers, and other staff participate in school decision-making and rule-setting? Diagramed on an organizational chart, would decisions flow only from the top down and accountability only from the bottom up, or would there be interactive feedback loops? In short, is the learning environment one of *hierarchies of domination* ultimately backed up by fear, or is it a combination of horizontal linkings and *hierarchies of actualization*, in which power is not used to disempower but to empower?

Partnership content is *what* we learn and teach. It is the *educational curriculum.* Does the curriculum effectively teach students not only basic academic and vocational skills but also the life skills they need to be competent and caring citizens, workers, parents, and community members? Are we telling young people to be responsible, kind, and nonviolent at the same time that the curriculum content still celebrates male violence and conveys environmentally unsustainable and socially irresponsible messages? Does the curriculum present science in holistic, relevant ways? Does what is taught as important knowledge and truth include – not just as an add-on, but as integral to what is learned – both the female and male halves of humanity as well as children of various races, ethnicities, and abilities? Does it teach young people the difference between the partnership and domination systems as two basic human possibilities and the feasibility of creating a partnership way of life? Or, both overtly and covertly, is this presented as unrealistic in "the real world?" In short, what kind of view of ourselves, our world, and our roles and responsibilities in it are young people taking away from their schooling?

Much of progressive education has focused primarily on process, and to some degree on structure. This is very important. But partnership education is not only a matter of more self-directed learning, peer teaching, cooperative learning, more individualized assessment tools, and other partnership pedagogies. Nor is it only a matter of a more democratic and participatory structure. It emphasizes the importance of narratives, and specifically what kinds of behaviors and values are presented as valuable in curriculum narratives.

One of the goals of progressive education is to give young people more choices. Yet even in many progressive schools the curriculum offers few alternative narratives. At best it does so in bits and pieces, mostly as add-ons to conventional narratives we inherited from earlier, more domination-oriented, times. So all too often there is a conflict between the worldviews and values progressive educators talk about and try to model, and the implicit, and even explicit, messages of the narratives or stories that consciously and unconsciously mold what people consider normal and desirable. Hence attention to narratives is a major component of partnership education.

THE POWER OF STORIES

We humans live, and all too often die, by stories. No one can ever tell me that the kinds of stories people are told don't matter. I was almost killed as a child because of stories—stories that said that Jews are evil and subhuman. So what stories are children told today?

On all sides, they hear stories that portray Jews as bad, cruel, violent, and selfish. Video games, action adventure movies, and TV shows present violence as the way to solve problems. Situation comedies make insensitivity, rudeness, and cruelty seem funny. Cartoons present violence as exciting, funny, and without real consequences. As in the journalistic motto of "if it bleeds, it leads," even the stories that make top headlines focus on the infliction and/or suffering of pain as the most significant and newsworthy human events.

And rather than correcting this false image of what it means to be human, much of what children still learn in schools reinforces it. Not only do history curricula still emphasize battles and wars, but classics such as Homer's *Iliad* and Shakespeare's kings trilogy romanticize "heroic violence." Scientific stories tell children that we are the puppets of "selfish genes" ruthlessly competing on the evolutionary stage.

If we are inherently violent, bad, and selfish, we have to be strictly controlled. This is why stories that claim this is "human nature" are central to an education for a domination system. They are, however, totally inappropriate if young people are to learn to live in democratic, peaceful, equitable, and Earth-honoring ways.

Partnership education offers empirical evidence that our human strivings for love, beauty, and justice are just as rooted in our biology as our capacity for violence and aggression. Young people learn how, by the grace of evolution, biochemicals called neuropeptides reward our species with sensations of pleasure, not only when we are cared for, but also when we care for others. The study of evolution from this larger perspective does not leave young people with the sense that humans are inherently violent and selfish – in which case, why bother trying to change anything! On the contrary, partnership education is education for positive social action on all levels – from our communities to our community of nations.

A NEW VIEW OF OUR PAST—AND POTENTIAL FUTURE

Partnership education offers young people a broader understanding of history that is essential if they are to more effectively participate in creating a more equitable, peaceful, and sustainable future. It shows that the struggle for our future is *not* between capitalism versus communism, right versus left, or religion versus secularism, but rather between a mounting movement toward partnership relations in all spheres of life, strong dominator-systems resistance, and periodic regressions.

Using the analytical lens of the partnership/dominator continuum, young people can see that along with the massive technological upheavals of the last three hundred years has come a growing questioning of entrenched patterns of domination. The 18th century rights of man movement challenged the supposedly divinely ordained right of kings to rule, ushering in a shift from authoritarian monarchies to more democratic republics. The 18th and 19th centuries feminist movement challenged men's supposedly divinely ordained right to rule women and children. The movement against slavery during both the 19th and 20th centuries culminated in worldwide movements away from the colonization and exploitation of indigenous peoples and toward their independence from foreign rule. This period also included anti-domination movements challenging economic exploitation and injustice, the rise of organized labor, anti-monopoly laws, and economic safety nets such as Social Security and unemployment insurance. The 20th century Civil Rights and the women's liberation and women's rights movements were part of this continuing challenge. So were the 19th century pacifist movement and the 20th century peace movement, the first organized challenge to the violence of war as a means of resolving international conflicts. The more recent movement challenging traditions of violence against women and children in families and other intimate relations is also a challenge to deeply entrenched traditions of domination and violence. The family planning movement has also been critical for women's emancipation as well as for the alleviation of poverty and greater opportunities for children worldwide.

And the environmental movement has frontally challenged the once hallowed "conquest of nature" that many young people today recognize as a threat to their survival.

But history is not a linear, forward-moving movement. Precisely because of the strong thrust toward partnership, there has been resistance from fierce dominator systems and periodic regression. So we also have seen over the last 300 years resurgences of authoritarianism, racism, and religious persecutions – from the Nazis in Germany to the more recent emergence of so-called religious fundamentalism, be it Eastern or Western, Muslim, Christian, or Hindu. In the United States we have seen the repeal of laws providing economic safety nets, renewed opposition to reproductive rights for women, and periodic violence against those seeking greater rights. In Africa and Asia, even after Western colonial regimes were overthrown, we have seen the rise of authoritarian dictatorships by local elites over their own people, resulting in renewed repression, exploitation, and, in some places, genocidal violence. We have seen a recentralization of economic power under the guise of economic globalization. Under pressure from major economic players, governments have cut social services and have shredded economic safety-nets—an "economic restructuring" that is particularly hurtful to women and children worldwide. We have also seen ever more advanced technologies used to exploit, dominate, and kill—as well as to further "man's conquest of nature," wreaking ever more environmental damage. We have seen a resurgence of violence against different races, religions, and ethnicities—including terrorist attacks against the United States. And the backlash against women's rights has been particularly violent, as in the government-supported violence against women in fundamentalist regimes such as those in Afghanistan and Iran.

GENDER AND EDUCATION FOR A PARTNERSHIP FUTURE

The subordination of women is a key to domination systems, which is one reason a major focus throughout *Tomorrow's Children* is a more gender-balanced curriculum. Many of us are so used to this subordination that we do not even notice that most of what children are taught is still extremely male-centered, from textbook illustrations of primate and human evolution with only male figures to how the canon in just about every field (from art to science) primarily features males. But we must take notice, and change this—not only for the sake of the female half of humanity, but for the sake of us all.

This marginalization, and often invisibility, of the female half of humanity perpetuates domination systems. Consider that a male-superior/female-inferior model of our species is a template for learning to associate difference – beginning with the most basic difference between male and female – with superiority or inferiority, dominating or being dominated, being served or serving. This difference can, of course, be applied to different races, religions, ethnicities, and so forth. That is why regressive regimes or would-be regimes focus so heavily on getting women back into their traditional or subservient place.

Of course, we have to change our textbooks to be more gender balanced, and we have to pressure textbook publishers to do so. In the meantime, every teacher can do her or his part by introducing narratives about girls and women in their classes – and *Tomorrow's Children* provides many materials for courses ranging from math and reading to literature and social studies.

Moreover, in addition to materials that can be integrated into existing curricula, *Tomorrow's Children* provides an exciting new curriculum loom and learning tapestry for those who want a whole-systems approach.

My hope and goal is that, adapted for different regions and cultures, partnership education can be a blueprint for refocusing, reframing, and redesigning education to help children grow up to be active agents of social transformation. It's our job – your job – as educators not only to help children meet the challenges of our difficult and increasingly dangerous times but to show them that a partnership future is not a *utopia* or no place, but a *pragmatopia*, a possible place – and to provide them with the knowledge and skills to build partnership cultures worldwide.

Sincerely,
Riane Eisler

NOTES

[1] Johann Pestalozzi, *Leonard and Gertrude* (New York: Gordon Press Publishers, 1976; originally published in 1781); John Dewey, *Democracy and Education* (New York: The Free Press, 1966; original 1916); Paulo Freire, *Pedagogy of the Oppressed* (New York: Seabury Press, 1973); Maria Montessori, *The Montessori Method* (New York: Schocken Books, 1964; original 1912), Nel Noddings, *Caring: A Feminine Approach to Ethics & Moral Education* (Berkeley: University of California Press, 1984).

[2] Riane Eisler, *Tomorrow's Children: A Blueprint for Partnership Education in the 21st Century* (Boulder, CO: Westview Press, 2000). For more resources on partnership education and the differences between partnership and domination systems, see e.g., Riane Eisler, *The Chalice and The Blade: Our History, Our Future* (San Francisco: Harper & Row, 1988); *The Power of Partnership: Seven Relationships that Will Change Your Life* (Novato, California, 2002); and *The Real Wealth of Nations: Creating a Caring Economics* (San Francisco: Berrett-Koehler, 2008), as well as other books and resources at www.partnershipway.org.

AFFILIATION

Riane Eisler
Center for Partnership Studies

ANA CRUZ

26. THE PERPETUAL FLAME OF CURIOUSITY

Asking Questions, Seeking Answers and Sustaining the Passion
for Teaching

Winter 2011

Dear Aspiring Teachers:

As I start writing this letter to you, I realize what a challenging task it is to write to those who have chosen the same path in life as I did: teaching!

I find the writing of this letter challenging for several reasons: (a) I do not want it to become just words on a piece of paper; (b) I want it to be a fun, but thought-provoking, letter that can also challenge you as you read my ideas; (c) I want it to spark your curiosity for the teaching profession as I reveal to you the passion that has kept me in the teaching profession for more than 20 years.

For those of you who are reading my words but never met me, you are probably picturing me as an "old lady," close to retirement. Not really! I started teaching, in an elementary school, when I was barely 20 years old. My own fears and worries about teaching then are not so different from the fears and worries of today's aspiring classroom teachers.

In my college education courses, I usually ask my students during the first weeks of class what they want to know about the teaching profession and what kind of concerns could impact their decision of becoming a teacher. The students' main concerns and fears are usually related to: classroom management (particularly discipline); dealing with parents; managing content-specific material; adequate preparation to teach diverse students; motivation; and assessment. Although these are all valid concerns, I do not want you to limit your views of teaching to a "skills-based," mechanized profession. I always tell my students that teaching cannot and should not be approached as a "static" task, where "recipes" can guarantee successful teaching. Teaching is indeed a fluid process! So you might then ask me, what is it that you want aspiring teachers to know about the teaching profession? I would say that I would like them to know that teaching is the hyphen between knowing and learning; it is a commitment to continuous learning. Teaching encompasses thorough understanding of the marriage between theoretical and practical knowledge. Teaching is a shared act – between teachers and students – of discovery guided by curiosity.

T. M. Kress and R. Lake (Eds.), We Saved the Best for You: Letters of Hope, Imagination and Wisdom
for 21st Century Educators, 119–122.
© 2013 Sense Publishers. All rights reserved.

CURIOSITY

As I reflect upon my path to become a teacher, my thoughts wander back beyond the years of my formal pre-service teacher preparation to the time when I, as a young girl, observed my mother teaching in her classroom. My mother, now enjoying retirement, was an elementary school teacher in the Brazilian private and public school system. The close geographical proximity of my own school and my mother's school allowed me to make frequent visits to her classes. I remember sitting either at the very front or in the back of my mother's classroom. The memories of these days are still very vivid in my mind. I remember curiously observing every detail of how teaching and learning took place in the classroom. I observed the content my mother taught; how she taught challenging subjects; what techniques and technologies she used to keep students' attention; how she dealt with disruptive students, shy students, dominating students.

I also was confronted with the reality faced by some of her students, a reality of poverty and social inequalities; the same reality that drove some of these students to school, primarily because of the free lunch they would receive (perhaps their only meal of the day). I observed how much my mother loved to teach and to interact with her students. I never knew what exactly would happen in my mother's classroom on a particular day and, therefore, I understood very early how dynamic and fluid teaching was. I also could see how curious my mother was about her students' day-to-day activities outside the classroom and how she would adjust her teaching to her students' lived experiences. Please note that I intentionally chose to use the word "curious" and not "interested" to describe my mother's interaction with her students. Yes, she was genuinely curious to get to know her students and as much as possible to make her teaching meaningful to them. I believe I can say that with her attitude, my mother also instilled in her students the curiosity to learn how a particular subject would help them in their own lives; consequently, driven by the curiosity to make teaching significant and the curiosity to learn, teaching-learning was fun and important to all involved in the process. The curious girl that once observed her mother's classroom still exists inside of me; this girl makes me – the professional I am today – appreciate even more the power of an education guided by curiosity. Paulo Freire (2007) remarked that "[education] must be a courageous, curious education, one awakening of curiosity, and for that very reason, an education that, as much as possible, keeps on preserving the girl [boy] that you were, without allowing your maturity to kill her [him]" (p. 68). I also want to emphasize to you, aspiring teachers, that there is no acquisition of knowledge and no understanding of learning without curiosity....."All knowledge begins from asking questions"... curiosity is asking questions! (Freire & Faundez, 1989, pp. 34–35).

ASKING QUESTIONS

In the teaching profession, the act of asking questions should go beyond a mere technique used to cover a specific subject matter. I have advised pre-service teachers that before they teach their first class and face their first students, they should be asking themselves: Who am I? What are my values and beliefs, and how will they influence my interactions with my students? Therefore, the act of asking questions should start with the teacher posing questions to himself/herself in the process of pursuing critical consciousness. This would trigger "an awareness that our ideas come from a particular set of life experiences, an ability to trace our ideas to their sources in our experience, and an acknowledgement that others will have equally valid, if different, life experiences and ideas" (Freire, 1974, p. 25). After dealing with questions to understand oneself, then teachers can move on to questions that deal directly with student learning.

The whole concept of students "asking questions" in class is perceived by many teachers as intimidating, challenging and sometimes even disrespectful. I frequently talk to pre-service teachers about the "power of silence" that students have in their hands. For many teachers, there is nothing more intimidating than receiving the "silent treatment" from students after posing a set of questions to them; the initial reaction from teachers is commonly to provide the students with the answer to their own questions and eliminate the "silence" as soon as possible! Questions can be also very challenging for teachers – they can challenge their knowledge about a specific subject and/or can challenge their authority – which can be perceived as disrespectful! In many instances, questions are perceived as unwelcome and the message that is passed to students is that "…it is not always convenient to ask questions" (Freire & Faundez, 1989, p. 35). If you, as an aspiring teacher, ever feel intimidated, challenged or disrespected by the act of "asking questions" from your students, please remember that it is by asking questions that students try to relate to gained knowledge and try to make sense of the world. This process involves silence to think and reflect, this process also involves doubting authoritative knowledge. It is through asking questions that critical thinking can manifest itself through re-imagining, re-inventing, and re-creating what is being learned.

A PASSION

To be curious, to ask questions and seek answers, to constantly strive to become a better teacher, and to fully commit to student learning can only occur in the presence of passion for teaching. There is no sustainability in teaching without passion! The realities of the teaching job will make aspiring teachers soon realize that there are numerous obstacles to be overcome. The limited and inequitable distribution of resources, frequent disruptions to class time, disengaged students, and vast demand of bureaucratic work can lead to worn out and underappreciated teachers. It is only with passion for the process of teaching that aspiring teachers will gain the strength and energy to see such obstacles "only" as challenges to be overcome, rather than walls that would block a committed teacher. I also want to let you know, aspiring teachers, that many times I was profoundly challenged during these 20+ years of teaching, to the point that I asked myself why exactly I chose the teaching profession.

Ironically, every time I asked myself this question, I would have a student come to my office or experience a teaching moment in one of my classes where I would see the shining eyes of a student or would read a student's note saying "I got it!" "I can see now, what you were trying to teach us – it just makes so much sense!" The dialogue between the student(s) and me that followed such statements was usually so rich, so involving, and genuinely grounded in learning and growth that the passion for teaching (and learning) was once again renewed!

Yes, the passion for teaching, curiosity, and asking questions will be your guiding light in the challenging moments of your profession, especially as you find ways of overcoming your concerns about teaching (like those listed in the beginning of this letter). I also want you to remember that the places you will be and the students with whom you will work will always be touched by you (hopefully always in a positive way) and, therefore, think of the teaching profession not as "a career path, but as a life path" (Darder, 2011).

With best wishes for your future,
Ana Cruz

REFERENCES

Darder, A. (2011, November). *Neoliberalism and the academic borderlands: An on-going struggle for equality and human rights*. George Kneller Lecture from the American Educational Studies Association 2011 Annual Conference. St. Louis, MO: AESA.

Freire, P. (1974). *Education for critical consciousness*. New York, NY: Continuum.

Freire, P. (2007). *Daring to dream: Toward a pedagogy of the unfinished*. Boulder, CO: Paradigm.

Freire, P., & Faundez, A. (1989). *Learning to question: A pedagogy of liberation*. New York, NY: Continuum.

AFFILIATION

Ana Cruz
Behavioral Sciences
St. Louis Community College Meremac

SUSAN VERDUCCI

27. THE IMMENSE VALUE OF DOUBT

Dear Teachers,

When confronted with the difficulties of the present, most Americans nostalgically long for the past – the "good old days" when life was simpler, more moral, and less troubled. When we closely examine those former times, however, we see within our rose-colored glasses obscure cracks of extreme and institutionalized racism, sexism and homophobia. We wonder about the ways in which the future will view our present. No time is without its problems, but if we are to live responsibly in any time, we must cultivate in ourselves and in others abilities that make it likely that we learn and progress as we move forward, both individually and collectively. As a teacher in a public university, I'm interested in cultivating an ability that allows for the possibility of progress and learning – the ability to doubt one's self. I suggest that as teachers we ought to move away from the question, "Am I right?" If we are to live responsibly in a global world, we ought to highlight the question, "Am I wrong?"

The Oxford English Dictionary defines doubt as "to be uncertain or divided in opinion about; to hesitate to believe or trust; to call in question; to mistrust" ("Doubt"). Self-doubt, although commonly conflated with a lack of self-confidence, primarily means: to be uncertain about, to hesitate to believe or trust one's self; to call into question one's beliefs. But why should we doubt? What value does it hold? I believe its primary value lies in its ability to initiate and extend inquiry. It motivates questioning and searching for answers and truths. Charles Sanders Peirce describes how and why. Doubt is:

> an uneasy and dissatisfied state from which we struggle to free ourselves and pass into the state of belief; while the latter is a calm and satisfactory state that we do not wish to avoid, or to change to a belief in anything else. On the contrary, we cling tenaciously, not merely to believing, but to believing just what we do believe. Thus, both doubt and belief have positive effects upon us, though very different ones. Belief does not make us act at once, but puts us into such a condition that we shall behave in some certain way, when the occasion arises. Doubt has not the least such active effect, but stimulates us to inquiry until it is destroyed (Hartshorne & Weiss, 1931, p. 230).

In this way, Peirce describes doubt as an "irritant" that "provokes inquiry" (Ibid). Inherent in doubt is a valuing and a search for answers and truths: "When we want to be as sure as it is humanly possible to be, we usually resort to logic which

T. M. Kress and R. Lake (Eds.), We Saved the Best for You: Letters of Hope, Imagination and Wisdom for 21st Century Educators, 123–126.
© 2013 Sense Publishers. All rights reserved.

relies on contradiction and doubting" (Elbow, 1986, p. 265). Self-doubt does not shut down or narrow inquiry in the way belief and certainty can. It challenges the comforts of these two in its initiation and extension of questioning.

Doubt also highlights our human epistemic fallibility; it recognizes what Nietzsche calls "the whole marvelous uncertainty and interpretive multiplicity of existence" (1974, p.), and connects to his notion of intellectual conscience. It does this in at least two ways. First, it acknowledges and negotiates the partial, situated and positional aspects of human knowledge. We are not omniscient and "[w]e can never get out of our skins, and lose our 'I.' We can never stop filtering what we know through our contextuality of time and place" (Thayer-Bacon, 1995, p. 59). Second, it connects to our epistemic fallibility by redirecting us to attend to what Nussbaum calls "certain interpretive possibilities" (1990, p. 144), possibilities that are closed when doubt is absent. Self-doubt acknowledges and negotiates the "incompleteness and inadequacy of our attention" (Ibid.). It allows us to "notice the way we are inclined to miss things, to pass over things, to leave out certain interpretative possibilities while pursuing others" (Ibid.). It "reminds us that, even when we do attend, our attention, like all human attention, is interested and interpretive" (Ibid.). In addition to initiating and extending inquiry, self-doubt actively recognizes and can help negotiate these human epistemic limitations.

Finally, doubt connects us to the virtue of humility. When humility refers to modesty and a healthy respect for human and personal limitations, it disconnects from concerns for greatness, honor and pride. Nor does it connect to their extremes: self-disgust, low self-regard, or low self-confidence (Emmons, 1999). Rather it aligns with a forgetting or transcending of the self (Pieper, 1966) and the moderation of ego. Self-doubt manifests humility and alerts us to the danger of humility's opposites – pride, arrogance, dogmatism and self-righteousness.

Although doubt initiates inquiry, recognizes our epistemic limitations and relates to humility, it is also commonly considered, "a thing to be dreaded; a danger, risk" ("Doubt"). As teachers I suggest we ought to uncouple the notion of dread from doubt and embrace the positive connotations that its inherent risk and valuing of truth has for growth. As teachers, we ought to shift the educational conversation from valuing "freedom from doubt" to "freedom to doubt."

Of course, we cannot "live" in doubt; it is unstable, and at times it moves us to reflection when action may be necessary. Self-doubt is not without its problems and is not for all times and places. As Peirce details, it requires an interactive coupling with belief. My point is not that we should always doubt, but that we should be as selfishly interested in cultivating self-doubt as we are in cultivating and expressing beliefs. We should be interested because the discourse in contemporary American politics, media and life is characterized by doubt's opposite, an entrenchment in particular beliefs and positions. We feed our beliefs and certainty by selectively picking and choosing to expose ourselves only to what confirms our beliefs (for example, with news sources). We are so "certain" that we are unable to communicate, much less act across difference and disagreement. In an interview for his Pulitzer Prize winning play and film, *Doubt*, John Patrick Shanley sums up the situation: "There's been this evaporation of doubt as a hallmark of wisdom" (Falsani, 2008). Differences and challenges cannot be addressed and negotiated without the ability to engage in open and meaningful ways – ways characterized by inquiry, recognizing our epistemic limitations and humility. If we cannot doubt ourselves, we do not allow ourselves opportunities for learning and for growth, both personally and as a society. As teachers, you and I are doubly responsible. In our influence over large numbers of impressionable children and young adults, we ought to embrace the freedom to doubt so that others might consider its value.

Sincerely,
Susan Verducci

REFERENCES

Doubt. (n.d.). In *Oxford English Dictionary* online. Retrieved from http://www.oed.com/.
Elbow, P. (1986). *Embracing contraries: Exploration in learning and teaching*. New York: Oxford University Press.
Emmons, R. A. (1999). *The psychology of ultimate concerns: Motivation and spirituality in personality*. New York: Guilford Press.
Falsani, C. (2008). Beyond the shadow of a doubt. *Huffington Post*, December 12. Retrieved from http://www.huffingtonpost.com/cathleen-falsani/beyond-the-shadow-of-a-do_b_150496.html.
Hartshorne, C., & Weiss, P. (Eds.) (1931). *Collected papers of Charles Sanders Peirce*. Cambridge: Harvard University Press.
Nietzche, F. (1974). *The gay science* (Books I-IV: 1882; Book V: 1887). (W. Kaufmann, Trans.). New York: Vintage Books.
Pieper, J. (1966). *The four cardinal virtues: Prudence, justice, fortitude, temperance*. South Bend, IN: University of Notre Dame Press.
Thayer-Bacon, Barbara J. (1995). Doubting and believing: Both are important for critical thinking. *Inquiry: Critical Thinking Across the Disciplines, 15*(2): 59–66.

AFFILIATION

Susan Verducci
Department of Humanities
San José State University

TINA WAGLE

28. MAKE THE BEST OF WHAT'S AROUND[1]

Dear future teacher,

As the editors wrote in the introduction, we are living in "dark times" in a time of war, of economic downturn, and contextually for this letter, at a time in which education continues to change and is abject to intense criticism. While they are correct in their assessment, they also acknowledge that it is more important than ever to uncover places of hope and inspiration—inspiration for ourselves and for those we hope to educate. I hope to demonstrate this sentiment in my letter to you by encouraging you to "make the best of what's around."

The use of letters as the vehicle for communication in this book offers educators everywhere an informal yet inspirational space that may generate self-reflection, openness and dialogue, all of which we desperately need. I would like this particular letter to you to support such a collective space so as to help rescue you from any experience of isolation or self-doubt you may feel as an educator, especially as a new educator. Of course, it's important to recognize that every teaching situation is different, but it's also important to recognize that we have a common goal: to strive to develop your own identity in the classroom – an essential ingredient to good practice. Knowing yourself as an educator (not such an easy process!) will only encourage your self-confidence necessary to create a successful classroom.

From an educational perspective, we often feel as though we live in a constant state of flux. No Child Left Behind evolves into Race to the Top, which we know will become something else, to which we educators will be expected to adjust. Because policy tends to drive educational pathways, educators may feel as though their domain (that is, the day to day life with our students in the classroom) is secondary, a mere afterthought, thus begging the question: do we have any voice at all? Policy changes often do not allow the time for complaining and careful consideration of why any particular changes are taking place. We must instead view them as opportunities to engage students and to help them reach their maximum potential. We must remember that the most powerful voice we have is the one inside our classrooms. That voice, your voice – the distinctiveness of which you are trying to create for yourself – manages, presides, supports and engages. You must also be aware, however, that the very same voice that can inspire also has the potential to offend, damage and silence. Be conscious of your potential as a leader who has

T. M. Kress and R. Lake (Eds.), We Saved the Best for You: Letters of Hope, Imagination and Wisdom for 21st Century Educators, 127–130.
© 2013 Sense Publishers. All rights reserved.

the capability of advocacy for and simultaneously of fracturing the spirit of your students. Take this as a cautionary note to be careful.

Today there is much talk about the Common Core Standards, a set of standards already adopted by many individual states that, over time, may evolve into national standards applied to every classroom in America. These standards seem to be privileging English Language Arts and Mathematics above all other subjects, so it is important to keep in mind the need for interdisciplinarity and critical thinking in all of the work we do. I am reminded of educational philosophers like Maxine Greene who have devoted time, attention and their own important voices to support a wider curricular vision including too often neglected areas such as the arts. Greene eloquently speaks of the need for holistic development that underscores individual students' learning styles, preferences and strengths. Imagining new, inclusive curricula can help students negotiate their own spaces of learning and methods of achieving their learning goals.

Perhaps surprisingly, even now, with mandates at every corner, innovation really is not dead! In these times of significant political and economic change, educators also find themselves in a space that offers opportunity. Be inventive in trying to apply mandated changes to daily classroom life. Now is not the time to find yourself in a silo. Reach out to other teachers and team members to share strategies for best practices. Encourage and take the time to join in collaborations and cross disciplinary planning. Isolation can be paralyzing; collegial solidarity will give you courage to continue to develop your identity, create an engaging classroom, and help your students learn.

Discovering one's own identity in the classroom is critical to one's ability to manage, engage and guide your students in their learning. Not only is your identity in question, however. What about your students'? What happens to youth and adolescents as they grow and develop? As a future teacher, you will play a key role in your students' personal development at the very same time that you are developing your own. You may not realize until years later just what an impact you have had on these children and, in turn, how they affected (often without your conscious awareness) your values, strategies and basic assumptions about teaching and learning.

It is in the classroom space that you must be true to yourself and teach how you must teach. Only you and fellow teachers will know your students well enough to be the best judge of their idiosyncrasies and thus, how they learn best. Despite policies in place that may be counterintuitive to your "gut", remaining true to yourself and the first-hand knowledge you have of your students is essential to your students' best chances for success. I encourage you to embrace your own observations and your insights because these are the moments that will help define you as an educator and that you will carry with you throughout your career.

Part of the reason I encourage identity development in educators is because I am still going through my own. In my position, I have been straddling the line between teacher and administrator for the last year and a half, struggling with my own roles, responsibilities and place. I do not think this feeling is unique to nascent teachers. We begin to ask ourselves: what comes first? To whom do I owe my best attention? Which side of various arguments should I take? Questions such as these invariably arise and we're often confused and unclear about appropriate answers. But I assure you it is okay, maybe even necessary, to become frustrated. But I encourage you to seek the space to work through these questions in a way that is comfortable for you so that burnout does not invade your life. One can lose steam but I humbly ask that you not lose heart. Our profession needs you. We need you to be free to think about your own space and education more broadly. We need you to be creative and to help us generate ideas for positive change. To that end, it is important to have a support system in place that allows time for decompression. You can and will make a difference. Please remember this particularly in times of trial—in those moments when you feel most disempowered.

I have been inspired by many, including John Dewey (1902), whose book *The Child and Curriculum* had a significant impact on me. One of the many lessons I took away from his notion of "learning by doing" was that learning and education mean something different for everyone. What does education look like? Are we so sure that our way, or better, "their way," is the only way? Who is educated? What assumptions are we making at every turn? While I believe formal education is valuable and important, I urge you to continue to rethink what knowledge looks like, whose interests it serves, and how it is measured. Howard Gardner reminds us that we all learn differently and have different strengths and limitations; the creation of knowledge is undeniably personal and individual. How can you become more aware not only of your own style but of the ways in which each of your students thinks and acts? We all need to continue to fight for agency and democracy. We need to share opinion and voice. What better location to initiate and develop your vision than in your own classroom?

To conclude my letter, I would like to revisit an old friend, a common driving force for teacher educators, and that is idealism. Why do we often refer to those we describe as "idealists" with cynicism and skepticism? Why have cynicism and skepticism dominated our field- a field that should be filled with idealists? It is my belief that educators should struggle (it's not always so easy!) to retain their great sense of idealism after entering the profession. Isn't this why you wanted to teach in the first place? We need to see the best in you and in your students; indeed, it is in recognizing our students' potential that we glimpse the potential of education itself. It is essential to recognize and remember that every student in your class has and brings value to his or her surroundings. Remember, you are about to become an inspiration to your own students. Make every day count and "make the best of what's around" even at a time when it seems as though many may not be listening to you.

All the best to you,
Tina Wagle

NOTE

[1] Dave Matthews Band. (1994). Best of What's Around. *Under the Table and Waiting (album)*.

REFERENCE

Dewey, J. (1902). *The Child and the curriculum*. Chicago, IL: University of Chicago Press.

AFFILIATION

Tina Wagle
Teacher Education
State University of New York, Empire State College

KURT LOVE

29. TO DARE BE AN INSPIRED, SATIATED, SOULFUL TEACHER

Dear Teachers,

Why do we teach? Our profession is not entirely a unique one. Many other professions have a teaching component to them. Other professions, whether they focus on medical, holistic, technical, artistic, religious, or community based practices, inspire "learners" to grow, become more confident, and build themselves with greater depth, purpose, and fulfillment. As teachers, these qualities can be at the heart of our work continuously.

To teach is to help someone else learn, perhaps one of the most sacred acts in life. In other words, to be a teacher is to help others (and ourselves) grow as people, and to explore the local and global communities and their infinite relationships. To teach is to support, nurture, and help someone stretch. Teachers who understand their practice deeply see that learning is a very personal endeavor for their students, which is inextricably linked to becoming their individual selves. To be a teacher who truly helps another person learn, whether they are 3 years old or 93 years old, is to help them consider new relationships and new questions. We merely offer many paths for students to explore and witness for their own development. Our personal growth, our development, our levels of soulful exploration, our abilities to see beauty and oppression, and the extent to which we are inspired people create the bounds in which we teach. We cannot teach what we do not think, see, know, or question.

Too often, the climate and general practices in mainstream schools are antithetical towards a learning experience that is divergent, explorative, and humanizing, preferring instead one that is convergent, limiting, and imprisoning. Fully liberated learning experiences are denied in schools so regularly that it almost seems natural to the uncritical eye to omit them completely. Honors students are routinely praised for the level of adherence, if not docility, with curriculum, while students who resist (and are wounded by) school are frequently described as burdens by narrow-minded teachers who uphold dominant social norms. The treatment of learning as a process of memorizing and regurgitating the "right" answer can only be seen as form of violence in contrast to liberated learning because it mentally and emotionally rationalizes that conformed thinking is natural and right while dissent, creativity, and divergence are ultimately problematic. Denying someone a liberated learning experience is akin to imprisoning their mind, spirit, and soul.

T. M. Kress and R. Lake (Eds.), We Saved the Best for You: Letters of Hope, Imagination and Wisdom for 21st Century Educators, 131–134.
© 2013 Sense Publishers. All rights reserved.

Learning is not about cramming laundry lists of definitions and bold faced words into our heads and retaining as much of them as possible for a series of tests so that we can eventually go to college. Yet, this is the dominant, normed view that politicians and business leaders routinely use to describe "successful" schools. Too often, schools are places where deep, critical, and creative thinking processes are prohibited in favor of conformity, sameness, and the loss of self. This is not learning; this is schooling. Learning is truly a liberating process. It is a powerful way that we can understand our deeper selves, perhaps even our own personal souls. Learning is the process by which we are fueled to explore this life, its beauty, our profound interconnected relationships that go beyond what we think we see everyday. Learning is the fundamental core living experience.

Schooling does not necessarily produce learning. Schools produce false impressions of learning, especially if a school's overall climate and tone is test-focused, controlling, and repressive. In this type of school climate learning is decontextualized from the living community that is just outside the doors and perhaps even visible through the classroom's windows. If a teacher reproduces decontextualized and irrelevant learning in her or his classroom, students are more likely to disengage, guard themselves, and resist that teacher. Many students who are disenfranchised with schooling do so because their cumulative educational experience has marginalized them, telling them that they are not worthwhile human beings. Why would students be open to a climate that dehumanizes them and tells them that learning is about conforming to decontextualized curricula that often reject or marginalize a student's own living experiences? In a democratic society these "disruptive behaviors" are generally called protest or civil disobedience in order to interrupt something that is unjust. Yet, students are rarely ever considered justified when they "act out" even though these can be legitimate tactics used to resist a process that is experienced as hurtful and dehumanizing.

Learning can most certainly be experienced as enriching, meaningful, and connective on a regular basis. When learning is rooted in one's community and related to real world issues, community problems and accomplishments that connect with our lives, this may be a fully liberated learning experience that can make one's whole body ring with joy and fulfillment. How do we do this kind of teaching and learning in an overall climate that is doing just the opposite? Can it be done? We can most certainly take education back from the business mindset that has gutted it. We can truly recover and heal from this toxicity, but we have to decide that this is a necessary process to take on and commit to seeing it through. We can succeed in making public education a deeply moving experience for teachers and learners, which will collectively shape our society towards dialogue, peace, and cooperation.

One of the most important steps a teacher can do is to clearly articulate a vision of why she or he teaches. This vision is what grounds you and will help you to remain focused on teaching with purpose. Write that vision and keep it in a place where you can see it every day. Maybe it is something as simple as writing a few key phrases down on a piece of paper that you tape on the inside of your desk where you know you will see it continuously. Or maybe you put it in the footer of every handout that you give to your students so that they are aware of it, too. Whatever you decide, just make sure that it does not become forgotten. Having it physically present in your classroom means that you can continually remind yourself why and how you are teaching your curriculum, but you will also be more able to see whether or not your vision needs to be restated. As you teach your students, you may find that your vision needs to be updated or clarified even more. On my office door are my office hours where I have written: "I teach about how to ask critical questions, not how to repeat back 'right' answers. I teach so that students may be empowered to build themselves, not conform to me, a dominant mindset, or each other. I teach so that I may help to make this a more connected, caring, and sustainable world." I make it known to all that pass by (students, professors, administrators, support staff, and visitors) that this is why I teach. I want it to be public because I want it to constantly be part of the culture and climate of where I teach. As the Secondary Education Division Coordinator for our department, I have even encouraged my colleagues to do the same and post their vision statements.

Teaching is a deeply personal and meaningful action. We generally teach because we care about our students and the world in which we live. The clearer we are about our reasons for teaching, the more our teaching practices and relationships with our students will be closely aligned. Despite the larger, systemic challenges imposed on teachers from politicians, billionaires, and business minded people with disproportionate amounts of power to make sweeping (and generally ignorant) policies, teachers have the power to push back and demand that their classrooms be a sanctuary for meaningful learning rooted in the living histories and experiences of their communities.

To teach with compassion, conviction, and purpose is to choose a lifestyle, a mindset, and perhaps even a spiritual path. The richness that we seek is not financial, but is achieved when our students explore the world with new eyes and connect with their deeper purposes and sense of self. For so many, teaching is a higher calling. We seek to build a better community. Teaching can be a daily practice of supporting and inspiring students towards their own individual and communal empowerment, creative expression, cultural connection, and community contribution. Teaching is inextricably interwoven into the foundations of a society, even at the very fibers of an individual's construction of reality. We teach people the beginnings of how to see their world, and if done well, we teach how to truly question that which they see and to search for what they do not see.

Kurt Love

AFFILIATION

Kurt Love
Teacher Education Department
Central Connecticut State University

DONNA DEGENNARO

30. YOU ARE NOT ALONE

Radically Redefining 'Place' as Community

Hope is essential to any political struggle for radical change when the overall social climate promotes disillusionment and despair (hooks in SECP, 1998).

Dear Teachers,

There is no way to say this gently. You are different. And because you are different, you often feel alone.

You sit in a room looking around at your colleagues as you reflect on your experiences. Your studies provided you with tools to see the world through multiple lenses and thus to see possibilities of creating learning environments that transcend rigidity, conformity, and hierarchy. You could choose to fall back into the gravity of traditional norms, but the experiences that have changed you so deeply don't allow you to do so; you feel you would be selling your soul. You hold steadfastly to the principles of emancipation, conscientization, critical conversation, and the quest of humanization (Freire, 1970; 1973) that have become so visible in your education. While you recall the theories and scenarios that opened your eyes, you sit in awe listening to their discussions of prescribing learning and ignoring culture, history, and local knowledge. You feel like you are floating outside the reality of other individuals who instead are held hostage to the very system that they know perpetuates ignorance, inequality, and the status quo (Parsons, 1959). The reality of this perplexes you. Silently you will wonder: *How could it be that others who had similar theoretical and practical groundings could not be equally changed by this deeply transformative educational preparation?*

In the wake of your resistance you will become labeled a radical thinker, an innovator, and a pioneer. You will, above all, be passionate about inspiring true learning, rather than automating human participation (Zuboff, 1988). Those who possess these characteristics are viewed not as an asset, but rather as irrational and insubordinate. As bell hooks writes, "I am passionate about everything in my life – first and foremost, passionate about ideas. And that's a dangerous person to be in this society... because it's such a fundamentally anti-intellectual, anti-critical thinking society" (1994, p. 39). Thinking and questioning, and teaching others to do so, liberates. Liberation is unpredictable. Unpredictability is terrifying.

T. M. Kress and R. Lake (Eds.), We Saved the Best for You: Letters of Hope, Imagination and Wisdom for 21st Century Educators, 135–140.
© 2013 Sense Publishers. All rights reserved.

Thus organization of educational practices tends toward prescription and control (Tobin, 2005).

You will hear their common justifications as they spew phrases such as: *Leave well enough alone; Why fix it if it isn't broken; We have to teach them to succeed in the current system, we can't change it*. Because you have embraced the importance of questioning, you will ask what constitutes well enough and for whom, when, and to what end? You will ask who decides and who benefits from this so called "well enough"? You will also ask what it means to not be broken. You will challenge these expressions by inquiring how this so-called unbroken system continues to generate a society that moves further away from being able to think, question, and foster this unfounded inability to change. The majority who chose to maintain the system will overshadow your voice. They live in fear – a fear of losing their job, of disrupting the system, or of falling from power.

You remember the words you once read: "Dominator culture has tried to keep us all afraid, to make us choose safety instead of risk, sameness instead of diversity. Moving through that fear, finding out what connects us, reveling in our differences; this is the process that brings us closer, that gives us a world of shared values, of meaningful community" (hooks, 2003, p. 197). This and other texts have profoundly awakened you in your journey and you cannot imagine that they do not see. You hold strongly to your values of inquiry, alternative structures, and new possibilities. You are stunned by the fact that people feed into the maintenance of reproducing education, culture and society (Bourdieu & Passeron, 1977). And in the process, you will be othered; the masses will consciously or unconsciously marginalize you.

I speak authoritatively on this subject because I have lived this journey. My transformation began in what was perhaps my first truly educative experience. In my first graduate degree, I was fortunate enough to be mentored by one of the most inspirational and visionary graduate program leaders I ever witnessed. This woman, in her 70s at the time, was beyond her time. She led an Educational Technology program with a leadership focus. She organized the program to not only include technology skills, but also reflections on rethinking learning, teaching, and the organization of education. We questioned everything, especially history's adherence to a positivistic existence (Giddens, 1974).

We read books about and by visionary innovators. Each shook the core of our conditioned notion of maintaining the machine (Weber, 1922). These texts challenged the very notion of the hierarchal mechanism. Such texts brought to light the importance of relationships and interrelationships as foundational to successful, yet continuously evolving, organizations. At the core of that successful learning institutions were the principles of "community, meaning, dignity, purpose and love" (Wheatley, 1994, p. xliii).

Change became something exciting, informative, productive, and collective. But to embrace change meant we as leaders would need to rethink the dominant class methods of deciding what norms, values and rules were essential to social order and how education should instill them (Durkheim, 1995). More than anything, we would need to release and reconsider our obsession with control. Instead, we practiced how to empower others in order to cultivate structures that emerged and evolved with input from all of our constituents. Leadership, we recognized, was not within the held power of one dictating individual, but rather comes from individual and collective agency developed by "leaders without followers" (Dede, 1993).

We lived this as students as we drew on these theories to think about the organization of schools, from administrative structures to the design of learning environments. We incorporated these theories with concepts such as socio-cultural learning theory (Vygostky, 1978), social constructivism (Glasersfeld, 1989) and distributed expertise (Hutchins, 1995). In our program, these ideas of integrating organizational theory with learning were not simply espoused; they were practiced. The learning "structure" was fluid. It built on student's cultures, experiences, and knowledge (Bransford, 2000). We were expected to contribute to our learning. Thus professors became learners as well as teachers. I worked not separated from my classmates, but rather in conjunction with them (Scardamalia & Bereiter, 2006). For the first time in my education, I felt that I was truly learning. I was contributing to my learning, not simply taking in and restating information. I was part of creating goals and purposes within myself and for myself and with my peers. It seemed so clear to me that learning was organic and organizational structures that fostered true learning would need to be as well.

Following this I held several positions, leaving each in search of *the* great place that inspired others to create teaching environments that emulated what I had learned. In each location, I watched as pawns in the game adhered to the assertive power to control the system. I watched them adhere to "learning" designs that did nothing but input information in order to output youth able to pass externally imposed tests. I witnessed behavior that eludes my comprehension. I saw people contributing to an educational system and organization that does not teach our students, let alone our aspiring teachers, to be intellectual and curious beings. This, I thought to myself, is all at the expense of generating and recreating a socially just and conscious world.

Although I have yet to find what I search for, I continue to seek it. But this search is now different. Initially, I thought I would find the perfect place that sees the significance of that practice and recognizes the importance of the values I have embraced. I have come to realize the "place" is less a matter of a location than a frame of mind, an attitude. It is continuing to make change in my corner of the world, with my students, where and how I can. And to keep my spirit and visions as strong as they were when I exited my transformative educational experience, I have found that seeking a community of people instead of seeking a utopian place that does not exist is the more viable. This community is one that I now aim to foster and keep close. It is the one that I reach out to when the larger system overcomes me. I have held several positions and in each location there exists at least one person who shares my charge to inform and reform education into an equitable learning community that values and liberates. In the wake of the dominant system that has so much inertia to keep you down, this community is essential.

You will have plenty of days that you ask why you chose this path. You will remember the bliss of living happily in ignorance. But you can't go back, because now that you see and think, you are compelled to continue the quest of truly educating your students and others. In this quest, in this struggle to keep positive, you feel alone, but you are not. You are, however, among the few who strive for the simultaneity of difference (Appiah, 2006). You are among the few who aim to transcend binding structures and see the world as a constantly changing and collectively organizing structure. At times, the days will be long and the fight will be exhausting. Yet you will find the courage to reach deep within and continue on.

The words of wisdom that I have for you are to find those with vision along the way. Those who are like you are out there. Find them, find your networks that do think like you, who transcend the normative structures, who choose to find purpose in rising above the chains that bind. Find them through the Internet, through social networks, conferences, and your work. They will keep you energized, invigorated and on your path. They will keep alive the hope that what you are doing is worth the struggle, worth the time, and worth the feeling of loneliness. They are there, they understand, they live what you live. They will be your support and help you to realize that this journey that you are on to make the world more aware is more than worth it. It is the very core of why you chose to teach.

You will realize too, that the change you seek to foster may not happen in your lifetime, but that every step is worth it, because you know that you are part of the momentum that has initiated this change.

Donna DeGennaro

REFERENCES

Appiah, K. A. (2006). *Cosmopolitanism: Ethics in a world of strangers*. New York, NY: W. W. Norton & Co.

Bourdieu, P., & Passeron, J. C. (1977). *Reproduction in education, society, and culture*. London: Sage Publications.

Bransford, J., Brown, A., & Cocking, R. (2000). *How people learn: Brain, mind,experience, and school committee on developments in the science of learning*.Washington, DC: National Academy Press.

Dede, C. (1993). Leadership without followers. In G. Kearsley & W. Lynch, Eds. *Educational technology: Leadership perspectives* (pp. 19–28). Englewood Cliffs, NJ: EducationalTechnology Publications.

Durkheim, E. (1995). *The elementary forms of the religious life*. London: Allen and Unwin.

Friere, P. (1970). *Pedagogy of the oppressed*. New York: The Seabury Press.

Freire, P. (1973). *Education for critical consciousness*. New York, NY: The Seabury Press.

Giddens, A. (1974). *Positivism and sociology*. London: Heinemann.

Glasersfeld, E. Von. (1989). Cognition, construction of knowledge, and teaching. *Synthese, 80*: 121–40.

hooks, b. (1994). "What's passion got to do with it?" in *Outlaw culture: Resisting representations*. New York, NY: Routledge.

Hutchins, E. (1995). *Cognition in the wild*. Cambridge, MA. MIT Press.

Parsons, T. (1959). The school class as a social system: Some of its functions in American society. *Harvard Educational Review, 29*(1): 297–318.

Scardamalia, M., & Bereiter, C. (2006). Knowledge building: Theory, pedagogy, and technology. In K. Sawyer (Ed.), *The Cambridge handbook of the learningsciences* (pp. 97–118). New York: Cambridge University Press.

South End Press Collective (Eds.) (1998). *Talking about a revolution: Interviews with Michael Albert, Noam Chomsky, Barbara Ehrenreich, bell hooks, Peter Kwong, Winona LaDuke, Manning Marable, Urvashi Vaid, and Howard Zinn*. Cambridge, MA.: South End Press.

Tobin, K. (2005). Building enacted science curricula on the capital of learners. *Science Education, 89*: 577–594.

Vygotsky, L. (1978). *Mind in society*. London: Harvard University Press.

Wheatley, M. (1994). *Leadership and the new science*. San Francisco: Berrett-Koehler.

Zuboff, S. (1988). *In the age of the smart machine: The future of work and power*. New York: Basic Books.

AFFILIATION

Donna DeGennaro
Department of Curriculum and Instruction
The University of Massachusetts Boston

PART IV

LETTERS OF CLASSROOM PRAXIS

NEL NODDINGS

31. TEACHERS AS CRITICAL THINKERS

Dear Young Educators:

I'm not sure that I agree with the title of this book; I'm not sure, that is, that "we have saved the best for you." It seems to me, rather, that we have made a mess of things—some of us by actively pressing anti-educational "reforms," others of us by not fighting the reform movement hard enough.

There has never been a "golden age" in education, however, and I still have hope that young educators can study and analyze the best of the past, rework it, and create something new and fine for the future. In most educational talk today we hear an endorsement of three great aims for 21st century education: cooperation, critical thinking, and creativity. I wish policymakers would take these aims seriously and drop the dull project of standardization, the ill-conceived demand for higher test scores, and the sick enchantment with GPAs and rankings.

In this brief letter, I want to encourage you to think seriously about all three aims, but I can address only one here, and I'll choose critical thinking. Critical thinking is a wonderful aim for education. It is at the heart of a deliberative democracy, and of course it is powerful in directing individual lives. But can we teach people to think critically? I'm not sure that everyone can become a critical thinker, but I do believe that everyone should have opportunities to develop that capacity. Those opportunities can be provided in every subject we teach, but to provide them we must be allowed to discuss controversial issues. There is little incentive to apply critical thinking to dull memorization and routine exercises. Critical thinking is induced by critical lessons on critical issues. I have written about this need in several places, most extensively in a book titled *Critical Lessons: What Our Schools Should Teach.*

Unfortunately, we have bequeathed you a system in which the teaching of controversy is frowned upon. For example, few teachers today feel able to discuss questions such as: Was the United States founded on Christian principles? Can you think of a way to address such a controversy and yield a rich, honest answer without disrespecting those on either side? Where would you turn to find a definitive answer? (Hint: Start with George Washington.)

This is your challenging task—to become a critical thinker and to model that thinking. Perhaps it would be best to start by thinking critically about teaching itself. You are today urged on all sides to adopt certain teaching methods and reject

T. M. Kress and R. Lake (Eds.), We Saved the Best for You: Letters of Hope, Imagination and Wisdom for 21st Century Educators, 143–144.
© 2013 Sense Publishers. All rights reserved.

others. Must you accept any method whole hog or reject it completely? If you are a critical thinker, you should be able to analyze and evaluate a method, asking: Where might this be useful? Under what conditions? For which students? How does it fit with other strategies and a system of instruction? Might it undermine larger, more important aims?

Over the years, educators and researchers have come up with a host of promising ideas, among them: discovery, intuition, mastery learning, task analysis, object lessons, role playing, behavioral objectives, group work, Socratic questioning, spaced practice, guided fantasy, mnemonic devices, wait time, drill, stage theories, incidental learning, ability grouping, open education, learning to learn, audio-visual methods, activity methods, readiness, whole word and/or phonics, online learning, spiral curriculum, overt thinking,...

Your job as critical thinkers is not to look over this list and decide which idea will dominate your approach to teaching. Your task is to explore each idea analytically through questions of the sort asked above. If you think critically, you will probably not use teacher-centered methods exclusively; nor will you reject them. The question is when you might wisely use teacher-centered or student-centered methods. You are entering a field in which the theoretical possibilities are rich. I hope that the foolishness of the present generation of policymakers will not foreclose those possibilities for you.

Are there any ideas that you should embrace or reject fully? Of course. But you should think about these deeply and ask yourself, first, why you are committed fully to certain ideals and, then, how those ideals lead you to reject some methods, movements, and pedagogical ideas. If one of your ideals is to support the development of critical thinking, you may reject—for example—scripted lessons, zero-tolerance rules, and empty slogans such as "no excuses"—all of which tend to cut dialogue short and thus undermine critical thinking.

While on a break from writing, I listened to a re-broadcast of Steve Jobs's 2005 commencement address at Stanford. He advised the graduates not "to settle," to keep looking for work they will love. Terrific advice! And if you have found that work in teaching, make teaching better, stronger, more inspiring so that others will be able to love it. I wish you the joy I have experienced in teaching at every level from fifth grade to graduate school. I'm still thinking about it...

Nel Noddings

AFFILIATION

Nel Noddings
Professor Emerita
School of Education
Stanford University

BRIAN D. SCHULTZ

32. OF KIDS AND COKES

Learning from, with, and Alongside Children

Dear Jennifer,

I have been meaning to get back in touch with you for some time. I sincerely enjoyed reading in your last letter that some of the ideas we discussed in class related to developing progressive practices and sharing authority with children are playing out well in your new classroom. Your stories reminded me of two recent experiences. The first was a somewhat alarming experience that occurred while I was teaching a graduate course and the other was a splendid conversation with a woman living in a retirement community. I'll start by recounting the more sobering class experience and then move to what I hope you will think is an uplifting anecdote from an elder. Whereas the stories are not overtly connected, I think the latter certainly supports my continued encouragement for students to try to live up to democratic ideals in their future educational spaces.

As you may recall, the graduate class, Development of Educational Thought, is part of a social foundations portion of a professional educational sequence that includes many students who are career changers. Whereas this course has always been one of my favorites to teach, I was struck by the perspective and tone of one of my students last semester. To recount, the course readings promote students to contemplate various historical and philosophical tenets of progressive education. One of the more vocal students sharply contested the idea that curriculum, teaching, and learning could start with students and that teachers may learn alongside their students. She insisted that students simply do not know enough and "do not have it in them" to understand choices and make wise decisions about how their education or schooling can be constructed. Further, she could not believe that curricula could realistically revolve around the needs, wants, interests and desires of young people. How I wish, Jennifer, you could have been in the class to challenge her by sharing your teaching experiences with young people in your classroom.

As you are well aware, protests from students are not unusual, yet the fervor this particular woman demonstrated appeared more profound than previous classroom deliberations. What stood out to me was her casting of doubt about children—even for her own four-year-old daughter!—and what she seemed to perceive as young people's inherent lack of ability, insight, curiosity, and imagination. Her agitation,

T. M. Kress and R. Lake (Eds.), We Saved the Best for You: Letters of Hope, Imagination and Wisdom for 21st Century Educators, 145–148.
© *2013 Sense Publishers. All rights reserved.*

perhaps even what appeared to be pride, that her daughter would not know what interests her and would not be able to self-direct any learning, left me at a loss for words. Apparently, reading John Dewey, W.E.B. Dubois, and Paulo Freire, as well as exposure to the ideas of Carter Woodson, L. Thomas Hopkins, and Caroline Pratt did not offer enough encouragement.

My advocacy for learning from, with, and alongside young people is often cast—especially by many of my university students who have attended Chicago Public Schools—as a radical concept. Many think this is some new-fangled idea. Many find these ideas challenge their normative views of teachers as keepers of knowledge and children as docile recipients of someone else's wisdom. Seldom do students come to class familiar with the rich theorizing from the last 100 years for which my construction of listening to and learning from students are based. My hope, though, is that these future educators will take such ideas to heart—as you have done—so that they can embrace the promise and potential of the young people they will encounter.

Maybe this particular former graduate student and other skeptical students could have benefitted from being a fly on the wall following a recent talk I gave at a local nursing home. The lecture focused on educational policy and how curriculum may connect to the lives of students. The audience listened intently and even called out during the presentation to share their approval. Many residents approached me after the talk. Each of the seniors that waited to speak to me following the session was a former teacher. Each had fascinating stories of their time in the classroom. Perhaps most profound, though, was one woman in her nineties—I'll call her Mrs. Bidder—whose story struck a chord with me. I have found myself telling and retelling her classroom's strategies every chance I get.

Having waited patiently in line clutching her walker with both hands, I am so glad that Mrs. Bidder was willing to endure the others' tales from their experiences so she could tell hers. Mrs. Bidder recounted her time teaching in a Chicago suburb; she identified herself "as a pioneer in a special education classroom." She indicated that she was appreciative of my talk not so much because of the narratives I shared about my experiences teaching young people, but because of the theories I described. Mrs. Bidder said hearing the theories affirmed that what she had done for so many years so many years ago as she made her classroom curriculum responsive to her students was not only good practice, but also had a theoretical basis to boot. She said she had always tried to respond to her students and had figured out a way to do it effectively.

To be honest, I was uncertain at first where Mrs. Bidder's tale was headed. She was slow to start as she described how she had given each of her students a bottle of Coca-Cola during one of the first classes of the school year. As Mrs. Bidder continued her account, she described how her students were always the children deemed struggling learners incapable of inquiry or sophisticated problem solving. She saw them differently. In the late forties and early fifties, Mrs. Bidder noted how having a teacher give her students a Coke was quite a treat. As her students sat around the classroom sipping on their cold beverages, Mrs. Bidder listened intently to their conversations with each other. Not knowing their teacher was keenly noting what they were talking about, they spoke about their interests, their fascinations, and what they would be doing after school. Mrs. Bidder said that whatever they mentioned with excitement and intensity became their curriculum. She knew they were interested because it was what they discussed when they had the time, space, and opportunity to do so.

As she reveled in the simplicity of her curriculum design model, so too, did I. Clearly, Mrs. Bidder was able to capture the imaginations of young people not by prescription or repetition, but instead by following their lead. The children's ideas became the curricular centerpiece. Mrs. Bidder then told how her class sessions were exciting and how her students actively participated in their curriculum throughout the year—challenging the expectations of those outside of the classroom. As you and I both know, this may sound novel to some, but the basis for such a practice is rooted in rich progressive education history. I plan to tell Mrs. Bidder's story of learning from, with, and alongside her students in upcoming courses—perhaps it may help to persuade some of the naysayers of the future.

I would love to hear your thoughts on these stories and hope to hear some more accounts of your own when you write back.

With warm regards,
Brian

AFFILIATION

Brian D. Schultz
Department of Educational Inquiry & Curriculum Studies
Northeastern Illinois University in Chicago

MELISSA WINCHELL

33. "YOU DIDN'T CONNECT WITH ME"

Teaching as Radical Contemplative Practice

Only if in teaching you experience yourself as still learning do you have what people call authority. Only if that is the case do you touch people's hearts.[1]

Dear Future Educator:

"You didn't connect with me."

The words, by the time I read them, a few months after the graduate course had concluded, were sterilized—anonymous and word processed, tucked into the pages of course evaluation data in my inbox. I knew they were coming, knew in the way that most of us who teach know when we've had a particularly tension-ridden class filled with strong personalities, a few of whom finish our courses unhappy. Even still, the knowing that I would receive a few hard-to-hear comments from a few disgruntled graduate students did little to mediate the impact of those words. I read them again. And again. And I felt the words settle into me, an accusation, a judgment, a failure. A truth. A student's truth. And mine.

As I sat there blinking at my computer screen, I returned again to my memories of the class, its conflicts and tensions, its rich insights and moments of profound learning. I thought back to that previous semester, to my personal life then, to my spiritual life. And I realized with startling clarity that I had been a disconnected *person* that fall. Stresses in my own life had left me disconnected from the core practices of my spirituality, the rhythms that kept me most sane, most feeling, most human. And for the first time, I could perceive how the connectedness of my own self, to myself (or, if the reader will allow, to spirituality, or spirit, or God), fostered in me a capacity for connectedness with others, and most particularly, for connection within my own classroom.

There is a lot of talk these days about our classrooms and schools as "third spaces" (Zeichner, 2010). As we labor together to construct and imagine new forms of hybridity, it seems to me that one of those hybrids must certainly be the connection between our bodies and an open, spiritual, contemplative personal practice. Our classrooms are deeply affected by our ability as educators to access such places within our lived experiences. Freire himself wrote about his own personal practice of contemplation, a practice that resulted in his positionality of "critical optimism" and proved foundational to his model of praxis (Freire, 1996, p. 14).

T. M. Kress and R. Lake (Eds.), We Saved the Best for You: Letters of Hope, Imagination and Wisdom for 21st Century Educators, 149–152.
© *2013 Sense Publishers. All rights reserved.*

Since the student feedback that pointed to my inability to connect, I have given a lot of thought to contemplative practice, and have ventured a return to the spiritual practices that moor me and remind me of my connectedness to myself and to others.

Contemplative practice is a radical choice, especially given the busy, stress-filled lives we lead. Like you, my life is very full, mine with full-time teaching, doctoral studies, a marriage, and three children (one with significant special needs). Even still, the student evaluation unsettled me and ultimately prompted me to return to some core contemplative practices. I swam again, using the hour of repetitive pool laps to train my mind to recall gifts of my life, giving thanks as I stroked. I began keeping my personal journal in my minivan, lingering behind the wheel a few mornings a week in the college parking lot to write, to remind myself to seek out open spaces within the busyness of the day. I continued to observe a one-day retreat every three months for journaling, spiritual reading, and prayer. And I've explored new contemplative practices—meditation, yoga, acknowledging my breath throughout the day, dancing, and slow walking. All of these are simple ways that I grow my memory—remembering that I am a human be-ing (not just a human do-er) and that I am connected to the people I meet throughout my day, and to Love. This act of remembering, this contemplative practice, is a radical departure from the disconnected, stress-filled, fear-ridden way I was living that fall semester, a way I think we are all prone to living.

It is, it seems to me, our default to live crazed and disconnected existences. And not just in our personal lives. Our teaching practice is threatened by similar drives of fear, control, and anxiety. We teach in a milieu that is becoming more and more results-obsessed, data-driven, and mechanical. Education in our schools is growing into a monster of positivism that reduces us and our students to cogs in a large machine—a machine that is expected to run as an efficient mass producer of learning (Kincheloe & Tobin, 2009). In such a system, contemplation is a radical stance, and to be a contemplative person in the face of such a monster seems rather preposterous. Contemplation does not seem to answer the burning questions of our day: Why is there an achievement gap? How do I help my students to pass national exams? How do I make more time for learning? Do I teach for depth or breadth? How do I differentiate for English language learners, students with special needs, and gifted students?

On the other hand, contemplation does offer us a third way. And it does so when we begin to extend our view of contemplation beyond the personal and into our classrooms, when we begin to re-imagine our classrooms as practice-places for contemplation. When we enter our classrooms not as workers in the grand machine but as people present to, and connected with, the bodies and souls that surround us, we discover new ways of moving through our workday, new ways of envisioning our students, our jobs, and ourselves. In this view, the ordinary and everyday become sacred space. Our teaching, like our other core practices, becomes a site of contemplation.

The class that semester in which my student perceived my disconnection was for me a site of *doing*. It was the first time I had taught a graduate-level course for that particular state university. I was obsessed with what I would teach, not what my students knew, or wanted to know, or would come to know. I carefully planned the syllabus, designed challenging assessments, and crafted each 3-hour class to incorporate a variety of best practices. I thought I created a model for these educators of how to teach well; if they watched me, they would encounter an educator who was not just telling them how to teach, but showing them. Underlying this process, however, was a deep-rooted fear. What I was really doing, I realized only in retrospect, was trying to prove to the students and the department that I belonged, that I could teach a class of that caliber, that I could perform as expected. Whenever fear and anxiety are the hallmarks of my teaching, I have learned since, they signal my default—education as hierarchy, education as proof of intelligence, education as doing, education as mechanical. And in a great irony, for some of these students, such a positivistic practice resulted in exactly the opposite of its intended effect, as I hindered student learning and provided for these perceptive few a model of how *not* to teach.

A couple months after the student evaluation confronted me on my computer screen, the university called and asked me to teach the same course again. I nearly declined; I was not sure if I had deepened my spiritual practice enough to be less fearful and anxious, less craving of control, approval, and power in a graduate-level classroom. But when I considered contemplation and its many practice forms, and when I considered that teaching the course could be a way for me *to* practice, a way for me to improve, I accepted. After all, I reasoned, I was an imperfect contemplator in all of my other practices—I sometimes fell out of a yoga pose and crashed to the floor, or suddenly realized that I had lost minutes of a meditation while obsessing over that evening's supper plan, and often a week would go by without any journal entries at all. Contemplation, properly understood as process and a continued becoming, allowed for me, a nervous new professor, to teach the course and to keep at the contemplative practice of education.

I re-designed the course with the idea of "connection" in mind. I allowed for more time in class to come to know the graduate students, and for them to know one another. I came to class with objectives and an itinerary, but was much more open about slowing the pace and welcoming participant voices, even if it meant that an activity never began. I focused on learning, and expressions of learning, and I listened more than I spoke. I added an entirely new assignment in which the course participants read biographies of their choice as a way of connecting our course content to actual lived experiences within histories and contexts. And one night—as a group of students presented on their biography, and a handful of students began to cry, and a rigorous discussion of justice in our schools ensued—I felt the sweetness of the sacred, the connected, the relational. Students left that class—and the course— telling me it was the best course they had taken in their graduate program. It was my best course, too, because each meeting had taught me more about slowness, and presence, and listening, and quiet. And when one student sent me an email during our last week that read, "I have never met a professor so entirely *present* to her students," I knew it was contemplative practice that had helped me to make my way. I had experienced a joyful hybrid of intellectual rigor and meditative practice.

As you know, our growth as teachers is measured in fits and starts. I wish I could tell you that since that course—now nearly 8 months ago—I am a consistently present, aware, open, and connected teacher. It is not so. I work now at a new-to-me college where I teach writing. I am painfully aware of the ways in which my teaching of writing is sometimes mechanical, other times connective. I can only say that I have a trust that continuing to approach my classrooms as sites for contemplative practice, to grow in my awareness of the ways in which I default to the mechanistic cog of education, will continue the growth of my teaching—and my life—practice. Like you, I work in a clamorous, fast-moving machine of education where I continue to quietly and slowly envision ordinary spaces as extraordinary places for connection. Like you, I seek to learn. And like you, I find it all wonderfully, joyfully, radically sacred.

Yours in contemplative solidarity,
Melissa Winchell

NOTE

[1] This quote was copied from my personal journal and is attributed therein to Ayya Khema, *I Give You My Life: The Autobiography of a Western Buddhist Nun*, as quoted in Faith Aidele's *Meeting Faith: The Forest Journals of a Black Buddhist Nun* (2005).

REFERENCES

Freire, P. (1996). *Letters to Cristina: Reflections on my life and work*. (D. Macedo, Q. Macedo, & A. Oliveira, Trans.). New York: Routledge.

Kincheloe, J., & Tobin, K. (2009). The much exaggerated death of positivism. *Cultural Studies of Science Education, 4*: 513–528.

Zeichner, K. (2010). Rethinking the connections between campus courses and field experiences in college- and university-based teacher education. *Journal of Teacher Education, 61*(1–2): 89–99.

AFFILIATION

Melissa Winchell
Humanities & Fine Arts
Massasoit Community College

CHRISTOPHER EMDIN

34. THE NATURE AND PRACTICES OF URBAN SCIENCE EDUCATION

Dear Educator,

I write to you from the back of a science classroom housed in a building that holds four schools, but is designed for one. Outside of the classroom, through the bars on the windows, I hear the exciting sounds of the city. Cars drive by playing music and animated conversations from the street below can easily be heard. I sit in the last seat of a row of six chairs observing a novice teacher who recently graduated from an Ivy League school with an extraordinarily high grade point average struggle to keep the interest of the youth in front of her. Before the class, I sat with her as she hurriedly printed off worksheets and told me of how she was recruited to teach in urban schools because of her passion for caring for those who are less fortunate. Her science class is neat. Posters adorn almost every inch of empty space on the walls, and as I sit to write this, students are seated silently.

This teacher, like many of you who will take the helm of an urban classroom, or who are currently teachers, comes to the classroom with stellar credentials and good intentions. She heard about the terrible physical conditions of urban schools, the achievement gaps between urban youth of color and their counterparts from other settings, and decided that she would teach in a "tough urban school" and "make a difference." She was an undergraduate science major, and today teaches biology to students in one of the poorest neighborhoods in the country. She is a good person, a caring educator, and an ineffective teacher.

As I soak in the happenings in the classroom today, and reflect on what I have learned about this teacher's experiences prior to, and after becoming, an urban science educator, I realize that the scenario that I am witnessing in this classroom is an all too familiar one. Situations in which teachers are placed in urban classrooms armed with college degrees, good intentions, and poor preparation for how to connect the lively world outside of the classroom to science teaching are rampant. I have witnessed these scenarios from the vantage point of a student, teacher, school administrator, and researcher. I have written about them to fellow researchers, advised school districts about them, and talked to school administrators about how to create the structures that avoid them. At the end of it all, I am convinced that I have been speaking to the wrong audience all along. Affecting any true change in education begins with you, the new educator.

T. M. Kress and R. Lake (Eds.), We Saved the Best for You: Letters of Hope, Imagination and Wisdom for 21st Century Educators, 153–156.
© 2013 Sense Publishers. All rights reserved.

I write to you today to share the inner-workings of teaching science in urban settings. More specifically, I write to share what I have learned about the traps that you may fall into on the course towards being an effective urban science educator. In particular, I write to share how science teaching in urban settings has become a haven for the well-intentioned teacher, who has become burdened with guilt about their privilege, and conditioned to use this guilt as a crutch for teaching in ways that maintain achievement gaps and youth alienation from school and science.

With all that having been stated, what I hope to leave you with after reading this letter is that you do not have to fit into an established mold of "science teacher in tough schools." You do not have to become a cog in the machine that transforms good intentions into ineffective pedagogy and forces passion to dwindle into empty guilt. You can become the creator of create new possibilities, the spark that ignites a passion for science, and the provider of ammunition to fight the cycles of complacency that have become the norm in teaching within urban classrooms. However, all this comes by breaking the mold, being innovative, and finding a Muse that drives you.

One path towards breaking the mold you have been placed in as urban science educator is to fully embrace the beauty and complexity of science. An educator who truly understands the nature of science and how it applies to the way science is taught is not easily convinced that the approach to science teaching and learning adopted in most urban schools (which silences youth and reduces science to fact memorization) is the best way to teach youth. Furthermore, this type of educator recognizes that youth have a certain science mindedness even before they set foot in the science classroom that must be enhanced and not stifled. When the teaching of science becomes a quest to embrace the nature of science and enhance the science mindedness that already exists, teaching can no longer be a process of pinning down students to feed them a bitter elixir of science. It cannot be giving empty tasks with a goal of memorizing facts. Instead, it becomes the creation of a path to discovery.

For educators who come to the teaching profession committed to sharing their passion for science and "making a difference" in the lives of urban youth, moving beyond traditional approaches to teaching science requires that we consistently question not just ourselves, but the nature of urban science teaching. Embracing the nature of science means that we cannot walk blindly into classrooms and begin teaching. We cannot take curricula we have been handed and blindly begin following them. We have to ask why existent curricula do not give youth an opportunity to *explore*, and *think*, and *question*. And we must ask ourselves, what am I, or will I be doing, to make sure that my teaching allows youth to do those three things?

The unfortunate reality that I am hoping will come to you as you read this piece is that there have been no genuine, long-standing efforts to move beyond teaching science in ways that disengage youth. Much of the thinking surrounding urban science teaching is rooted in a simplifying of everything that concerns education. In particular, each factor in science teaching and learning has been reduced to a singular method that plays on the desire of the teacher to do well, and the provision of "easy" ways to be a better teacher. This move towards simplifying education, or making education easy, means that teachers get a package of knowledge to give to students; this process renders teachers powerless in the effort to truly affect change in the lives of youth.

For picking a science teacher, the formula has been to recruit someone with some content knowledge, provide this person with a highly scripted curriculum, and train the person to see youth as needing to be controlled in order to get very specific science content in the curriculum. In deciding what science content to teach, the formula has been to reduce the discipline to a very static scientific method and a bunch of facts to be memorized. For teaching, the process has been reduced to a test preparation activity. These formulas for science and teaching have created a population of teachers who are driven by a need to serve the "underserved," yet are trapped in a system that limits their ability to translate their passion into action.

The nature of science, despite its lack of a concrete definition, lays out for the world that science is complex, social, not authoritarian, imaginative, and requires evidence. It reminds us that science is ever growing and evolving, and consequently, is completely antithetical to the static and prefabricated version of it that is found in traditional urban science classrooms. It shows us that "science" and "school science" are in a conflict that cannot be resolved with the implementation of existent science curricula. It shows us that traditional school science and its simple answers to complex questions erode any hope for truly affecting change in urban science classrooms.

To write the closing paragraph of this letter, I have moved to a different classroom. Once again, I am sitting in the back of a science class. This time, I am observing a different teacher in a different urban school. The students are so loud that I can't hear the sounds from the street. In fact, I heard the students in the classroom from the hallway before I even got to the class. As I sit in the back of the class, I see students in groups creating posters based on experiments that they conducted at home. They understand the scientific method, but are obviously not memorizing the steps. They are using scientific language, collaborating with their peers, arguing, drawing, and writing. I can assess their content knowledge just by listening closely to some of the conversations. One young man looks up at me from the right corner of the room, interrupts my writing, and asks me if I can help settle an argument he was having with a friend about dependent and independent variables. At one point, I couldn't find the teacher because he was seated on the floor in a group of students engaged in a discussion about their work. In this classroom, students were doing science. It did not look like the traditional classroom, but I knew that the teacher had created a backdrop that welcomed the nature of science. As you walk into your own classrooms, fight to create that environment as well. Translate your passion for change into action.

Sincerely,
Dr. Emdin

C. EMDIN

AFFILIATION

Christopher Emdin
Teachers College
Columbia University

ROBERT W. SIMMONS

35. LOOKING BACK ON TEACHING IN DETROIT

Believing in our Students and Ourselves

Dear Future Educator:

Their eyes were locked onto the formula on the board and riveted by the model we created at the beginning of class. As we progressed through the first period of the day, I was watching my students' eyes. I was watching my students' body language. I happened on a set of eyes that spoke volumes. His eyes looked back at me during the lesson and he blurted out—"I don't get this shit, Mr. Simmons!" Another set of eyes darted back and forth, a neck cocked to the left, and a pencil was snapped by another: "Yo, Mr. Simmons, I ain't about to try this." In an effort to avert a crisis, I stopped the class and walked over to Thomas and Michelle to help them work through their frustration. I recognized that middle school science was challenging for both of them, but I also knew that my response to these moments would determine their success or failure and their willingness to engage further. As such, I always told my students, "I believe in you" at the beginning of class and during tough moments. At the end of the class, and during moments of class discontent or discourse associated with failure, I would say, "I believe in us." It is with this perspective of believing in my students and believing in my solidarity with them that I entered into my portable classroom on the East Side of Detroit day after day.

The current rhetoric associated with public education in Detroit has placed despair, hopelessness, and dysfunction at the center of the student and teacher narrative. As many teachers currently work in overcrowded classrooms and in schools that are inadequately funded (Gaston, Anderson, Su, & Theoharis, 2009; Howey, 2006; Murrell, 2007), the educational experiences of students and teachers in the Detroit Public Schools has been referred to as ground zero for educational reform by the Secretary of Education Arne Duncan (Welch, 2009). While Duncan has asserted that the best way to reform the schooling situation in Detroit is to close the failing schools and fire all of the teachers, he fails to address the ways that administrators have disenfranchised teachers by being caught up in politics and inefficient bureaucracies (Noguera, 2003). I could further challenge the premise associated with Duncan's version of school reform, serve up a scathing critique of the oligarchs who leave their high-powered executive jobs at General Motors to fix a "broken" system, but

T. M. Kress and R. Lake (Eds.), We Saved the Best for You: Letters of Hope, Imagination and Wisdom for 21st Century Educators, 157–160.
© *2013 Sense Publishers. All rights reserved.*

I will not. Instead I want to offer words of hope for those who do the most important work in the entire system—teach.

I BELIEVE IN YOU & I BELIEVE IN US

At the beginning of the school year my students and I would talk about dreams. We discussed their dreams. We discussed my dreams. We didn't focus on the testing associated with this era of hyper-accountability. While I was very aware of the state test that some politician seemed to think was the best way to determine if I was a good teacher, or if our school was failing or not, it wasn't the lens through which I viewed the educational experiences in my classroom. The lens that focused all teaching and learning in my classroom was grounded in my students' dreams—their dreams of going to college, their dreams of going to beauty school, their dreams of becoming a police officer, their dreams of becoming a teacher. Through their dreams I was better prepared to collaborate with them during our educational journey.

Despite my efforts to probe their dreams and expose my own, some of my students lacked self-efficacy and self-confidence. These students would approach learning by asking, "Why is this important to me?" while also publically stating, "I can't do this shit, Mr. Simmons." Early on in my career I wasn't quite sure how to respond to the various iterations of these types of statements. The moment that I knew how to respond was when Marcus walked into my classroom. His story was like mine— raised by his mother and grandmother, struggling to deal with an incarcerated father, and struggling to fit in. Marcus and I had our struggles—I struggled to reach him and Marcus struggled with being reached. Finally, Marcus said to me, "Has anyone ever believed in you?" I responded in the affirmative and our discussion lasted for an hour after school.

At that moment I recognized that my students needed more than my knowledge of science to be successful, and more than a surface commitment to the premise that "all students can learn." My students needed me to not only believe in them but they also needed me to tell them that I believe in them, and most importantly demonstrate that I believe in them through my actions. I told my students every day that I believed in them. I told my students every day that I believed in us. And I told them that if they ever felt I wasn't acting like I believed in them, they had every right to call me on it. This challenged me to the very depths of my soul because I had days when I didn't believe in myself. I had days when the lesson didn't seem to work out. I had days when I didn't believe in the system. I had days when I didn't believe that education would change the violence that many of my students experienced daily in their neighborhoods. I had days when I had to attend a student's funeral. I had days when I wanted to quit.

But then there was Marcus. Marcus believed in himself. Marcus believed in me. And Marcus made it. Marcus gave a speech as his high school valedictorian. During his speech he said the following: "I would be selfish if I attributed my grades to being smarter than the rest of you. I would be selfish if I didn't remind myself of the days in middle school that I didn't want to be in school. I would be even more selfish if I didn't thank my middle school science teacher and mentor, Mr. Simmons, for not only believing in me but for always telling me that he believed in me. For that I am forever grateful. And that is why I stand here today – because someone believed in me."

With Marcus in mind, I challenge all teachers to tell your students daily: "I believe in you." With Marcus in mind, I challenge all teachers to tell your students daily: "I believe in us." With Marcus in mind, I challenge all teachers to not only tell your students that you believe in them but also demonstrate your belief through your actions. Despite all of the rhetoric associated with school reform in urban schools, and the associated elements of hyper-standardization and hyper-accountability, it is our collective belief in our students that will help us make it from day to day. It won't be easy but it's something that we can do.

Sincerely,
Dr. Simmons

REFERENCES

Gaston, A., Anderson, N., Su, C., & Theoharis, J. (2009). *Our schools suck*. New York, NY: New York University Press.

Howey, K. (2006). Urban context and urban schools. In K. Howey, L. Post, & N. Zimpher (Eds.), *Recruiting, preparing, and retaining teachers for urban schools* (pp. 1–22). New York, NY: American Association of College for Teacher Education.

Murrell, P. (2007). *Race, culture & schooling*. New York, NY: Lawrence Erlbaum Associates.

Nogurera, P. (2003). *City schools and the American dream*. New York, NY: TeachersCollege Press.

Welch, S. (2009, May 13). Detroit called ground zero in effort to improve education in U.S. *Crain's Detroit Business*. Retrieved from: http://www.crainsdetroit.com/article/20090513/FREE/905139975/detroit-called-groundzero-in-effort-to-improve-education-in-u-s

AFFILIATION

Robert Simmons
School of Education
Loyola University Maryland

HELENA WORTHEN

36. LABOR EDUCATION AND "OPPOSITIONAL KNOWLEDGE"

Dear Future Educator:

I am a labor educator; my classes are a combination of strategy, history, political economy, law and communication because they are about how workers can make a decent living, improve their working conditions, and ultimately, survive their jobs by exercising control over their work. In order to do this, the workers have to draw on knowledge that is learned under conditions of struggle and conflict, that is emotionally charged, and is collectively created and held by workforces, colleagues, networks, families, and friends. What I teach is not job skills, which do not necessarily have anything to do with how fair or safe a job is or how much someone gets paid. I don't teach "soft skills." What I teach is sometimes called, by employers, "oppositional knowledge." It is opposed to the idea that labor should be squeezed to produce as much as humanly possible as cheaply as possible.

One of the great teachers of my generation, along with Myles Horton and Paulo Friere, is Staughton Lynd. A collection of his work, *From Here to There: The Staughton Lynd Reader*, came out in 2010 from PM Press, edited by Andrej Grubacic. Lynd, you may or may not know, was an active member of the radical left group SDS (Students for a Democratic Society) in the 1960s. In 1964 he was coordinator of the Mississippi Freedom Schools, which were church-basement schools for African-American students. These schools taught everything from literacy and nonviolence to political economy during the hottest days and nights of the Civil Rights movement. Lynd went to Hanoi during the Viet Nam war, got fired as an academic and was blacklisted, became a legal aid lawyer in Youngstown, Ohio, in 1978, and fought the impact of the closing of the steel mills there in the 1980s. He and his wife, Alice, are currently deeply involved in the defense of men who participated in the insurrection at the maximum security prison in Lucasville, Ohio. In other words, he has made important contributions in many areas. But I want most to tell you about his work with non-violence and the labor movement.

I am writing this in summer 2011 when anti-union legislation has been introduced into over twenty state legislatures. Most of these are attempts to narrow the scope, if not entirely eliminate, collective bargaining rights for U.S. public sector workers. Aside from the fact that many otherwise educated people do not even know what "collective bargaining" means, the people who have introduced this legislation seem

T. M. Kress and R. Lake (Eds.), We Saved the Best for You: Letters of Hope, Imagination and Wisdom for 21st Century Educators, 161–164.
© 2013 Sense Publishers. All rights reserved.

to have forgotten that collective bargaining is a process that was invented and written into law in order to forestall labor conflict. It was the peace offering, as it were, of the labor movement to employers, a way of saying, "We will sit at a table with you and talk and negotiate an agreement, rather than close down your factory or throw up barricades on highways or call for a general strike." It was a way of bringing the confrontation between workers and owners indoors and making it happen during working hours, in an office, using words, calculators, charts and photocopiers rather than bricks and, in some cases, guns (although the guns were nearly always in the hands of the police or the National Guard, not the workers). Collective bargaining is the ultimate non-violent way of settling a labor dispute. Ignorantly, it is misunderstood to be the problem, rather like thinking that fire departments cause fires.

Lynd's article, "Nonviolence and Solidarity," was written in 1999 when Clinton was president and the mood of the country still took labor unions to be a more or less permanent feature of our balance of power. Yet even then Lynd wanted to point out that, if you make a list of all the different things that employers and workers can do to each other to try to satisfy the conflicting needs and interests of each, a remarkable number of the non-violent tactics that workers can use are illegal. The more nonviolent tactics are illegal, the more the remaining legal tactics risk being violent.

To put it very simply: the employer provides materials, tools, a plan for a product, a location; the worker comes with skills, strengths, intelligence, willingness; they agree on schedules, goals and compensation. Into each of these factors an element of power enters. At one extreme is slavery or prison labor, in which the worker has virtually no say in the agreement. At the other extreme is the professional, who may have virtually everything to say about the agreement. In between (but skewed toward the powerless) lie most jobs and most workers. What are the tactics that these workers can use in order to bring the power that they have to the making of their agreement?

Imagine that workers, though their union, and their employer, are in the middle of negotiating a contract. What are workers legally allowed to do to put pressure on the employer? You might think that if employers can withdraw tools, material and locations—that is, close up a factory and move it to another city or country—workers could just as legally withdraw their labor – that is, stop working, any way they might want whenever they want.

Wrong. Lynd makes a list of things they can't do (I am expanding his list a bit here). Withdrawing your labor is called a strike, of course. Striking is ringed around with legal prohibitions. You can't strike, for example, in the middle of a contract. You have to wait until the contract expires. In some industries (healthcare, for example) you have to give advance notice. Under the Railway Labor Act, there's a "cooling off" period. Many unions have no-strike clauses in their contract, in fact. How about sympathy strikes? If the maintenance personnel at a university go on strike, do you think the clerical workers can go on strike out of sympathy and to increase pressure? No—they have to cross the picket line (or call in sick, which can be cause for discipline). Mass picketing is prohibited. Your strike has to be about "economic self-interest"—it can't be because you're a dock worker and you and your colleagues don't agree with loading bombs onto a ship that is heading for an undeclared war zone, for example. A sudden strike to address a critical problem at work—a sudden laying-down of the tools or walking off the job in protest—is called a "wildcat" strike, and it's the union steward's job to prevent or condemn it. And what happens when a strike actually takes place? Does the establishment stay struck? Do the workers have in fact the right to withdraw not just their own labor, but labor itself, from the plant? No. The employer can hire replacements—not just temporary replacements, who will be laid off when the labor dispute is resolved, but permanent replacements. Which means that going on strike is tantamount to quitting your job—a job where you may have been working for twenty years and out of which you were planning to retire. And of course, quitting your job means losing your healthcare access, if you even had employer-based health insurance.

Lynd's point is that, when non-violent actions like the above are criminalized, violence is what remains: "All these prohibitions cut off possibilities of nonviolent action and channel workers toward a choice between violence and surrender" (p. 190). But then he makes a jump that has the logic of a Zen kōan —a whack on the head to make you blink. Non-violence illegal? So he advises "young people who are considering a commitment to the labor movement" to practice nonviolence. Is he telling young people to break the law? Or is he simply rejecting outright the possibility of surrender?

As an example, he mentions the Pittston strike: "When one hundred striking miners occupied Pittston's Moss 3 coal preparation plant, they were instructed that if fired upon, they should kneel and wait for further orders" (p. 189).

Kneel and wait, under fire? What kind of discipline did that require? He tells about the occupation by angry workers of the U.S. Steel administration building in 1979 when the company announced the closing of all its Youngstown facilities (p. 192). He mentions the hunger strikes of imprisoned pacifists during World War II, protesting racial segregation and other abuses such as censorship of mail (p. 193). He describes the daily confrontation between indigenous women, some carrying babies on their backs, with soldiers in riot gear who are guarding the attempts by the Mexican government to construct a highway into the autonomous communities of Chiapas (p. 197).

These examples have much in common. First, they are not individual actions; they are collective. Second, they may be illegal but they are not aggressive. Third, they pose real danger to the people who undertake them – the miners may be fired upon, the hunger strikers may really starve. But fourth, their power flows from the fact that they signal a warning, a threat of what might happen next. They are like a mighty fist raised in the air, ready to strike in an unpredictable direction; they are frightening.

As you can imagine, they are also not easy to do. They are not easy to plan, easy to organize, easy to sustain, easy to manage. If running a factory is hard, running a factory occupation is harder. But teaching and learning is an essential part of non-violent action.

Teaching in the labor movement today, in other words, means teaching in a context in which the old curriculum of labor-management cooperation has been yanked. Instead of teaching how to come to an agreement, we have to teach how to raise the stakes; how to engage the public; how to establish solidarity across long-established racial, ethnic and gender divides; how to prepare a whole community for the consequences of a protracted labor dispute; how to create a threat. Herein labor education comes more to resemble the disciplines of the arts and humanities than the technical and legal content of its early industrial relations. But in order to open those gates and draw on the treasures of those disciplines, the next generation of teachers needs to be ready to step across the line of what's legal or illegal and think about what's good about "oppositional knowledge."

Helena Worthen

REFERENCE

Grubacic, A. (2010). *From Here to There: The Staughton Lynd Reader*. Oakland, CA: PM Press.

AFFILIATION

Helena Worthen
Center for Labor Research and Education
University of California Berkeley

ROBERT DANBERG

37. SOMETHING FROM NOTHING

The Writing Teacher's Work

I want to talk to you about your work, the writing teacher's work.
For the time it takes to read this
I want to close the door on curriculum,
The common syllabus,
Outcomes and assessment,
Strategies for effective peer review,
Grading policies, and the calendar,
And evoke instead something else,
The something and the nothing
Out of which learning in the writing classroom takes place,
An else that often feels like making sculpture from smoke.
To evoke this thing I rely on an old media,
The voice in your head.
If you are reading this you've lent it to me,
As students lend me the voices in their heads.
Thank you. I will assume with you, as I do with them,
The storyteller's imperative to bring news from far away,
A far away that is quite close,
And as mysterious as a house cat to Christopher Smart
And as familiar as a tiger to William Blake.
Of course, if I set aside the calendar
And which readings,
And which themes,
And how to assess,
And our syllabuses,
What is left?
This is the "Nick the Chopper" question.
In the Wizard of Oz
the Wicked Witch of the East cursed Nick
To keep him from marrying his beloved, Nimmee Aimmee.
She cursed his axe so it chopped off his limbs as he worked;
Ku-Klip replaced them, one at a time, even his head

T. M. Kress and R. Lake (Eds.), We Saved the Best for You: Letters of Hope, Imagination and Wisdom for 21st Century Educators, 165–170.
© *2013 Sense Publishers. All rights reserved.*

Until, Voila—
Nick the Chopper became The Tin Woodsman.
As an aside, Ku-Klip kept Nick's "meat head" in a cabinet.
Nick's head insists that he,
Not the Tin Woodsman,
Is Nick the Chopper.
Do you get where I'm going with this?
Chop chop chop.
I set aside syllabus.
Chop chop chop.
I set aside the assignment sheet.
Chop.
I set aside the problem of citation.
Chop chop.
Etcetera etcetera.
Chop chop chop.
What of writing class is left?
A little bit of nothing?
A little bit of something?
What I would say is left is the work.
Gary Snyder uses the phrase, "The real work"
To describe some of what I mean.
He uses the phrase here and there— in poems and essays.
An interviewer asked him
"What is the real work?" Snyder answers,

> I think it's important, first of all because it's good to work— I love work;
> Work and play are one. And that all of us will come back again
> To the hoe in the ground, or gather wild potato bulbs with digging sticks,
> Or hand-adze a beam, or skin a pole, or scrape a hive—
> We're never going to get away from that...

He continues,

> We've been living a dream that we're going to get away from that...
> Work is always going to be there. It might be stapling papers,
> It might be typing in the office. But we're never going to get away from that work,
> On one level or another. So that's real. The real work is what we really do.
> And what our lives are. And if we can live the work we do know that we are real,
> And it's real, and that the world is real, then it becomes right.
> And that's the work: to make the world as real as it is,
> And to find ourselves as real as we are within it

What is the *real work* of the writing classroom?
Teachers must transmit what our students need to know,
Yet what we transmit is hardly even the half of it.

There is another knowledge, which we also address in our plans
and intentions:
Stuff you can only learn through experience,
Stuff that is manifest to others and apparent to ourselves
Only through the act of making something
And so the real work of teaching writers involves a fundamental tension
Between what we must tell students and what they can only know for themselves.
Let me put it another way:
My son made his first roast chicken recently.
According to the recipe I told him,
The one he's watched me make for years.
He called to ask me,
How will I know when it's done
And I had to think for a moment.
I have cooked a thousand chickens
How do I know when it's done?
When it smells done.
When the time has past that I know it is done.
And finally, when you prick the thickest part of the thigh with a fork
And the juice runs clear.
And he, who had never done it on his own before
Asks, *what is clear?*
We—writing teachers—know it is our responsibility,
To transmit the traditions, the tools, and forms we value,
But we also know that such knowledge hardly describes
What it means when we describe what and how a writer knows.
To know how, as the philosopher Gilbert Ryle puts it,
Is not to check first than act, but to act spontaneously,
Not to ask how and what first, then act,
But to be deeply imbued by what it is to act.
This does not mean we do not critique or reflect,
Especially when we are learning something new,
But that even those moments of deliberation and reflection
Move toward spontaneous action
When we are able to forget ourselves in the work we do,
Which allows us to create something right for each unique time
and place.

So, the writing teacher creates a place,
Out of the clock and the calendar,
Out of the once and the now
Out of the assertion and the reason why,
We draw a circle around rooms full of writers,

Who receive an invitation to the work:
Of tools, materials and forms,
Of perceptions, thoughts and feelings,
Of efforts at attunement,
That make a writer capable of her own work,
"Work" is a peculiar word for these peculiar classes we teach,
Though whenever I think about the writing teachers' art,
I begin and end with thoughts on our work.
"Work" stands for the product.
And "work" stands for the "process"
But in the writing classroom,
The process is the product,
And so it—the process—is kind of artifact, too.
Work also refers to "the work."
When I am in a classroom,
By the third or fourth week,
If I have done my job well.
"the work" emerges.
It emerges in a way that is not mysterious but elemental,
Each student sets down, in a sense, "my work"—
By "my work" I mean the personal struggle—
And glimpses the common struggle.
We, the two of us or the ten of us, or the twenty five of us,
Turn toward it, and regard it
As if we'd driven over a rise
To find our city pooled in mist
And the mist dissolves as we approach
And first we regard it at a distance
And then as we approach it may disappear
And then it is all around us.
Each class is an invitation to inhabit
Its forms of attention and attunement

Patterns of caution and regard,
Machines of consideration,
Rhythms of what's done.
If all goes well, it is no more mysterious than
The heart and mind, that tangle we are always entangled in,
The heart and mind, for which there is no word that doesn't,
inadvertently,
Evoke separation: the heartmind, which we hesitate to name
knowledge,
But is knowledge—

My materials are words and forms and time and attention.
I shape experience, enter conversation strategically and
spontaneously, And direct a periodic return to some elemental act or event, (the adze,
the axe, the digging stick)
That repeats and elaborates upon itself.
The classrooms pile up behind me like the lifetime of beds I've
slept in, But I draw a circle around each one, and
Rather like my grandmother,
Who could make any kitchen her own
Simply by drawing a circle around it with her work,
Hand around the sharp knife, hand at the cutting board.
I invite my students to do the same as I,
Hand at the keyboard, hand around the pen,
Screen and paper, the stapler,
Through which the work makes
The world clear and real and apparent,
A circle they can draw anywhere
At anytime simply by taking up the work
As long as the work persists.
And so I enter every odd classroom,
Like the tailor in the Yiddish folk song,
Who seems to make a something from a nothing,
That is never really a nothing.
First, he sews his newborn daughter a blanket,
And when the blanket became worn and frayed at the edges,
And he saw her leaving it here and there,
He trimmed it and sewed it again,
And made her a little vest to wear,

And soon, she grew too big for it,
As she was bound to,
So, he cut it a bit and hemmed it,
And made her scarf,
Which, when it became too short to keep out the cold,
He trimmed and stitched
Into a handkerchief for her.
When it too, became worn and threadbare,
He made it into buttons,
A row for a pretty school dress.
And when the buttons were lost, one by one,
And there was no fabric left
To make something from a button
That was once a scarf,

That was once a vest,
That was once a blanket—
He made this story—which I learned,
And which I have now told you.

Robert Danberg

AFFILIATION

Robert Danberg
Writing Initiative
Binghamton University, State University of New York

THOMAS LAKE

38. LETTER TO A WRITING TEACHER

Dear Teacher,

One morning you'll find yourself standing alone at the front of a room across from twenty-five or thirty children who would rather be asleep, and you'll have to make them care about writing. In time they may come to appreciate the narrative sweep of the *Iliad*, or the untrammeled confidence in Melville's voice, but if there's a canyon between you on this first morning you'll have to be the one who crosses the bridge. So: Ask them about their preferences. What are your favorite movies? (Those had to be written.) Television shows? (Written. Even *SportsCenter*.) Comic books? (Written.) That boy near the back with the wires partially concealed beneath the hood of his sweatshirt—he's listening to some guy angrily singing written words. That girl who stares straight ahead even as her thumbs furiously conspire on the keys of the cell phone hidden under her desk—she's writing right now, with astonishing hand-eye coordination and clarity of thought. Show of hands around the room: Who uses MySpace? Facebook? Twitter? Who keeps a blog? Writing, writing, writing and writing.

Anyone here going to college?

(You'll need a good application essay.)

Who likes money?

(Money flows from work, and most good jobs require a well-written cover letter.)

Raise your hand if you've ever been in love, or want to be.

(Few things are more romantic than a good love note.)

There's no escaping it. Many times in your life, if not every day, you will be known by your writing. Might as well make it good.

Well, how do you do that? You have to give it life.

This might sound crazy, but stick with me for a moment. Just play along. Imagine two puppies. Let's say they're golden retrievers. Now, help me describe them. They have these shiny fur coats, almost the color of butter. Black eyes shining like the moon on the ocean. Tails waving side-to-side like grass in a shifting wind. Constant shallow breaths, this audible panting, *hehuhhehuhhehuhhehuh*. High plaintive voices, yelping at their mother for food and attention.

T. M. Kress and R. Lake (Eds.), *We Saved the Best for You: Letters of Hope, Imagination and Wisdom for 21st Century Educators*, 171–174.
© 2013 Sense Publishers. All rights reserved.

These two dogs look almost identical, right? But what if you could put them both through an X-ray machine to see what was inside? First one goes in. What do you see: Bones insulated with cartilage, lungs, a beating heart. Everything you'd expect to see inside a living, breathing animal. Then the second dog goes in, and this time you're very surprised. What do you see in the second X-ray? Metal gears. Wires. Circuit boards. Semiconductors. Gadgetry. On the outside the dogs both look real. But it seems that one is actually a robot.

Now, as long as we're imagining things, think of good writing as that second dog. The writing is not really alive. When you get right down to it, it's only a trail of black shapes on the page or screen, just as the robo-dog is only a mass of wires and circuits. But it's a convincing simulation. The best writing puts the reader in the middle of an experience—whether real or imagined by the writer—so that when you're finished reading you're left with a memory just as clear as if you had been there yourself. Raise your hand if you've ever been to Hogwarts School of Witchcraft and Wizardry. Nobody? But I'll bet half of you remember some good times you had with Harry Potter and his friends.

So. How does the writer do it? How do you breathe life into a machine?

I can think of two good starting points. Two sets of skills you can start building today.

The first has to do with the machine itself. The technical side. To understand the circuitry of good writing, you need to read a lot of good books. Forget the robotic dog for a moment—some authors out there have built entire robotic neighborhoods, cities, civilizations. You should study them for clues to the work. Now, I'm not saying you have to go home and finish *War & Peace* tonight. But you need to know what good writing looks like. So maybe you start with something like *The Pearl*, by John Steinbeck, an action-adventure story that you really can finish in one night. Or *Tuck Everlasting*, by Natalie Babbitt, a riveting short novel about a family cursed with eternal life. Or, if you prefer true stories, maybe you read Tom Junod's story about Fred Rogers, the guy from *Mister Rogers' Neighborhood*. It's so good it might knock you over.

Here's something you'll notice when you read great works like these: The grammar is perfect. The punctuation is perfect. The verbs and the nouns are in the right place, and so are the commas and periods. Going back to the idea about robots, these robots are technically perfect. All the circuits and wires are placed correctly. You may not enjoy textbooks on English grammar, you may get sick of reading about subjects and objects and gerunds and semicolons, but those books are important. They're like the technical manuals for your robot. Your robot won't work if it's wired incorrectly, and your writing won't work if your grammar is off. People notice this stuff, even on text messages or the Internet. If your robotic golden retriever has a faulty circuit board, it'll never have a chance of coming to life. So you have to learn the technology.

Now, let's move on to the second set of skills. This one is much more fun. Think of it as the ON/OFF switch for your robot. Ernest Hemingway, one of the great writers of the twentieth century, talked about this set of skills in his book *By-Line: Ernest Hemingway*. In the passage he's talking to a young apprentice before they go on a fishing trip:

> Watch what happens today. If we get into a fish see exactly what it is that everyone does. If you get a kick out of it while he is jumping remember back until you see exactly what the action was that gave you the emotion. Whether it was the rising of the line from the water and the way it tightened like a fiddle string until drops started from it, or the way he smashed and threw water when he jumped. Remember what the noises were and what was said. Find what gave you the emotion; what the action was that gave you the excitement. Then write it down making it clear so the reader will see it too and have the same feeling that you had (Hemingway & White, 1998, p. 215).

He's talking about the spark of life, the magical power that puts the reader in an experience. Your writing can have this power, but to get it you have to become a very good observer. You have to practice taking the details of real life and putting them into words. Does anyone here keep a journal, or a diary, or a blog? Good. That's a great way to start. Now let's try taking it to another level. You could just write, "I love dessert." But that doesn't tell us much. We need the details. So try this: "I love chocolate cake, especially with shreds of coconut in the frosting and a cold glass of milk on the side, on my birthday, June 16, a hot Saturday afternoon, as my three best friends and I stand on the back porch with blades of grass stuck to our bathing suits after two hours on the Slip 'N Slide."

You could write, "Coach O'Toole is mean," but what if you tried this: "Jackson wouldn't shut up in gym class. He kept whispering to me about girls while Coach O'Toole was talking, and I tried to keep a straight face, and finally I just said, 'Shhhh,' and Coach O'Toole heard me, and he made me run thirty-four wind sprints while everybody watched and Jackson just stood there."

Your powers of observation will improve with practice. Try keeping a notebook in your pocket and writing down what you see, feel, and hear. You could even narrate the scene to yourself: "White threads of rain on the windowpane. Elm tree shivering in the wind. Goldfish turning circles in the bowl, waving its translucent fins. Air-conditioner humming. Dull ache in my legs from running all those undeserved sprints in gym class. Face getting hot just thinking about it. Doorbell rings. I limp down the stairs and open the door. Through the screen I see Jackson. I slam the door. Now he's pounding, pounding, and I finally open the door again. 'I'm sorry,' he says, and those might be tears on his cheeks or it might just be the rain. He turns to leave, and I say 'Wait—' but then he starts running, and when he gets to the street he turns around and he runs back to the door, and then back to the street, and his sneakers are soaked, and he's slipping, falling in the mud, red-brown stains all over his jeans, but he keeps running, back and forth, back and forth, ten times, twenty, thirty, thirty-four."

And then you flip the switch, and your golden retriever comes to life.

Thomas Lake

REFERENCE

Hemingway, E. & White, W. (1998). *By-Line Ernest Hemingway: Selected articles and dispatches of four decades*. New York, NY: Scribner.

AFFILIATION

Thomas Lake
Sports Illustrated

ROSER GINÉ

39. ACTUALIZING AN ETHIC OF CARE IN THE (MATHEMATICS) CLASSROOM

Dear twenty-first century educator,

As a mathematics educator, I have encountered numerous challenges in school teaching. These have ranged from a lack of collegiality among adults in a school community, a lack of resources, and flawed leadership structures, to a rigid focus on testing, not for the sake of student growth, but rather for school evaluative and ranking purposes. In response to such limitations of school communities and in the face of unrealistic demands on schooling from various constituents, demands that are unable to meet our students' needs, I have fought back and resisted. In formal leadership positions, I have proposed change (e.g. interdisciplinary curriculum, depth over breadth, teaching of concepts and ideas rather than teaching to a test) to advocate for our students, who have often been rendered voiceless in their own educational process. However, various resistances to change have also led me to try new school settings, only to be faced with different problems--hierarchical organizational structures serving only to alienate teachers and the work of the classroom that ultimately interfered with the attention given to students. This is not to say that there are no school communities that value our students—in fact, I have found the most inclusive and innovative visions for education in member schools of the Coalition of Essential Schools (CES), even when the adult communities faced conflict and crises. In these settings, I was inspired by the caring relationships between adults and their students, and most of all, by the ways in which student diversity was honored and even nurtured. As a teacher and a school leader in this context, I have actualized an ethic of care in my corner of the world, in my classroom—an ethic put forth by Nel Noddings (2005) that has provided a measure of hope in my life's work of teaching mathematics.

In *The Challenge to Care in Schools,* Nel Noddings (2005) places care at the center of the educational process. She first explores the notion of caring as a relational construct, where two parties engage with one another as givers and recipients of care, and characterizes the carer as one who can "hear, see, or feel what the other tries to convey" (p. 16). She further explains that, at the other end of this kind of relation, one must be willing to receive care. It is such a mutuality that typifies a mature relationship, one composed of "strings of encounters in which parties exchange places; both members as carers and cared-fors as opportunities

T. M. Kress and R. Lake (Eds.), We Saved the Best for You: Letters of Hope, Imagination and Wisdom for 21st Century Educators, 175–180.
© *2013 Sense Publishers. All rights reserved.*

arise" (p. 17). In schools, and in the mathematics classroom in particular, teachers can provide care and model what it means to care for others in a relational sense, while honoring and caring for ideas, and communicating their passion for learning. The most fulfilling teaching moments in my life have embodied this vision for education. I have attended to my students' needs while deferring to the authority of the discipline of mathematics to convey my respect for and belief in the power of the ideas of the giants who have developed and advanced a body of knowledge that helps us explain the world in which we live.

I taught mathematics and led the math department at the North Central Charter Essential School (NCCES), a member school of the Coalition of Essential Schools (CES) in Fitchburg, MA, where the school structure and culture allowed me to develop and refine who I would be as a teacher. I created the school's first pre-calculus course, followed the next year by a calculus class for the same students. The students' general disenchantment with the discipline can be perceived from the following communication with one very capable and talented young student: "Through most of high school, mathematics rarely excited me. I most often felt that what I was required to learn had no relevance or context. For this reason, I approached it as requirement only and consequently lacked ambition. This attitude of lethargy seemed to be endemic amongst most of my classmates." The task on which I embarked was to find ways, delving deeply into mathematics, that would engage students and integrate their interests with the concepts and ideas of pre-calculus and calculus.

Several students in this course participated in the school's music group. This deep interest in music was a resource for me in choosing ways to teach functions: we explored sound using logarithms and then moved into waveforms and trigonometry, remaining within the context of creating sound and music (in another setting, my students had designed musical instruments using mathematical laws). One student was interested in design, and in our calculus class, we built model roller coasters with maximum thrill (we determined "thrill" based on height of paths and angles of steepest descent). We also explored conic sections in pre-calculus, by designing a whispering gallery that showed the dynamics of sound reflected from one focus point to another. This project work served to enrich our classroom community and rendered each person within the classroom, including myself, as explorers and learners—some with expertise in areas that I could not alone provide. Each of these experiences contributed to creating a classroom community built on care towards ideas and towards one another, and each gave me practice in understanding how to respond differentially to students' needs. The student quoted above continues his account of what resulted from our classroom learning: "When I began learning [in this class] my perception changed. Roser approached teaching with a fresh and interactive method. She molded the curriculum to better suit our learning styles and she always stayed organized and relevant. What had been a dull classroom became a learning community where we were encouraged to participate creatively. What was a lifeless order of symbols became a way to understand and connect with a vibrant and complex world. Roser's love of mathematics was contagious and what was a dreaded subject became one of my favorite classes" (letter written by Samuel King).

I also had the privilege of teaching students at the Francis Parker Charter Essential School, the flagship school of CES. Teachers worked collaboratively to design a mathematics unit that would allow students to see and apply the power of linear programming. We based our curriculum unit on the Interactive Mathematics Program unit, in which two bakers have to make decisions on the number of different types of cookies to bake in order to attain a maximum profit, given constraints on time and costs of ingredients. The class applied understanding of linear programming to other similar (somewhat artificial) problems. As is common in Essential Schools, towards the end of the year, students designed their own projects for an exhibition that would be used to help determine promotion. Ann Harvey, a tenth grader at Parker at that time, approached me with her project idea: she was interested in minimizing the cost for flying volunteers from her church to New Orleans for a rebuilding effort after the hurricane Katrina disaster. Her experience with linear programming earlier in the year had been significant: she understood such an approach could inform an effort she was deeply invested in. With some guidance, Ann determined the number of children and the number of adults that would go on this trip as she considered constraints including costs of plane tickets, children needing to be accompanied by adults, and the hours children and adults could work on rebuilding homes during the weeklong trip. While as teachers we often cannot predict or even experience the effect that our work might have on students, this student thoughtfully integrated her understanding of a problem-solving approach to give shape to an idea in order to fulfill her need to care for others.

While I have addressed the power of creating a classroom space built on mutual caring relationships by getting to know our students well, I would be remiss in my communication to you if I did not present an argument for de-compartmentalization in schools. With respect to teaching the disciplines, we must carve out space to attend to ways of thinking and specific language and tools that have served to develop and communicate new understanding. This can be well accomplished within the existing school structures. Even in our approach to teaching in such contexts, we can communicate our passion for ideas and care for student growth. However, students need opportunities to apply and integrate specific disciplinary knowledge and understanding in more realistic contexts, cognizant of the limitations we must often impose on a real problem in order to tackle some aspect of its complexity. This kind of exposure necessitates adults working together in a school setting to share expertise and to choose problems and projects for students that will enable such integration—an approach to education that breaks down disciplinary boundaries and results in the re-structuring and de-compartmentalizing of school settings. Such restructuring is consonant with the conceptualization of care in schools presented above. I believe there is a need in our profession for the de-compartmentalization of traditional teacher roles, to allow for our students to witness teacher passion, caring capacity, and love of learning.

It was with the same group of students from my calculus class at NCCES that I had the opportunity to further share my world by co-creating a celebratory experience in the form of planning an end-of-year trip to Europe (we went to my native home of Barcelona and to Paris). Students staged every aspect of the trip, from its initial planning stages to raising needed funds. The school principal allowed me to teach a course for interested students that involved learning about the culture of Catalonia, learning essential words and phrases in French and Catalan, designing school-wide experiences for all students that would help us raise money towards the trip (e.g. a morning bagel bar, dinners at local restaurants for the members of the school community), and planning an itinerary. As part of this course, I invited my parents to our class to share the history of Catalonia through their eyes, having grown up just after the Spanish Civil War. Our work finally led us to a long-awaited trip, when we had the opportunity to visit museums (the Louvre, among others), cathedrals (we marveled at the unfinished Sagrada Familia in Barcelona), other historical buildings, and to experience the French and Catalan cultures. When we went to Barcelona, we shared a meal with my parents prior to heading to the countryside to visit and tour my cousin's vineyard. At the vineyard and accompanying cellar, my aunt prepared a traditional luncheon for our group, which we were able to enjoy as we looked upon the Priorat countryside – this experience is one that neither my students nor I will ever forget.

I share this story as an example of what I believe it means to share and explore the world with our students, by together making sense of how people who have come before us have developed and refined ideas, embodied in cultural-historical artifacts. For me, teaching meant getting to know students well and opening myself to being known as a teacher and as a caring adult in their lives. It meant sharing my own world and aspects of it that continue to inspire and move me. It meant remaining open to my students' interests so that we might uncover the intersection between their passions and my own. This is what I refer to as de-compartmentalizing the teaching profession—as teachers, we can share the path we pave in becoming who we are, and, as we get to know our students well, confirm their efforts in discovering who they are and in realizing who they want to become.

There are currently few school communities that have broken the boundaries of the disciplines; rather, many continue to support and sustain structures that "work against care" (Noddings, 2005, p. 20). I have experienced first-hand the isolation of teaching, the reactions to (harmful) interpretations of standardization, the machine-like (positivist) model for schooling that moves kids in and out of schooling establishments. When I begin to lose perspective or question what I might offer my students in such settings, I think of what a friend once said to me:"Light your own corner." I would expound on his words by encouraging you to light your corner by caring *for* ideas, *with* your students – you will then light the world.

Roser Giné

REFERENCE

Noddings, N. (2005). *The challenge to care in schools: An alternative approach to education.* New York, NY: Teachers College Press.

AFFILIATION

Roser Giné
Graduate School of Education
The University of Massachusetts Lowell

DENNIS LITTKY

40. KEEP THE FAITH

Real Learning will Win in the End

Dear 21st Century Educators,

After 42 years of working in public education and innovating constantly, I am saddened by what I see today. Things seem to have gotten worse. Innovation has taken on a more cautious meaning. It is no more, let's try something new or let's start over now that we know more how students learn. Instead of this, innovation is giving way to methods that only *seem* to be working in a utilitarian sense. How is that looking to the future? That's not innovation but repetition. I started a school, The Shoreham Wading River School when I was 27. The school had advisories, an integrated curriculum, with students working in the community…that was in 1972. Are those innovations being furthered? In 1981 these innovations were advanced at Thayer Junior/Senior High School in New Hampshire where I was the principal. We were on the cutting edge with advisories, integrated curriculum, team teaching and internships, portfolios, performance evaluation and exhibitions. We were praised everywhere we went. We were the first school in a new high school movement, Ted Sizer's Coalition of Essential Schools. Other schools began to use this design to innovate at their own school.

Then Elliot Washor and I had an opportunity to start a school from scratch in Providence, Rhode Island. We didn't just try to replicate what others had done in the past. We built on what we learned by framing the question, "what's best for kids?"

Many of the so called innovations of today just tweak the old model of education. Subjects become integrated but the same content is used. Advisories are set up but typically they only meet for around 15 minutes in order to give priority treatment to "important subjects". Students are pushed to do projects, to construct their own knowledge, again around the same state- mandated curriculum.

In our present school, *The Met Center* (a coalition of six high schools in Providence, Rhode Island) we took what works in learning theory, brain research and practice and designed a new program. In this model, teachers serve as general educators becoming advisors and staying with their students for 4 years. The curriculum content is built around students' interests. Each student has to read, write, and think like mathematicians and scientists while developing their own range of personal skills.

T. M. Kress and R. Lake (Eds.), We Saved the Best for You: Letters of Hope, Imagination and Wisdom for 21st Century Educators, 181–184.
© 2013 Sense Publishers. All rights reserved.

Students follow their interests in internships two days a week and come back to campus the other days expanding on their work, reading, writing and researching while working toward tangible goals within their internships. They could be writing a newsletter or a grant or designing a healthier menu for a restaurant. All work has some value beyond the school itself. Once again, during the 1990's these innovations became acknowledged as important. The data started coming in that revealed increased attendance and graduation rates, better attitudes and even better test scores. The Bill and Melinda Gates Foundation saw this and funded *The Big Picture,* a nonprofit coalition of schools. Our goal was not just replicating the program in a cookie cutter fashion. We took what we had learned and individually designed each school around the country and internationally in innovative ways according to the specific culture and needs of the region. What is of utmost importance is that students' needs are met and each has an individualized curriculum that leads to a successful college and work life.

Our goals are laid out in my book, *The Big Picture* students should:

Be lifelong learners

Be passionate

Be ready to take risks

Be able to problem-solve and think critically

Be able to look at things differently

Be able to work independently and with others

Be creative

Care and want to give back to their community

Persevere

Have integrity and self-respect

Have moral courage

Be able to use the world around them well

Speak well, write well, read well, and work well with numbers

Truly enjoy their life and their work. (Littky & Grabelle, 2004, p. 1)

But then around the turn of the 21st century, something happened. The work of funding small schools was not changing things fast enough for The Gates Foundation – so their money started going to school systems and research. A major push to turn around schools began but the only measures for success were improved test scores. Individual states began to focus more and more on high stakes tests, but if the students didn't pass all content areas they didn't graduate, regardless of whether they were brilliant writers that were just behind on their math.

Then charter school companies started springing up and advertising themselves with bold claims of "improving test scores". Consequently, "the teaching for increased standardized test scores agenda" took precedence in teacher training programs as well. So very quickly, learning got a new definition. Instead of the definition known by every parent and businessman which was creativity, integrity, applying knowledge and solving problems, learning became a number on an English or math test, all under the rubric of closing the gap between the white and students of color, the poor and the rich.

These goals are fine but not by themselves. Just seeking to increase test scores will not keep students in school or make them more prepared for the world. This will only close the gap by an answer or two marked correctly on a bubble sheet.

Those of us who work with marginalized students every day are left to wonder how long it would take policy makers to stop this testing madness if the poor and students of color did better on standardized tests than the middle class. The goals for students have been so narrowed. Do people really believe a few points difference on our standardized tests will solve our education problems?

The story gets worse: now, not only is education narrowly defined and based on how well students do on test scores, researchers are looking at how to make teachers more efficient at raising those test scores. They are watching videos of teachers teaching in the front of a room and picking up techniques that they feel will increase learning. We have fallen back to how we saw education in medieval times by assuming every student is the same.

What about all the research on how our brains work, including what we know about motivation and how people learn? What about a history of successful schools? Why don't private schools put the same emphasis on standardized tests? Why does Obama tell stories about his children and standardized tests and then say no child should be judged by one test. This is what the president said.

> ...[O]ne thing I never want to see happen is schools that are just teaching to the test. Because then you're not learning about the world; you're not learning about different cultures, you're not learning about science, you're not learning about math. All you're learning about is how to fill out a little bubble on an exam and the little tricks that you need to do in order to take a test. And that's not going to make education interesting to you. And young people do well in stuff that they're interested in. They're not going to do as well if it's boring (2011).

So you can see how sad the times are for me. It is sad to see people not even acknowledging the work in past innovation in schools and in research studies.

The newest addition to education is the use of the internet- which is important. But instead of using our new capacity to work with others and access information individually and internationally, we are bringing lecturers to the students virtually. Lectures don't work in person, why do we think they will engage students online?

183

I'm not sure what needs to happen to turn things around. It must be something that helps those in power to admit that teaching to a test is not the answer. Will 10 more years of students dropping out raise eyebrows? Will it be the breakthrough in technology that engages students like gaming does and forces teachers to stand back and stop lecturing?

Personally, I keep doing what I think is best for students and continue to help our students be good thinkers, entrepreneurs, leaders as well as learning the basic skills. I know of no other way to act. I am even trying to create a different kind of college called *College Unbound*. After 2 years, we have seen if you change the curriculum and build it around students' interests and use internships, college students of all ages, races and classes stay engaged.

I hope to write to you a more upbeat letter when I celebrate my 50 years in education, and in the meantime I will never stop trying to help change the way the world thinks about education and our youth.

So, keep the faith! The No Child Left Behind policy is finally being seen for what it is. Testing will prove to be not a mechanism to improve education. Real learning will come to the top as technology allows every student to have a personalized curriculum and the real world becomes the textbook.

Peace,
Dennis Littky

REFERENCES

Littky, D. & Grabelle, S. (2004). *The big picture: Education is everyone's business.* Alexandria, VA: ASCD.
Obama, B. (2011). Univision town hall meeting on education (transcript, March, 28, 2011). Retrieved from:http://standardizedtests.procon.org/view.source.php?sourceID=011661

AFFILIATION

Dennis Littky
The Met Center

PETER APPELBAUM

41. A GAME AND A DARE

Dear Friends,

It's a lost cause. Don't even try. And by this I mean, celebrate! Yippee!

There was a time not too long ago when educators believed that their job was to help learners make sense of things – to make sense of their world, to make sense of mathematics and language, static electricity and genocide, how to string a longbow, or how to sew just the right number of pleats in a skirt. Then, a shiver slithered up and down a few spines and the title of an ancient rock album, the sound track to a film of the same name from long-ago 1984, throbbed over and over in more and more minds: *Stop Making Sense*.

> In the desire to pull learners along a smooth path of concept development, we've planed off the bumpy parts that were once the precise locations of meaning and elaboration. (Davis 2008, p. 84)

Before this apocryphal phrase, "stop making sense," was common, a dangerous sense-making mania dominated teacher-education as well as teachers' educating: people were constantly focused on making sense of their work and taking responsibility for careful planning of well-designed mechanisms for efficiently riveting learners to mastery of learning objectives. Well-meaning, earnest benefactors would identify the easiest ways to the easiest methods of easing the leap to "best practices", "test score increases", and, in general, a simplification of all that matters.

Yet there is another theoretical thread winding its way through history.

At the cusp of the fourth and third centuries before the Common Era, Plato wrote dialogues starring a character named after his teacher Socrates, who noted that any serious effort to actually understand anything is going to lead to the realization that we can at best say that we don't really know anything at all. Visitors to the Fredericksberg Gardens in Copenhagen are greeted by a statue of Søren Kierkegaard (1992), who in his "Concluding Unscientific Postscript to the Philosophical Fragments" described sitting there in the mid-1800's and realizing that it was his job to balance those well-meaning benefactors by devoting his efforts to complicating everything, to creating difficulties everywhere. People would soon be seeking out the difficulties of life, and he would be there ready. In 1978 Bernard Suits re-wrote Aesop's fable of the ant and the grasshopper and helped us see that it is the grasshopper, the game-playing aesthetician, who has much to teach us, not the industrious, hard-working,

T. M. Kress and R. Lake (Eds.), We Saved the Best for You: Letters of Hope, Imagination and Wisdom for 21st Century Educators, 185–192.
© *2013 Sense Publishers. All rights reserved.*

goal-driven ant. In 1982, the French philosopher Jacques Derrida wrote that obliqueness leads a better hearing than simplistic readings: Simplistic readings and writings lead to ignorance rather than wisdom,

> An ignorant person does not hear. Awakening non-listeners "risks permitting the noisiest discourse" (1982, xiii).

What we need is a way to keep us away from that seductive desire to make sense of everything, to enable us to complicate things over and over again. Only in this way might we be prepared for the difficulties of educational life. *This* is *not* a lost cause: I have a suggestion for you. It has helped me; maybe it'll help you.

THE GAME

What I offer is a game because games are specifically about doing things in a way that does not make the most sense (Appelbaum, 2007). For example, if one wanted to move a tiny ball across a great distance and place it in a small hole hardly bigger than the ball itself, one would probably not think of hitting it with a golf club. Yet it is precisely the absurdity of the rules of golf that make it worthwhile and engaging in the first place. Personally, I don't play golf, but it's a good example: people who play golf find it challenges them to understand a great deal about themselves and to confront a host of complex issues in order to become good at the game. I do like to play *Fluxx* (Looney Labs, 1997) – a card game where one tries to have the right combination of cards on the table at just the right time before someone else changes what the goal of the game itself is. You might like to try this one. I find *Fluxx* provides a great metaphor for what it might mean to cope with a constantly changing world where the rules seem to be shifting without me even realizing it.

But back to our game here: we need a way to complicate educational theories and practices. And I think I have just the thing. To play this game, you start with a lesson or unit plan, one that you think is very good. Or, you start with a learning objective or institutional policy. Then, you shuffle the two decks of cards (instructions for preparing the cards ahead of time appear below – we'll get to that once you have a feel for the game), and deal out one from each deck, face up. Now the fun begins! You have a choice of how to proceed:

a) You may take your turn by identifying all the ways in which your lesson or unit plan, learning objective, or institutional policy satisfies the expectations of both cards at once; or,

b) You may take your turn by identifying all the ways in which your lesson or unit plan, learning objective, or institutional policy, would need significant modifications to satisfy the expectations of both cards at once.

The next turn in the game, played either by you (the solitaire version, when you play at home) or by a friend or friends with whom you are playing (the best version of the game, for two or more, played ideally at a coffee house or bar after school), is to rewrite the lesson, unit, objective or policy, in the most amusing yet genuine spirit of the two cards just played. If this game gets routine or too easy, some players have enjoyed adding a third card for this turn. Yet another version has each player create their own new card for the deck before play begins, emphasizing the issues and concerns that he or she is bringing to the game on that particular day.

Play proceeds by the fastest player grabbing the decks and dealing out two cards before anyone else gets the chance.

The Cards

So what goes on the cards? You might make them out of cardboard or paper napkins, beer coasters ... some people have been known to craft them out of fine cedar or to use linoleum block printing on framed silk. The important thing is the content, not the material. Even so, it is fun to google the names of the people on the cards to find a nice image that might be reproduced on the card – not essential, but players of the game do end up taking pride in their decks.

The European thinkers deck:

Jacques Rancière—Rancière is a French philosopher who was once known for his writings on political discourse, but who has more recently been writing and lecturing on art and aesthetics in relation to his earlier interests in politics. In *The Ignorant Schoolmaster* (1991) he described the conundrum that directly trying to teach something often fails completely. In contrast, he tells the story of an educator who did not speak the same language as his students, yet set them to task in figuring out on their own how to explain in his language a text written in that language, by using a book that had a simultaneous translation. Based on the success of this approach, he went on to design curricula where the "teacher" is intentionally ignorant of his or her students' ignorance: the students are assigned the capability of learning themselves. For example, he created a program for illiterate peasants to teach their children to read. In *The Emancipated Spectator* (2011), Rancière critiques art that tries to move people to action: such art reproduces the pedagogic stance that is unlikely to make an impact. Instead of treating the audience as actors in the world, the act of teaching them that they need to act on something to make changes in the world turns them into people who need to be taught and shown what to think, which makes them in this way into passive spectators rather than actors transforming their world. At issue for us in this game is the ways that teaching turns students – often the "audience" – into passive people who "need" teachers to learn. This merely exacerbates the problem of a passive class who waits to be told what to do. The ignorant schoolmaster intentionally remains woefully ignorant of her or his students' lack of understanding in order to recognize all that they do bring to the classroom, and all that they are capable of ... in this way, the ignorant schoolmaster can facilitate learners' learning and using what they learn to make a difference in their lives and in the lives of others.

Gilles Deleuze—Deleuze was a French philosopher who wrote on psychoanalysis, literature, film, art, and with his co-author Félix Guattari, on the mental health system and social life. In his work, *Difference and Repetition* (1995), he attacked good sense and common sense: "Good sense" treats the universe statistically and attempts to optimize it to produce the best outcome; it may be rational, but it mainly reduces rather than amplifies the power of difference, turning every question into one of economics in which the value or worth of something is an average of expected values, and in which the present and the future might be interchanged. "Common sense" on the other hand is the ability to recognize and react to categories of objects. Deleuze suggested that common sense complements good sense, and in fact allows it to function; 'recognition' of the object enables 'prediction' and the cancelation of danger (along with other possibilities of difference).To both common sense and good sense, Deleuze opposes paradox. Paradox serves as the stimulus to real thought and to philosophy because it forces thought to confront its limits. Of interest to us in the play of the game are the ways that we can make paradox a greater presence in educational experience, so that we do not reduce learning to only common sense and good sense.

Deleuze also wrote with Guattari (1987) about the idea of "nomadic epistemology." This is a way of combating two-sided thinking in order to imagine more alternatives. For example, they use the idea of nomads as not fitting into the categories of homeless or sheltered: they are *both* homeless and have homes, yet are neither homeless nor without homes. The common sense categories simply do not fit, yet nomads like the Romani in Europe co-exist with the world in which most people seem to fit into one of the two categories. Similarly, in our game, we can use nomadic epistemology to coexist with common sense categories yet not be limited by them. What might our lesson be like if people were neither teachers nor students, yet are always both teachers and students? How might our students be neither readers of others' writing nor writers themselves, yet at the same time be writers and readers? Are our students mathematicians or students of mathematics? Maybe they could be something that is not best described as mathematicians nor as learners of mathematics, yet act like mathematicians and like learners of mathematics at the same time?

Johann Wolfgang von Goethe—Goethe was a German writer, pictorial artist, biologist, theoretical physicist, and more. He is often considered the supreme genius of modern German literature, living from the later 1700s to the earlier 1800s. In his book *Wilhelm Meister's Apprenticeship* (1795), he describes how a young man tricks his parents into thinking he is living the life of a decent apprentice while finding adventures off on his own. It turns out that his father and others have been intentionally following him behind the scenes like puppet masters steering his seemingly independent life. Via the adventures that only appeared independent at the time, the young man eventually comes to appreciate the life he was destined to live, and he saw those adventures as carefully designed to help him assume a responsible middle class existence. At issue for us in the play of our game is the ways that we feel it necessary as adults to be the puppet masters for the lives of youth. Must we be protecting them from all danger lurking behind the scenes, saving them from what might take place without us? Do they need to disobey and imagine they are off on their own without us in order to figure out that they agree with our values and goals all along?

Michel De Certeau—De Certeau was a French Jesuit and scholar whose work combined history, psychoanalysis, philosophy and the social sciences. In *The Practice of Everyday Life* (1984), he noted that everyday life is distinctive from other practices of daily existence because it is so routine and repetitive that it has become unconscious. His ideas help us think about how we and others navigate from streets and recipes to books to ideas to theories and back again, without necessarily actively making decisions. They also help us see the difference between what he called "strategies" – wielded by institutions and structures of power who are the "producers" of society, and "tactics" – actions and ways of behaving that are taken on or invented by individuals who might be called the "consumers" who are acting in environments defined by the strategies of the institutions and power structures. Of interest to us in the game are the ways that teachers and students might be subject to strategies such that their tactics are never fully foreseen or understood by the strategies of power – like people walking the city who take shortcuts and entertaining side routes not included in the map. Students, and sometimes teachers, live their everyday lives by poaching on the terrain of others, using the rules and products of our culture in ways that are influenced but rarely fully determined by those rules and products.

The North American thinkers deck.   Contemporary curriculum scholars are helping educators come up with new languages for thinking through important decisions every day. One aspect of contemporary scholarship is that none of these scholars is easily labeled by a specific, important theory or concept that they are known for. Nevertheless, we can pick out a few things for each of the following cards in our game:

Sharon Todd—(a) What if the content that students are officially learning were used in some way to help facilitate youth leadership, voice and participation in the educational space? (b) People present in a classroom are often acting on unspoken or even unconscious desires. Desires are not only handled or dealt with, but are also produced and constituted. (c) Differences among various members of an educational community – age, ethnicity, culture, gender, interests, and so on, are always constructed by our society differently, and these different kinds of differences are important to think about. Meanwhile, any attempt to create some form of democracy or citizenship, or even to think and act humanely, already seems to presume an implicit definition of what a human "is," so that educating as if we already know what people need, deserve, should strive for, etc., risks counting some people "in" while others are excluded or marginalized.

Kieran Egan—We are always not only facilitating the learning of "content" but also at the same time we always tell a story *about* the content. To use an example from the actual practice of storytelling, Cinderella might be about how being a good person pays off in the end, or about class structure (rich people have power in society), or about gender inequality (why does Cinderella need to marry a prince to be happy? Why did the wicked step-mother need to marry Cinderella's father to be happy?). So, to use this example as a metaphor, the experiences we have as we learn tell a back-story; and, the content on the surface and that which is officially in a scope and sequence chart for a school district is merely a means to an end of telling a more important story behind the story.

Marla Morris—(a) We are always arriving at what we are doing "in the middle of the conversation;" there is no "beginning" to what we are doing or learning or teaching. Instead, disorientation is a springboard for invention. (b) Sometimes, whether we are playing seriously or seriously playing with ideas, we become *blocked*, frozen and "unable to play;" taking *this* seriously, recognizing and valuing it, appreciating that peoples' attempts to understand this, ignore this, overcome this, even realize this, are as important, or more important, than what is specifically going on, on the surface of things. Furthermore, periods of such paralysis and blockage often reverberate and manifest themselves in unconscious ways years later, even in contexts that are not obviously related.

Anne Winfield—We have a long history of scientifically and rationally planning schools to be efficient in the ways that it serves the "needs" of learners, sorts students into categories to facilitate its goals, and uses forms of assessment and diagnosis in order to optimize the methods employed. But a historical perspective on these professional practices leads us to understand not only their origin in the eugenics, but also how our current practices often reproduce the same insidious beliefs and assumptions that perpetuate inequalities and injustice. For example, eugenicists believed ability was innate and that it was the job of education to successfully sort students and match them to the vocations for which they were best suited; by matching inborn ability with appropriate path, society would achieve a system of meritocracy where income and ability were directly correlated. Forms of tracking and sorting and categorizing are indications that eugenics is still alive and rampant. Historically and in the present these ideas may come from or be implemented by progressives, conservatives, leftists, fascists, and so on, but regardless of political standpoint, the theories and practices are racist and oppressive.

Deborah Britzman—Educators often go about their business as if learning should be no problem for the learner. But in fact, as psychoanalysts have helped us understand, important learning is accompanied by resistance to insight. In fact, the more important the self-knowledge, the stronger, ironically, is the resistance. The closer we get to understanding ourselves as teachers and as human beings, the more we will resist really understanding this. The closer our students get to really important knowledge, the harder it will be for them to learn. Learning can arouse anxiety, and defenses against learning. At the same time, teachers seem to have a desire to correct, as a form of a rescue fantasy they are looking for mistakes to correct so that they can feel good about saving a child from his or her errors. What if the mistakes do not come? What then? Maybe we need to confront our own fantasies about our work, instead of plowing ahead with our supposedly well-intentioned actions. Rescue the child from what?

	Jacques Rancière *Pedagogical Stance*	Gilles Deleuze *Nomadic Epistemology*	Johann Wolfgang von Goethe *Puppets or Danger?*	Michel DeCerteau *Strategies & Tactics*
Sharon Todd *Beyond Multiculturalism & Cosmopolitanism*				
Kieran Egan *Teaching as Story telling*				
Marla Morris *Play & Paralysis*				
Deborah Britzman *The impossible Profession*				
Anne Winfield *Legacy of Eugenics?*				

Figure 1. Possible card combinations in table-form.

THE DARE

Okay, so I didn't really mean "it's a lost cause" – yes, it's absurd to simplify everything so that we can believe we are doing the absolute best thing for our students at all times. In fact, it is ludicrous and maybe even damaging and harmful. But … *EDUCATION* … well, *that* is something that is happening whenever we act on the results of the game. It's *not* "just a game" but a *dare*:

Today or tomorrow, you have to try out the rewritten lessons, units, objectives and policies, so that these rewritten versions can be the starters for the next play of the game.

Let me know how it goes!
Peter

REFERENCES

Appelbaum, P. (2007). *Children's books for grown-up teachers: Reading and writing curriculum theory.* New York, NY: Routledge.

Britzman, D. (1998). Why return to Anna Freud? Some reflections of a teacher educator. *Teaching Education. 10*(1): 3–16.

Davis, Brent. (2008). *Huh?* In E. De Freitas & K. Nolan (Eds.), *Opening the research text: critical insights and in(ter)ventions into mathematics education,* pp. 81–85. New York, NY: Springer Verlag.

De Certeau, M. (1984). *The practice of everyday life.* Berkeley, CA: University of California Press.

Deleuze, G. (1995). *Difference and repetition.* New York, NY: Columbia University Press.

Deleuze, G, & Guattari, F. (1987). *A thousand Plateaus.* Minneapolis, MN: University of Minnesota Press.

Derrida, J. (1982). *Margins of philosophy.* Chicago, IL: University of Chicago Press.

Egan, K. (1989). *Teaching and storytelling: An alternative approach to teaching and curriculum in the elementary school.* Chicago, IL: University of Chicago Press.

Kierkegaard, S. (1992). *Concluding unscientific postscript to philosophical fragments,* Volume 1 (Kierkegaard's Writings, Vol. 12.1). Hong, Howard & Hong, Edna (trans.). Princeton, NJ: Princeton University Press.

Looney Labs. (1997). *Fluxx: The card game with ever-changing rules.* http://www.looneylabs.com/games/fluxx.

Morris, M. (1998). The Tao of Derrida. *Teaching Education. 10*(1): 23–33.

Morris, M. (2009). *On not being able to play: Scholars, musicians, and the crisis of psyche.* Rotterdam, The Netherlands: Sense Publishers.

Rancière, J. (1991). *The ignorant schoolmaster: Five lessons in intellectual emancipation.* Palo Alto, CA: Stanford University Press.

Rancière, J. (2011). *The emancipated spectator.* New York, NY: Verso.

Suits, B. (1978/2005). *The grasshopper: Games, life and utopia.* Peterborough, ON: Broadview Press.

Todd, S. (2008). *Facing humanity: The difficult task of cosmopolitan education.* http://www.philosophy-of-education.org/conferences/pdfs/Sharon_Todd.pdf.

Todd, S. (1997). Looking at pedagogy in 3-d. In S. Todd (Ed.), *Learning desire: Perspectives on pedagogy, culture, and the unsaid* (pp. 237–260). New York, NY: Routledge.

Winfield, A. G. (2007). *Eugenics and education in America: Institutionalized racism and the implications of history, ideology, and memory.* New York, NY: Peter Lang.

Winfield, A. G. (2010). Eugenic ideology and historical osmosis. In E. Malewski (Ed.), *Curriculum studies handbook – the next moment,* (pp. 142–157). New York, NY: Routledge.

AFFILIATION

Peter Appelbaum
Department of Education
Arcadia University

PART V

VOICES FROM THE PAST

SUSAN JEAN MAYER

42. JUST KEEP IT REAL

Dewey's Wisdom for our Classrooms

Dear those of you who have recently embarked on a career in education,

When I was working as a graduate assistant in my university's teacher certification program, a colleague told the students a story from the previous year that has stayed with me. At least at the time, all the teacher-education candidates taught summer school classes as part of their initial semester, mostly to students who had not managed to pass the same class during the school year. The idea was to forego the idealistic wheel-spinning by subjecting these prospective educators to the rhythms and demands of classroom life from day one.

As you might expect, the teacher-education students, many of them not terribly older than those in their charge, could find it tough at times to their get students to care in the summer about material that most of them had neglected during the school year. One teen, perhaps in a rush of sympathy, or even camaraderie (for who among them wanted to be whiling their summer days away in that classroom?), gave his novice teacher some parting words of advice. He said, *just keep it real*.

There was some talk in our gathering that day about what that young man might have meant to suggest with that phrase, and I am likely not the only one who has continued to ponder what keeping things real in classrooms looks like or how a teacher who wants to do so might proceed. I feel as though I could probably write a small book on the topic at this point, but here I just want to point out a few of the overlaps I see between keeping things real and the way in which John Dewey, devoted philosopher of democracy, thought about the possibilities of human experience.

Although the idea of representing the thirty-seven volumes of Dewey's collected writings with a single word may sound ridiculous, one could actually make a case for the word *experience* as Dewey uses it. This one revered word carries intimations of Dewey's passionate commitments to democracy as a form of human relation and to progressive education as the means by which democratic relations could be practiced and learned.

For public school teachers, particularly new public school teachers, Dewey's use of the word *experience* provides a needed touchstone in these times. When Dewey spoke of educative experience, *he* meant experiences capable of enlivening the hearts and minds of students and teachers alike and of deepening and expanding

T. M. Kress and R. Lake (Eds.), We Saved the Best for You: Letters of Hope, Imagination and Wisdom for 21st Century Educators, 195–198.
© *2013 Sense Publishers. All rights reserved.*

our sense of connection to each other and to our social and material worlds. Dewey believed that experiences of this nature make life feel more satisfying and worthwhile and that democratic schools can and should help to teach an ever larger number of people how to lead lives that feel satisfying and worthwhile in these terms.

How might those of us who agree with Dewey approach this challenge? How shall we imagine the work of engendering among our students ever more alert, caring, and discerning relationships with the content we teach and with each other? How can we ensure that our students acquire the dispositions and resources they will need to sustain their learning after they move on? Although Dewey felt that we must always hold these questions before us, he would have cautioned against trying to address either set of issues in final terms. Rather, questions such as these provide the fertile and fascinating terrain we tramp as educators: in grappling with such questions, we engage and enrich the deep meanings of our field.

We can never entirely know, of course, what our students' experiences with us will come to mean to them over the course of their lives: we can only do our best to make those experiences significant and memorable. In addition to teaching them how to calculate and communicate, this means leaving them with questions to which they will feel called to return. This means teaching them to notice patterns and perplexities that intrigue us and to trust their capacity to learn more about such matters themselves.

Along the way, Dewey's concept of experience returns our attention continually to the character of the interpersonal and intellectual transactions of classrooms. Do people seem self-possessed and focused? Are they listening with interest to others and hazarding to share their own views? Is something we might want to call *real* happening?

As both Dewey and the summer school student understood, you have to stay sharp to keep things real within any social world. You have to get out of your own head and into the hearts and minds of those around you. As teachers, this means attending thoughtfully to our students' responses to our challenges and providing them with opportunities to reveal themselves to us, to themselves, and to each other through the work that we ask them to do. It means helping them to view the work that feels pointless within a broader perspective.

Well beyond standardized test scores lies the challenge of teaching children to attend to each other with respect, to speak thoughtfully and cogently, and to value their own and each other's ideas. Well beyond standardized test scores lies the challenge of demonstrating to all children that what they can learn in schools truly promises to enrich their lives. Well beyond standardized test scores, and all too often in opposition to the pressures that those scores currently exert in our schools, lies the challenge of keeping things real in classrooms.

Should it seem, at times, as though all that the people around you can talk about these days is test scores, know that many dedicated and insightful educators concerned with these larger purposes have preceded you and continue to join you in this work every day. You only need to find a handful of them to get started together on the questions that matter.

Welcome to the field,
Susan Jean Mayer

AFFILIATION

Susan Jean Mayer
Brandeis University &
Northeastern University

MEGAN J. LAVERTY

43. PICTURE THIS

Written as if from Ludwig Wittgenstein

Dear Readers,

When the editors honored me by asking me to contribute a letter to this book, my first thought was to accept their invitation and my second thought was to communicate about a matter of urgent importance. I feel I shall have great difficulty conveying my thoughts and ask that you make my task easier by trying to get at my meaning. Remember, I do not offer theories but merely seek to clarify problems. My fear is that we are held captive by a vision of education. In what follows, I will say something about this vision and then put forward an alternative one that, I hope, will encourage you to see things differently.

Before I begin, let me make a few introductory remarks about my interest in education. I trained as an elementary school teacher in Vienna and spent seven years teaching in rural Austria in the 1920s. Ineffective as a school teacher, I only reluctantly accepted the position of university professor. I do not care for the strenuous demands of teaching and find myself deeply conflicted about it. I am torn between wanting to change my students' thinking *and* not wanting to have too great an influence. I expect my students to be intellectually independent, but I get frustrated when they only half-understand philosophical ideas. I am offended by their superficial cleverness, and yet I worry about their aspirations of becoming professional philosophers. I care about my students deeply and want them to have useful and fulfilling lives.

In thinking about my own teaching, I rely heavily on analogies. In particular, I favor the image of the London tour guide. I imagine, that just as the London tour guide helps visitors orient themselves to the city by taking them up and down its streets—from north to south and east to west—I help my students know their way around a concept by introducing them to its many and varied uses. My aim, like a good tour guide, is to familiarize them with those uses which are most important while suggesting possibilities never previously considered. By the end, my students should have a perspective on an entire conceptual field.

Philosophically speaking, education raises as many intriguing philosophical paradoxes as it resolves. You will notice that the words "pupil", "child," "teaching" and "learning" appear throughout my work. We know that children acquire language and yet we understand so little about it. We find it difficult to identify what linguistic mastery

T. M. Kress and R. Lake (Eds.), We Saved the Best for You: Letters of Hope, Imagination and Wisdom for 21st Century Educators, 199–202.
© *2013 Sense Publishers. All rights reserved.*

consists in; we cannot specify precisely how to convey the meaning of words; and it is impossible to isolate the moment when an individual can be said to have grasped a concept. Our powers of explanation run dry. I will return to this later in the letter but for now I want to introduce the image that dominates our educational imaginary.

We are inclined to view education as a conjointly negotiated endeavor of parents, governments, school administrators, teachers and students. Put differently, education is something that these stake-holders set out to achieve by strategically partnering with one another in its requisite and constitutive activities. They undertake certain calculated risks with a view to acquiring greater control. Education is something that individuals *do*. The picture's specialized or secondary words include: "learning outcomes," "multiple intelligences," "learning disabilities," "standardized assessments," and "dispositions."

As one among many, the picture is fine. I am troubled by its omnipresence, an effect of which has been to inflate the significance of learning outcomes and put untold pressures on teachers and students to fulfill escalating academic expectations. Imagine that newly developed cognitive-enhancing drugs allowed individuals to exceed academic expectations with no effort? Could we defend our current educational practices then? And, would we even want to? Some individuals will no doubt embrace such a pharmacological invention, while others will be inclined to speak about the integrity of presence, the transcendence of teaching and the joy of classrooms. It would be a mistake to dismiss these latter efforts as an exercise in nostalgic sentimentalism. They seek to make explicit the qualities of the teaching and learning relationship that are not reducible to intended measurable outcomes. Such accounts gesture at the mysterious and the ineffable as they come up against the limits of a certain picture of education. What we need is an alternative picture.

Humans are cultural beings. Our world is normatively structured. Concepts are our principal medium of perception, understanding and communication. They give shape to our activities, interactions and lives.

Changes in conceptual understanding reflect changes in life—and vice-versa. Individuals enter this world by learning a language or, alternatively, participating in language-games. Language settles for us our forms of experience, ways of life and world-pictures; we must strive to use it *well*. Ironically, language and language-use remains one of life's sublime mysteries. We do not know how individuals come to use words correctly. How is is that they express what they want to say and are able to grasp the meaning of what others say to them? We mostly rely on the ways that the community is collectively inclined to go on. Put in a different way, we recognize an individual as having grasped the meaning of a word when he uses it in ways that conform to how the word is conventionally used.

Within the context of the teaching and learning relations, we read the adult in the child. When the child's speech or behavior deviates from the communal norm, we seek a causal—as opposed to a logical—explanation. We look to the disciplines of sociology, psychology, cognitive and neuroscience for systemic explanations for why the child fails to understand what others have no difficulty understanding. To *only* read the adult in the child is to overlook the possibility that the child's nonconformist speech or behavior might be equally authoritative. It is to fail to appreciate that the child's "deviance" might be normative and have a logical explanation. In other words, there is nothing about our grammatical norms that prevent a child from using a word differently in a new context. I highlight this point in my example of the student who reproduces the expected pattern of answers when adding 2, but upwards of 1000 produces answers: 1004, 1008, 1012 and 1016. When his error is pointed out the student is incredulous. He is convinced that he is going on in the right way, doing the same with numbers greater than 1000 as he did with the numbers below it. One response is to dismiss the student as clearly mistaken. Another response is to imagine the inherent normativity of his approach, that is, to try to think with him.

Extrapolating from this example, it is just as important for the teaching and learning relation to read the child in the adult and recognize the indeterminacy of our concepts. The criteria governing grammatical and behavioral norms are not impersonal and absolute; rather, they are provisional and improvisatory. Prompted by unique situations, individuals exercise their customary words, thoughts and habits in *creative* ways. Individuals do not simply subsume the new situation under an old idea; instead, they project familiar ideas in unfamiliar directions. Norms usefully provide guidance but they do not foreclose on new reaches of significance. Such improvisatory uses results in a modified or revised conceptual understanding expressed in changes to the individual's manner of speaking, behaving and interacting.

If what I have been claiming is true, then students must be taken seriously as attempting something meaningful. If the student's speech or behavior appears puzzling or deviant, then the educator must intensify his or her efforts to discover its inherent intelligibility. The educator must seek to discover what the student takes him or herself to mean in an acknowledgement of the student's equal claim to grammatical and behavioral authority. It is by imagining the student's perspective that the educator is able to elicit his or her agreement with community-based norms; the educator has an idea about how to make the proposed way of going on more intelligible to the student. This is not to imply that the student's agreement is a foregone conclusion. The student may continue to withhold agreement, offering the educator a glimpse of what community life might become. In summary, the educator exemplifies community-based norms and invites the student to adopt them in the process of recognizing that these community-based norms are contingent and limited.

In schools, students must be given the occasion to "speak for themselves," even at the risk of talking nonsense. They must be provided with opportunities to *use* their linguistic, mathematical, and historical modes of thought, even at the risk of misuse. They must be introduced to pedagogies that lack guaranteed outcomes, including speculative questioning, thought experiments, paradoxes, aphorisms, aporias and silence. To take up educating students in this manner places an ethical demand upon teachers. They must refrain from the authoritarian imposition of their ideas, having recognized that no one way of going on is more grounded than another. Teachers must seek to elicit agreement from students by providing and preserving those occasions when a concept is disclosed, ramified, or "forced upon" an individual. This picture's specialized or secondary educational words include: "meaningful" "deepened," "imaginative," "exemplary," "authoritative" and "necessary."

Education is difficult but not for the reasons that we normally think of. It is a process of coming to accept, and assume responsibility for, our own human finitude. It is difficult to live with nothing beyond our lives providing a secure justification. Practically speaking, we are committed to always having to disentangle the normative and causal elements of human speech and behavior. It is a task that requires patience, observation, conversation and imagination. We cannot afford, however, to pass up on such an endeavor. We only have ourselves. There is nothing to catch us. Language, and language alone, comprises our net of possibilities.

Megan J. Laverty
(as Ludwig Wittgenstein)

REFERENCES

Biesta, G. (2012). Transcendence, revelation and the constructivist classroom: or: in praise of teaching." In R. Kunzman (Ed.), *Philosophy of Education 2011* (pp 358-365). Urbana-Champaign, IL: PES.

Cavell, S. (1990). *Conditions handsome and unhandsome*. Chicago, IL: University of Chicago Press.

Cerbone, D. R. (2003). The limits of conservatism: Wittgenstein on 'our life and our concepts', C. J. Hayes (Ed.), *The grammar of politics: Wittgenstein and political philosophy* (pp. 43–62). Ithaca , NY and London, GB: Cornell University Press. pp 43–62.

Diamond, C. (1988). Losing your concepts. *Ethics, 98*(2): 255–77.

Hall, R. L. (2010). It's a wonderful life: Reflections on Wittgenstein's last words. *Philosophical Investigations, 33*(4): 285–302.

Metro-Roland, D., & Farber, P. (2011). Lost causes: Online Instruction and the integrity of presence. *Philosophy Of Education Archive, 0*: 205–213. Retrieved from http://ojs.ed.uiuc.edu/index.php/pes/article/view/3031/1106

Malcolm, N. (1958). *Ludwig Wittgenstein: A memoir*. London: Oxford University Press.

Mulhall, S. (2002). Ethics in the light of Wittgenstein, *Philosophical Papers 31*(3): 293–321.

Peters, M. A., Burbules, N., & Smeyers, P. (2008). *Showing and doing: Wittgenstein as pedagogical philosopher*. Boulder, CO and London, GB: Paradigm Publishers.

Pianalto, M. (2011). Speaking for oneself: Wittgenstein on ethics. *Inquiry 54*(3): 252–276.

Pope, D. C. (2002). *"Doing school": How we are creating a generation of stressed-out, materialistic, and miseducated students*. Yale, RI: Yale University Press.

Rhees, R. (2006). *Wittgenstein and the possibility of discourse*, D. Z. Phillips (Ed.). Oxford, GB: Blackwell.

Williams, M. (2011). Master and novice in the later Wittgenstein," *American Philosophical Quarterly 48*(2): 199–211.

Wittgenstein, L. (1980). *Culture and value*, (Peter Winch, Trans.). Chicago, IL: University of Chicago Press.

Wittgenstein, L. (1966). *Lectures& conversations on aesthetic, psychology and religious belief*. C. Barrett (Ed.). Oxford, GB: Blackwell Publishers.

AFFILIATION

Megan J. Laverty
Teachers College
Columbia University

BARBARA J. THAYER-BACON

44. CHILDREN ARE OUR HOPE FOR THE FUTURE

A Letter on Behalf of Maria Montessori to 21st Century Educators

Dear Ones,

I write on behalf of Maria Montessori.[1] I don't claim to channel her directly but I share her deep love of children and her faith that they represent our hope for a future that is more peaceful and harmonious. She was Italian, through-and-through, and I am from the country that first embraced her whole-heartedly, and then rejected her—the United States. She might resent my representing her voice for that reason, but I seek to make amends for our rejection of her ideas, and she would welcome that effort.[2] The greatest cause for concern by Montessori, that I would consider myself capable of writing a letter on her behalf, may be the fact that I am a philosopher of education. Dr. Montessori viewed herself first-and-foremost as a scientist, as the first licensed female medical doctor in Italy, and she fought hard to be taken seriously as a scientist in a male-dominated world that continually positioned her only as an attractive, graceful female educator. She especially did not appreciate being compared to other philosophers such as Rousseau. However, I am a feminist philosopher of education who has presented her case, in terms of gender biases she faced in her lifetime,[3] and I am a cultural studies scholar who has presented her case in terms of her political positioning within a tumultuous time in Europe.[4] Most importantly, I am a former Montessori teacher and a mother of four children: I began a career in education as a means of keeping my own children enrolled in Montessori schools.[5] I was seeking to find ways to help my children keep their love of learning alive, and by teaching in their school, I paid for their tuition as well as earned a minimal salary. For those reasons I would earn her respect and a possible invitation to speak on her behalf. Here goes:

Dr. Montessori was able to observe children with fresh eyes, due to her scientific training as well as her deep spiritual belief in their humanity. She was an astute observer of children's behavior and she was able to bring new meaning to their actions, thus revealing adult meanings we bring to our (mis)understanding of children's behavior. She held a deep level of respect for children, and that regard helped her to take note of children that others had removed from society and made invisible – children with special needs. She was able to see the children placed in the Roman mental institutions who were playing with crumbs on the floor after being fed like animals and translate

T. M. Kress and R. Lake (Eds.), We Saved the Best for You: Letters of Hope, Imagination and Wisdom for 21st Century Educators, 203–206.
© 2013 Sense Publishers. All rights reserved.

their observed behavior as intellectual curiosity and a need for stimulation, not as disgusting, animal behavior. Instead of seeing their situation as hopeless, Montessori saw potential in their curiosity and began to seek sources to help her find ways to possibly teach the children. By making that important observation and following up on it, she helped launch what we now call special education. We now understand that children with special needs have just as deep of a desire to learn as any other child and that they have the ability to learn, if we break down concepts into sequential steps, use manipulative materials to teach abstract ideas, and rely on all sensory resources available to the children to help them make connections between abstract ideas and their concrete experiences. We understand that children with special needs have the human right to an education and that they deserve to be treated with dignity and respect, thanks in great part to Dr. Montessori.

Dr. Montessori became internationally famous for her successful efforts to teach children with special needs how to read and write and pass Italy's examinations at the same levels as "normal" children. She could have stopped there and been content to help develop a new field in education. However, she didn't stop there; her scientific curiosity caused her to wonder why the "normal" children weren't doing better in school when they didn't have to face the challenges her special needs children had to overcome. Thus, she began observing "normal" children in traditional schools and when offered an invitation to work with some children, she jumped at the chance to test her ideas. This time it was preschool-aged, low-income children that became her focus, children who needed to be attended to while their parents worked as laborers during the day.

Once again, Montessori was able to observe behavior in children that adults were ignoring, preschoolers whom we would label today as "at-risk" due to their families' low socio-economic status. What other adults translated as destructive behavior, Montessori translated as bored, undirected behavior; the children were defacing the public buildings where their families lived. She hypothesized that the children wanted to learn. What other adults translated as nonsensical, whimsical play, she saw as preschool-age children in need of meaningful work. Montessori brought the same teaching philosophy to her educational experiments with preschool-age children, and helped to launch what we now call preschool education. Montessori trusted children's desire to learn, and her students gleefully went right to work at the task of learning, far exceeding anyone's expectations of what they were capable of doing as a result.

Thanks to her careful observations and willingness to question what most educators took for granted, we now understand that young children have incredibly absorbent minds and are capable of learning a great deal. We now know they will doggedly work on a task over and over again until they have mastered it, and that they have abilities to concentrate way beyond that for which we gave them credit. We understand that they have sensitive periods for learning skills such as ordering their environments, as well as reading and writing, and that if we trust children's desires to learn, and give them the opportunity to move freely around a room full of sensorial materials, they will choose wisely, based on their interests and needs, and they will work diligently to understand their world more completely. We also understand now that even young children have a human right to an education, and that we should support their efforts to learn.

Dr. Montessori treated children with respect and dignity, and they loved her for that. In a Montessori school, a child who is immersed in her work is not interrupted because of adults' scheduling issues unless interruption is impossible to avoid. They are allowed to work until they are satisfied that their work is complete. Children are forewarned about the need to put down their work to prepare for things such as time to go home. In a Montessori school, children are allowed to move freely around the classroom and choose what they want to work on as well as who they want to work with or, if they prefer, to do a task alone. Children are allowed to rest or fix themselves a snack when they need to. They are taught how to take care of their environment, given the necessary tools that fit their body sizes to be able to do so, and they are trusted to be able to do that care-work.

Montessori saw in children possibility and potential as well as deep spirituality. She reminds us that children are the hope for a better future, for a world where people can learn how to live in harmony with each other as well as their environment. For Montessori, the classroom is a community of little explorers who will grow up to become the future citizens of our various countries. A child who is cranky or inconsolable is treated like a child who is not feeling well and needs medical attention or intervention. The child is given sympathetic attention and gently led to a quiet place to rest. A child that is restless and causing disturbances for others in the room is treated like a child who is bored and in need of intellectual stimulation. That child needs to be shown a new material, one that is challenging and taps into that child's interests. Montessori observed that children want to learn and are interested in the world around them. They need adults to facilitate in their learning, offer them the tools and resources that will help them with their exploring, and to get out of their way and let them work.

Montessori's methods of educating children succeed at an international level. She led training programs for teachers from all over the world, up until her death in 1952. The teacher training programs she developed still continue today, including at the elementary and secondary level. There are now over 3,000 Montessori schools in over 80 different countries. Dr. Maria Montessori reminds us that children are dear ones and that there is much we can learn from them if we are wise enough to pay attention and open our minds and hearts to them.

Much love,
Barbara Thayer-Bacon

NOTES

[1] My biographical sources include: Kramer, R. (1976). *Maria Montessori: A biography.* New York, NY: G. P. Putman's Sons; Standing, E. M. (1957/1998). *Maria Montessori: Her life and work.* New York, NY: Plume, Penguin Group.

[2]   Thayer-Bacon, B. (in press). Maria Montessori, John Dewey, and William H. Kilpatrick. *Education and culture*.

[3]   Thayer-Bacon, B. (October 27–29, 2011). *Maria Montessori's gendered story*. Paper delivered at the Research on Women and Education Annual Fall Conference, Houston, Texas.

[4]   Thayer-Bacon, B. (September, 2011). Maria Montessori: Education for peace. *In Factis Pax*. 5: (2011): 307–319.

[5]   I am an elementary licensed Montessori teacher who taught in three different Montessori schools (lower and upper elementary) for several years. Between my teaching and my children attending Montessori schools, I have twenty-seven years of experience with Montessori education. For those interested in knowing more about Montessori schools, contact the American Montessori Society (281 Park Ave., New York, NY 10010) or the Association of Montessori International (1095 Market St., Suite 405, San Francisco, CA 94103). A key source for Montessori's method of education is: Montessori, M. (1909). *The Montessori method*. New York: Random House.

AFFILIATION

Barbara Thayer-Bacon
Department of Educational Psychology & Counselling
University of Tennessee Knoxville

TIANLONG YU

45. THE BEST IS YET TO COME

Confucius's Hope

Dear Teachers of the 21st Century:

I am Confucius, a teacher who lived and worked some 2500 years ago in China. What a privilege it is to address you from across the centuries and to share my thoughts about something we both hold dear: Education.

But first, let me say I am a little perplexed by the treatment I receive today in my home county and abroad. It seems I am being rediscovered. I am promoted as a new beacon of light and the symbol of the Chinese cultural tradition, as if one man could possibly symbolize something so vast, intricate and beautiful. I heard the Chinese government has founded several hundred so-called "Confucius institutes" around the world with the express purpose of spreading Confucian influence worldwide and as a way to showcase China. I have become a new super power's cultural capital which is of course an absurd reduction. I am even more troubled by what is showered upon me within the Chinese borders. I have been grabbed and dragged into a feverish national movement that can be summarized with the phrase "returning to tradition." My name and what I represented is repeatedly invoked by statesmen and politicians as a means to restore order to China's current chaotic transitional time. On national TV and in lecture halls, scholars are interpreting my theories anew. Students are reading my words, often simplistically rephrased and stripped of their richness. Self-styled "experts" have cashed in on the trend, becoming millionaires by reiterating what I said. There is even a Hollywood-style movie about me and there was talk of erecting a statue of my likeness during the opening ceremony of the Chinese Olympics! Thank goodness they didn't do it. All of this becomes even more ludicrous when I remember that a few decades ago in this same place I was demonized. I became the object of loathing, a source of national shame and denial. Contrast this with my new-found popularity among the political and financial classes as a means for their gain, and you can understand my reluctance to embrace it. I don't mind being presented as a cultural ambassador to promote international understanding; yet, I loathe any efforts in my name to strengthen nationalism or provincialism. Such an emphasis fosters competition and conflict among nations and communities. People seem to forget that I envisioned a "One World" shared by all where love, peace, and harmony would prevail.

T. M. Kress and R. Lake (Eds.), We Saved the Best for You: Letters of Hope, Imagination and Wisdom for 21st Century Educators, 207–210.
© *2013 Sense Publishers. All rights reserved.*

While it is true that every age, my own included, has its blind spots which may be best overcome by studying ideas from other ages, you will serve your own age best if you remain firmly grounded in your present. You must not heed the call to return to tradition in education policy today. Be mindful that there never was a "golden age" in education. You cannot go boldly forward while fixing your gaze on the past – you will surely stumble! Instead take the best from the past with gratitude, and discard the rest.

I long to restore your faith in yourselves as teachers. Historically, Chinese teachers have enjoyed respect from the larger public. In recent years, however, teachers' status seems to have declined rapidly in the midst of a national craze for economic growth. Teachers are not compensated well, enticing many bright young people to choose career paths with greater financial rewards. The American education system becomes fodder for political gamesmanship with each election season, and is blamed for every societal ill. The "Race to the Top" is undermining teachers' morale and pushing many good teachers out of their profession. I know it is unrealistic for you to rely on politicians to restore faith in you during this "open hunting season for education" when you have become targets, but you must continue to demand such respect and most importantly not to lose faith in yourselves. Remember that elections come and go, and when the rhetoric dies down you will still be in your classrooms, doing the most important work of any culture or country: shaping the characters of the next generation, enculturing and equipping young people to create a better world.

Education is the ultimate means for human flourishing and social renewal. It saddens me that it is not always highly regarded as such in present-day China and many other parts of the world. I'm particularly disheartened with a lack of educational opportunity for many of the world's children. When I opened my private school, one of the first such schools in ancient China, I had an "open door" policy. I didn't erect high-stakes requirements for admission. I was willing to teach anyone, whatever their social standing, as long as they were eager and tireless. Hundreds of students did come to me with nothing more than their love for learning. Today, many highly motivated and talented youngsters have their educational rights brutally denied due to poverty or discriminatory policies. Many Chinese children, especially in poor rural areas, never complete a high school education. In America many students, especially in the impoverished inner-cities, drop out at increasing rates from an education system that they see as irrelevant to their lives. Why is this so?

Government-mandated standardized tests have only made the situation worse, stifling creativity and innovation in their teachers. Such a system values conformity above all else, and the child who cannot conform is miserable. It is as if their uniqueness is something to be despised. The one-size-fits-all education for all students in all places imposes the idea that there is only one way to be, one way to live, one way to dream. You must resist this to the extent that you can. Our students' gifts are as numerous as our students. Allowing one path to success necessarily diminishes those students who see the world differently, in different shades, from different vantage points, with different goals. Worse, this emphasis on conformity promotes the idea that all education is a means to one economic end: that of material comfort. Our students see the moral hypocrisy in this, even if they don't articulate it. They want something more, something transcendent. Otherwise, why bother? To become educated should mean to become more fully human, not to become the first among your peers to own a flat-screen TV or the latest cell phone!

Which brings me to the issue of moral education. I have been lauded as a moral educator, and yes, I do believe every teacher ought to be a moral teacher. As economic orientation increasingly drives the reform movement, the moral purpose of education is forsaken.

But how can we work to educate for morality? In both China and America, there is an ill-placed emphasis on children, a "blaming the victims" mentality at work. Children are asked to better their morals and values, to be virtuous, and often this "virtues crusade" is launched under the banner of Confucian or Aristotelian virtue ethics! My theory of moral education does emphasize individual moral perfection to achieve social harmony, but in teaching, I always stressed dialogue, connection, and community. The interplay is complex, and students must be educated in the kind of thinking that produces moral behavior. The Confucian moral philosophy largely revolves around the concept of "Ren" or "compassion" and the best way to cultivate "Ren" is not through indoctrination or rote learning, but through personal reflection and application of the Golden Rule: "Do unto others as you would have done unto you." You may call this an "ethic of reciprocity." I also emphasized "Li" or "propriety" for self-restraint. However, "Li" doesn't mean suppressing one's desires entirely, but learning how to reconcile one's own desires with the needs of one's family and community. Students learn that their decisions do not occur in a vacuum – their decisions do indeed impact others. In addition, I believe that teachers teach with their own lives as moral examples. I always emphasized that moral teaching considers the context when arriving at the best course of action. The reflection required for this produces the maturity that education promises. My disciples knew how hard I tried to utilize different methods working with them, discovering the best in each and every one of them, helping them to achieve their inner balance, to pursue their personal happiness and humanity.

I have a lot more to say as an old person who has seen so much. Though I may sound quite disappointed with the state of education, I remain hopeful and optimistic for the future.Those of you pursuing education in the current somewhat hostile environment are by necessity dedicated to your life's work. The word "education" comes from an ancient word meaning "to lead out" (of ignorance). Finish this idea by leading *into* the fertile land of understanding, a land where cooperation and a high regard for others is the order of the day, a place where various thoughts are discussed and scrutinized, the best of them treasured. The torch is passed to you, my fellow teachers, to boldly light the way forward equipped with the condensed wisdom of the ages as you break new ground and forge a better world. The best is yet to come!

With peace, love and solidarity,
Confucius

AFFILIATION

Tianlong Yu
Department of Educational Leadership
Southern Illinois University Edwardsville

LOIS HOLZMAN

46. ON BEHALF OF VYGOTSKY

Dear 21st Century Educators,

I don't remember exactly when I made the following statement, which was repeated in print long after my death:

> To the naive mind, revolution and history seem incompatible. It believes that historical development continues as long as it follows a straight line. When a change comes, a break in the historical fabric, a leap – then this naive mind sees only catastrophe, a fall, a rupture; for the naive mind history ends until back again straight and narrow. The scientific mind, on the contrary, views revolution as the locomotive of history forging ahead at full speed; it regards the revolutionary epoch as a tangible, living embodiment of history. A revolution solves only those tasks which have been raised by history; this proposition holds true equally for revolution in general and for aspects of social and cultural life. (Quoted in Levitin, 1982, inside front cover).

During my short life of 38 years, the locomotive of history was traveling at full speed. The Bolsheviks seized power in 1917, and there was so much to do to support the Revolution and to transform the culture, support people to develop and learn, and create a truly Marxist psychology. Although I didn't know how to do it (it wasn't knowable; it was only creatable), I knew it would require a new conception of science, of method, and of human beings. I did what I could, with my dedicated colleagues. And then I died.

Looking at where we've come in 2012, I see how naïve I was. Yes, I was aware, in the last decade of my life, how politics and ideology contaminated science and education in my country. But I never dreamed that in capitalist America schooling would become utterly and completely politicized. That creating new understandings and new kinds of practices of learning and development—some of them done in my name—would have so little impact on how schools function.

It seems I was correct about revolution solving those tasks raised by history. But I was mistaken in putting my faith in science. I didn't foresee what science would become—a religious worshipping of the ahistorical and acultural particular. I applaud those of you who affirm the philosophical and political power of the ontological socialness of human beings, who insist that the creativity and joy of the learning-development dialectical unity of early childhood is a human right at any

T. M. Kress and R. Lake (Eds.), We Saved the Best for You: Letters of Hope, Imagination and Wisdom for 21st Century Educators, 211–212.
© *2013 Sense Publishers. All rights reserved.*

and all ages, and who recognize that this historical task cannot be solved by science "alone," because it is a cultural and political task.

I wish you the best,
Lev Vygotsky and Lois Holzman

REFERENCE

Levitin, K. (1982). *One is not born a personality. Profiles of Soviet educational psychologists*, V.V. Devydov (Ed.). Moscow, RU: Progress Publishers.

AFFILIATION

Lois Holzman
East Side Institute for Group and Short Term Psychotherapy

ANDY BLUNDEN

47. LETTER FROM HEGEL TO THE EDUCATORS OF THE 21ST CENTURY

Dear Educator,

In 1812, my friend, Friedrich Niethammer, Commissioner for Education in Bavaria, asked me to write a report on the teaching of philosophy in secondary schools. In part of my report I touched on the new-fangled idea of "content-free education":

> According to the modern craze, especially in pedagogy, one is not so much to be instructed in the content of philosophy as to learn how to philosophize without any content. That amounts to saying that one is to travel endlessly without getting to know along the way any cities, rivers, countries, men, etc... Thus in learning the content of philosophy one not only learns to philosophize but indeed really philosophizes. (Hegel, 1984, p. 279)

In the 21st century, when anything you might ever want to know is available to any child who can use Google, some teachers have come to the conclusion that one must teach children how to evaluate the information they find, but that there is no longer any need to teach a child any positive content. My report went on:

> The unfortunate urge to educate the individual in thinking for himself and being self-productive has cast a shadow over truth. As if, when I learn what substance, cause, or anything is, I myself were not thinking. As if I did not myself produce these determinations in my own thought but rather tossed them in my head as pebbles. As if, further, when I have insight into their truth, into the proofs of their synthetic relations or dialectical transitions, I did not receive this insight myself, as if I did not convince myself of these truths. As if when I have become acquainted with the Pythagorean theorem and its proof I have failed to know this theorem and prove its truth myself! As much as philosophical study is in and for itself self-activity, to that degree also is it learning: the learning of an already present, developed science. This science is a treasure of hard-won, ready-prepared, formed content. This inheritance ready at hand must be earned by the individual, i.e., learned. The teacher possesses this treasure; he *pre-thinks* it. The pupils *re-think* it. The philosophical sciences contain universal true thoughts of their objects. They constitute the end product of the labor of human thought in all ages. These true thoughts surpass what an uneducated young person comes up with thinking by himself to the same degree that such

T. M. Kress and R. Lake (Eds.), We Saved the Best for You: Letters of Hope, Imagination and Wisdom for 21st Century Educators, 213–216.
© *2013 Sense Publishers. All rights reserved.*

a mass of inspired labour exceeds their own effort. The original, peculiar views of the young on essential objects are in part still totally deficient and empty, but in part—in infinitely greater part—they are opinion, illusion, half-truth, distortion, and indeterminateness. (Hegel, 1984, p. 279–280)

Of course, children must actively seek out knowledge and know how to acquire it. But they must be encouraged to study the works of the great writers of the past, something they will not easily do of their own accord, since the old way of writing is foreign to them. And nor is it sufficient to direct students to the great thinkers of the present time and to learn about the past through their eyes. Students cannot re-think the thoughts of their teachers on the philosophers of the past, until they have some first-hand acquaintance with the content of what their teachers are criticizing.

This fascination with "thinking for oneself" is worse even than it was 200 years ago, in my day. A person can no more think for someone else than they can eat or drink for them (Hegel, 1975, pp. 36). *Before a child can think for themself they have to experience thinking the thoughts of the great thinkers of the past, which a teacher can guide them through, but cannot do for them. It would be a deception to give the child some skills for critically reviewing the information they find on the Internet and pretend that this is enough to prepare them to live up to their responsibility as citizens. The child should not simply find the wisdom of the past lying there to be picked up at will.* Unless the child retraces stages of a road which has been worked over and levelled out by past generations (Hegel, 1967, p. 16. §28) *and learns the long and arduous struggle by means of which we have learned how to think critically, then the child is unlikely to develop the critical eye for which the experience of the great thinkers of the past has prepared us.*

The child's right to education *flows from the child's responsibility* to realise his or her potential and to acquire for themselves the position which he ought to attain. They do not have it by nature (Hegel, 1975, p. 117). The school thus forms merely the transition from the family into civil society (Hegel, 1971, p. 61). *The school does have the responsibility to ensure that a child has the skills necessary to earn their living in civil society and find a vocation in which they can meet the needs of others in the community. But this is not enough.*

I once heard that when a father inquired about the best method of educating his son in ethical conduct, a Pythagorean replied: 'Make him a citizen of a state with good laws' (Hegel, 1975, p. 109). *The converse also applies: the school must prepare the child to be an active and effective citizen, so that the whole community will advance. That is the surest and only guarantee that the individual will have a better life.*

Experience of the market has shown that notwithstanding the efforts of philanthropists and the welfare state and despite an excess of wealth, civil society is not rich enough – its own resources are insufficient – to check excessive poverty and the creation of an impoverished rabble. *No amount of vocational education can abolish or even reduce poverty and* the concentration of disproportionate wealth in a few hands (Hegel, 1975, p. 150). *This is the reason that the school bears such a responsibility to impart to children the critical spirit, the ability to be active in the political domain, the knowledge of where the institutions of their state have come from, the conditions of previous generations. Schools must teach children to know how to effectively represent their interests in the political sphere.*

Andy Blunden
(on behalf of Hegel)

REFERENCES

Hegel, G. W. F. (1967). *The Phenomenology of Spirit.* (J. B. Baillie, Trans.). San Fransisco, CA: Harper & Row. (Original work published 1807).

Hegel, G. W. F. (1971). *Philosophy of Mind.* (W. Wallace & A. V. Miller, Trans.). Oxford: UK: Oxford University Press.

Hegel, G. W. F. (1975). *Philosophy of Right.* (T. M. Knox, Trans.). Oxford: UK: Oxford University Press.

Hegel, G. W. F. (1979). *Hegel's Logic.* (Wm. Wallace, Trans.). Oxford, UK: Oxford University Press. (Original work published 1830).

Hegel, G. W. F. (1984). *Hegel: The letters.* (C. Butler & C. Seiler, Trans.). Bloomington IN: Indiana University Press.

AFFILIATION

Andy Blunden
Independent Social Research Network

JOAN BRAUNE

48. PEDAGOGY OF DISOBEDIENCE

(Written as if from Erich Fromm)

Dear Teachers,

It would be hard to overestimate the importance of the teaching vocation. In fact, of the many teachers and mentors that I have had, I credit a high school teacher with first opening my mind to a question that dominated much of my later scholarly work and social activism. When World War One broke out, I was fourteen. Our English teacher had assigned us to memorize the English national anthem. Rebelling, we German boys refused to complete the assignment; England was our sworn enemy, we insisted. In a time of nationalistic pride and self-certainty, that teacher just casually replied, "Don't kid yourselves; so far England has never lost a war!" This calm, rational voice and simple statement of fact awakened me. I began to question the war. As the senseless carnage continued, I found myself asking again and again, "How is it possible?"[1] The question about the causes of violence and nationalism continued to haunt my adult life.

When I arrived in the United States in the 1930s, fleeing Nazi Germany with my colleagues in the Frankfurt Institute for Social Research, I was soon exposed to American philosophy, and especially to John Dewey and to "progressive education." I would like to begin by reiterating the Deweyan educational themes I laid out in my 1955 book *The Sane Society*, before addressing the ways in which the concept of "authority" provides an apt and related critique of current educational systems.

In the 1940s, I taught at Bennington College, which was famously founded by a Deweyan. I began to explore Dewey in my 1947 work *Man for Himself*,[2] but I concluded my 1955 book *The Sane Society*—a best-selling and controversial text, which argued that American society as such is insane due to its quiet acquiescence to the possibility of global nuclear annihilation—with some reflections on education based on my encounter with Deweyan "progressive education." There I offered essentially three claims:

1. There is a grave lack of meaningful and aesthetic communal rituals in modern capitalist societies.[3] Far from relegating art to the museum, aesthetic experience must be fostered and acknowledged in everyday life.
2. We must overcome the divide between practical and theoretical knowledge, by including work skills in educational programs and by training youth in a trade.[4]

T. M. Kress and R. Lake (Eds.), We Saved the Best for You: Letters of Hope, Imagination and Wisdom for 21st Century Educators, 217–220.
© *2013 Sense Publishers. All rights reserved.*

3. We must increase opportunities for adult education, since it is only at later ages that most people are really prepared for "understanding rather than…memorizing"[5]— education is experiential, in the present, as opposed to merely preparatory for the future.
4. Far from embracing such concerns as these, I argued, our current educational system is geared mainly towards the creation of compliant employees and adjusting the individual to a society that is essentially insane. The aim of the present educational system, I argued in 1955—and one could likely say the same today—is:

> to give the individual the knowledge he needs in order to function in an industrialized civilization, and to form his character into the mold which is needed: ambitious and competitive, yet co-operative within certain limits; respectful of authority, yet "desirably independent," as some report cards have it; friendly, yet not deeply attached to anybody or anything. Our high schools and colleges continue with the task of providing their students with the knowledge they must have to fulfill their practical tasks in life, and with the character traits wanted in the personality market.[6]

Actually imbuing youth with the values we claim to profess—the love, hope and faith of our religious traditions, the freedom we claim that our democracy values, and so forth—goes by the wayside, and critical thinking is subtly discouraged.[7]

Despite my enthusiasm for the many exciting experiments in progressive education going on in the United States in the 1930s and 40s, I realized some possible limitations of these projects, centering around the theme of *authority*. Before fleeing the rise of Nazism, I conducted for the Frankfurt Institute a massive sociological and psychoanalytic study of the German working class's attitude toward authority and of their likely acquiescence to Nazism. My early work on criminology had also focused on authority, including the way in which the state itself takes on the role of "educator" in disciplining the populace. I was very wary of the ways in which authoritarianism may be latent within a society that appears to profess a love of freedom.

In my 1960 introduction to A.S. Neill's book *Summerhill*, I discussed my distinction between overt and anonymous authority:

> Overt authority is exercised directly and explicitly. The person in authority frankly tells the one who is subject to him, "You must do this. If you do not, certain sanctions will be applied against you." Anonymous authority tends to hide that force is being used. Anonymous authority pretends that there is no authority, that all is done with the consent of the individual. While the teacher of the past said to Johnny, "You must do this. If you don't, I'll punish you"; today's teacher says, "I'm sure you'll like to do this."[8]

Anonymous authority is not just exercised by parents and by teachers—it ensures that bureaucracies operate smoothly, and it tricks us into thinking that we are "free" when we make decisions as consumers, picking from among a list of pre-selected, carefully marketed options. Even our fear of failing to conform with others in society stems from the force of anonymous authority:

> The same artifices [of anonymous authority] are employed in progressive education. The child is forced to swallow the pill, but the pill is given a sugar coating. Parents and teachers have confused true nonauthoritarian education with *education by means of persuasion and hidden coercion*. Progressive education has been thus debased. It has failed to become what it was intended to be and has never developed as it was meant to.[9]

I do not, of course, believe that anonymous authority should be replaced by overt authority, by the rigid system of punishment and enforcement that I experienced in the German school system, and which is probably not very different from that of many schools in the United States in the early twenty-first century. Rather, I find all training in obedience suspect—human history could only have begun through a courageous act of disobedience, and if it is ever brought to a bitter and final end, it will be through an excess of obedience. Our heroes should be figures like Antigone, who bravely defied an unjust law in the name of higher principles. Nevertheless, I do think education is essential and that good educators possess a certain kind of authority. I call this neither "overt authority" nor "anonymous authority" but rather *rational authority.*

The teacher who is a "rational authority" has little need for force, whether overt or hidden. A rational authority educates through her own genuine interest and ongoing engagement in the subject. She is in love with life, with process, with development and change. She is not concerned primarily with neat classifications, with order, or with imparting facts (what Paulo Freire would call the "banking model" of education), but rather with the experience of activity, hope, and aliveness. Such an educator exemplifies what I would call the "being orientation," to use the terms of my late work *To Have or To Be?* (1976). Such a teacher is motivated by *love* and by *faith*—not necessarily a religious faith, but a tradition of humanistic faith spanning thinkers as diverse as Karl Marx, Benedict Spinoza, and Meister Eckhart, a faith in the potential of all humanity, a faith that enables her to see in her students— and in society and all of human history—the possibilities for future liberation and fulfillment.[10]

To Life,
Erich Fromm

NOTES

[1] Erich Fromm, *Beyond the Chains of Illusion: My Encounter with Marx and Freud* (New York: Pocket Books, Inc., 1963), p. 7.
[2] Erich Fromm, *Man for Himself: An Inquiry Into the Psychology of Ethics* (New York: Henry Holt and Company, 1990), p. 207.

3   Erich Fromm, *The Sane Society* (New York: Henry Holt and Company, 1990), p. 347.
4   Ibid., p. 345.
5   Ibid., p. 346.
6   Ibid., pp. 344–5.
7   Ibid., p. 345.
8   Erich Fromm, "A Forward by Erich Fromm" in *Summerhill: A Radical Approach to Child Rearing* by A.S. Neill (New York: Hart Publishing Company, 1960), p. X.
9   Ibid.,xi.
10 Fromm, Man for Himself, p. 207.

AFFILIATION

Joan Braune
Philosophy
University of Kentucky

CURRY STEPHENSON MALOTT

49. LETTER TO EDUCATORS

Rethinking Educational Purpose in the History of Education

Dear Educational Community,

In this letter it is my intention to primarily speak to my likely audience, that is, those teachers and future teachers studying education in possibly a teacher education or doctoral program. As a student you are in the process of acquiring some form of degree or certification to work in an institution of education. Given the fact that you are about to give yourself over to an institution for the better part of your productive life, it seems reasonable that you might be at least a little bit interested in what exactly it is you are getting yourself into. The first thing you might consider doing is asking yourself a series of simple questions. Knowing how busy your lives are as students and, for many of you already, professionals in the field, let me give you a beginning. To get you started, I will consider what seems to be the most logical first question:

– What has been the official, primary, historical purpose of the institution in which I am seeking to exert my labor power?

Before Common Schooling in colonialist America, education primarily served the purpose of educating the children of the ruling class as a way of reproducing the hierarchical system of labor and capital (within slave plantations and early industrial factories). However, around the beginning of the second industrial revolution (mid-to-late 1800s), which included increased immigration, urbanization, large-scale industrial manufacturing, economic integration, a massive chasm between an emerging wealthy ruling class and a savagely exploited working-class, and the subsequent rise in a revolutionary-oriented labor movement, industrial capitalists began to realize that formalized education was going to be a necessary cost of production. In this view, education would both discipline labor and make technological advances to ensure American corporations maintained a competitive edge in the global market.

Consequently, early on in the process of industrialization and westward expansion, the federal government invested in universities to fulfill the purpose of making such advancements in the technologies of economic innovation and capitalist expansion (i.e. the railroad). Making this point their introductory text *American Education*, Urban and Wagoner (2009) note that the "largest universities…were translating

T. M. Kress and R. Lake (Eds.), We Saved the Best for You: Letters of Hope, Imagination and Wisdom for 21st Century Educators, 221–226.
© *2013 Sense Publishers. All rights reserved.*

[the] latest scientific advances into technology that would support America's new industries" (p. 274).

For example, the Morrill Acts of 1862 and 1890 granted states land for agricultural, mechanical, and military colleges. Similarly, the Hatch Act of 1887 funded agricultural experiment stations for research on farming, animal diseases, and so on (Foner, 2009; Smith, 1984; Urban & Wagoner, 2009). *However in this present time,* Mexico State University in Las Cruces, NM is one of these institutions playing a significant role in both agricultural science and military science. The institution is so committed to policing the official pro-capitalist purpose of the university that it has developed an "NMSU Position on Animals in Research and Emergency Preparedness Plan." The following excerpt is telling:

> An important part of the mission of a land-grant university is to conduct appropriate research to optimize the use of animals in the service of man... NMSU defends the right of free speech...regarding the use of animals in research...however, coercion, intimidation, and unlawful acts will not be allowed...Any organization using animals should be prepared for various protests...from animal rights' groups...Appropriate steps will be taken to limit disruption of NMSU activities. (2008, p.53)

What this policy alludes to is the interconnectedness between the technologies of capitalist expansion (i.e. military science and agricultural science and engineering) and the technologies of social control (i.e. controlling the ideas of labor through ideological indoctrination as well as physically censoring ideas through policy and police). But for now let us return to the 1800's.

During this period of rapid growth in industrial output there were virtually no regulations restricting capital's ability to extract surplus value from human labor power. As a result, "by 1890 the richest 1% of Americans received the same total *wealth* as the bottom half of the population and owned more property than the remaining 99%" (Foner, 2009, p. 567). During this time the life of the working class consisted of long hours, low wages, no pensions, no compensation for injuries, and the most dangerous working conditions in the industrial world with more than 35,000 deaths a year between 1880 and 1900 (Foner, 2009).

It was within this context that the labor movement was born, first emerging in Philadelphia, PA. The membership of the Knights of Labor exploded during this time. However, this more mainstream or *nativist* (i.e. U.S.-born whites) branch of labor had a reputation for being anti-Chinese (Urban & Wagoner, 2009) as they had not been able to overcome their own white-supremacist indoctrination as White, male Americans. The Industrial Workers of the World, on the other hand, represented a more counter-hegemonic, and thus anti-racist, branch of the revolutionary labor movement (discussed below). What is particularly striking about this early era of labor organizing is its vast militancy and revolutionary fervor. As future or current education workers, the lesson here is to engage your professional union with a critical eye, always challenging the organizations to assume more critical positions, such as challenging the hegemony of global capitalism rather than only being concerned with the interests of the rank and file and the students served. By placing this militancy in a larger context, Karl Marx highlighted the inherent savageness of competitive, market capitalism.

Dramatizing the barbarism of capital's insatiable quest for profit and the speed at which the first and second industrial revolutions subsumed the social universe within which they emerged (i.e. the accumulation of surplus value or unpaid labor hours), Marx focuses on the length of the working day, which he divides into two components: "...the working-time required for the reproduction of the labor-power of the laborer himself" (Marx, 1867/1967, p. 232) and the amount dedicated to the capitalist class' accumulation of surplus labor. Marx (1867/1967) hones in on the struggle between the capitalist class and the working class's determination for the length of the working day because at the dawn of the second industrial revolution "the capitalist has bought the labor-power at its day-rate" (p. 232). This is significant because when the laborer sells his commodity (i.e. his labor power) on the market to a capitalist, he forfeits control of this commodity (i.e. himself) during the time purchased. If the working day is three times longer than the amount of time needed to reproduce himself, then he or she can protest that they are being robbed of two thirds of the value of their commodity – their own capacity to labor (Marx, 1867/1967).

Because the capitalist is driven by the need to perpetually expand the rate of profit obtained from the purchasing of commodities such as labor power, it is in the interest of capital to extend the length of the work day as long as possible. Asking, "What is the length of time during which capital may consume the labor-power whose daily value it buys?" Marx (1867/1967) observes that, "it has been seen that to these questions capital replies: the working-day contains the full 24 hours" (p. 264). As a result, the laborer is "nothing else, his whole life, than labor-power", and all his or her time is therefore dedicated to "the self-expansion of capital" leaving no time for "education, intellectual development, for the fulfilling of social functions and for social intercourse, for the free-play of his bodily and mental activity" (Marx, 1867/1967, p. 264) and even for the necessary time to rest and rejuvenate the body for another day's work. The historical development of capitalism, especially during the second industrial revolution, has proven unequivocally that "capital cares nothing for the length of life of labor-power" (Marx, 1867/1967, p. 265). Communicating this destructive impulse of capital, Marx (1867/1967) summarizes:

The capitalistic mode of production (essentially the production of surplus value, the absorption of surplus-labor), produces thus, with the extension of the working day, not only the deterioration of human labor-power by robbing it of its normal, moral and physical, conditions of development and function. It produces also the premature exhaustion and death of this labor-power itself. It extends the laborer's time of production during a given period by shortening his actual life-time. (p. 265)

Marx (1867/1967) reminds us that this impulse toward barbarism has nothing to do with the specific personalities of market profiteers/capitalists. That is, it is not a matter of the "good or ill will of individual capitalists," but rather, "free competition brings out the inherent laws of capitalist production" (p. 270), trumping any generous impulse a human capitalist or CEO may or may not posses. What determines then the length of the normal working day or the rate of exploitation in an hourly wage system is "the result of centuries of struggle between capitalist and laborer" (Marx, 1867/1967, p. 270). The key factor determining the course of history in capitalism is therefore class-consciousness.

Again, it was within this context of industrial capitalist barbarism and working-class awakening that Horace Mann set out on a Protestant-inspired crusade for a system of Common Schooling. Mann, working as the Secretary of the Massachusetts Board of Education in the 1840s, saw educating the working class as an effective way to discipline labor and prevent rebellions and other "crimes." Mann, in fact, wrote reports outlining the merits of educated versus uneducated workers. His primary audience was industrial capitalists whose skeptical approval he had to gain. Essentially, Mann sought to convince them that a basic or common education was a necessary cost of production more effective in controlling labor than police, that is, physical force. In school workers would learn "respect for property, for the work ethic, and for the wisdom of the property owners" (Urban & Wagoner, 2009, p. 121). It was within this context – the need to discipline labor and the emergence of science as a theory of everything – that the managers of industry and academics sought to develop a human science as effective at predicting and controlling human behavior as biology and physics were at conquering the natural world. This explains why teachers' colleges opened to ensure future teachers were sufficiently trained with the most up-to-date techniques of social control and behaviorist pedagogy. Zinn (2003) accurately describes teachers, managers, engineers, and other constructors and regulators of the system as "loyal buffers against trouble" (p. 263).

These college educated *middle buffers against trouble* have been so important to the perpetuation of the ruling class because of the cyclical nature of crisis at the heart of the internal laws of accumulation. That is, because capitalism is driven by an insatiable appetite for wealth, the capitalist manager or corporate CEO is forever searching for new ways to reduce the cost of production. The variable cost of labor has historically been one of those areas from which capitalists have sought to cut costs or extract more wealth. As a result, there is a built-in drive that pushes wages down, deeper and deeper, until labor is no longer able to purchase the commodities flooding the market place. At the point when the potential value embedded within commodities is not realized, the cycle of capitalist production breaks down and the system goes into crisis. It is at these moments of increased suffering and hardships within labor that the potential for revolutionary change heightens.

We might therefore conclude that the current purpose of public schooling, reproducing the working and middle classes, was forged during the second industrial revolution as Horace Mann saw the rising tide of working-class discontent that threatened the elite class from which he came. U.S. colleges and universities, many of which were founded during this time, embodied a related purpose – that is, advancements in the technologies of social control. In this context of increasing indoctrination Marx's approach to class-consciousness and a serious discussion about a socialist alternative is imperative.

What this suggests is that while the official purpose of education has always been to serve the interests of capital, as educators, we do not have to accept it. That is, we can challenge this official purpose in our quest for a democratic socialist alternative, consciously not repeating the mistakes of Stalinism. In other words, by not falling victim to the false belief that real socialism can exist in isolation or in a single country, we will not be naïve enough to be led down the road of replacing private capitalism with state capitalism. We will know that an isolated socialism will not have the ability to socialize anything but poverty (Eagleton, 2011). Both state capitalism and private capitalism have relied heavily on an indoctrinating system of education to minimize descent and worker-led rebellions. As radical educators, our post-capitalist challenges must therefore always be situated in a global as well as historical context.

Sincerely yours in the struggle forever,
Curry Malott

REFERENCES

Foner, E. (2009). *Give me liberty!: An American history. Volume 2: From 1865* (2nd ed.). New York, NY: Norton.
Marx, K. (1867/1967). *Capital: A critique of political economy: Volume 1: The process of capitalist production.* New York, NY: International Publishers.
New Mexico State University. (2008). *Policy Manual.* Retrieved from: http://nmsu.edu/~safety/policies/policy_5.94.13_AnimalsUse_in_Research.html
Smith, P. (1984). *The Rise of industrial America: A people's history of the post-Reconstruction era.* New York, NY: Penguin.
Urban, W., & Wagoner, J. (2009). *American education: A history* (4th ed.). New York, NY: Routlege.
Zinn, H. (2003). *People's history of the United States: 1492—present.* New York, NY: Perennial Classics.

AFFILIATION

Curry Stephenson Malott
Department of Professional and Secondary Education
West Chester University of Pennsylvania

50. WHEN ORDINARY PEOPLE DO EXTRAORDINARY THINGS

In Memory of Howard Zinn

Dear Friends and Colleagues,

It is with enormous sadness and yet great hope that I write this letter. As many of you know, historian, academic, activist, and inspiration to millions of people, Howard Zinn, born August 24th, 1922, passed away on January 27th, 2010. His personal story and life's work are a call to all of us to make the world a more just and humane place.

Howard was born in Brooklyn, New York, the son of Jewish immigrants who escaped the oncoming mayhem of World War I; his father was living under the Austro-Hungarian Empire, and his mom made her way out of the insufferable conditions of Eastern Siberia. Howard's parents toiled in low-paying, manual labor jobs in the U.S. to make a better life for their family. Offering what little they could to raise and educate their kids, Howard got introduced to the ideas of such social critics as Charles Dickens, and he began developing his creative skills with the pen at Thomas Jefferson High School.

As a young man, Howard joined the U.S. Air force during WWII to fight anti-Semitism and fascism. After the war and living with the harsh reality of having committed atrocities as a bomber pilot, he was insistent on furthering his education and fighting against the propaganda embedded in vulgar nationalism and global capitalism. With the help of the GI Bill, he attended NYU and then went on to do his maters and doctorate in history and political science at Columbia University; subsequently doing postdoctoral work in East Asian Studies at Harvard.

Writing extensively on labor history, civil rights, and anti-war activism, Howard is perhaps best known for his book *A People's History of the United States*. It inspired countless people, including me, to be critical educators. As a young person, I was particularly moved by the fact that this book is not only critical in its view of U.S. history, but it is also about ordinary, everyday people taking great risks to fight for and achieve real social change.

Howard understood that teachers are activists, whether or not we want to be, as we inevitably influence people in our classroom exchange of knowledge and values and beliefs. This important point is the focus of his memoir *You Can't Be Neutral on a Moving Train* in which he describes his work at Spelman College where he

T. M. Kress and R. Lake (Eds.), We Saved the Best for You: Letters of Hope, Imagination and Wisdom for 21st Century Educators, 227–230.
© *2013 Sense Publishers. All rights reserved.*

was a history professor, participated in the Civil Rights Movement, worked with the Student Nonviolent Coordinating Committee, provided insight and guidance to student activists, and as a result of his politics and actions, was dismissed from his teaching position in 1963. In 1964, he took a faculty position in political science at Boston University where he eventually retired in 1988.

Howard believed that we as educators need to inspire young people to think about the world critically and realize their own agency. He understood that developing critical consciousness isn't an exercise to get people to think in a certain way, but rather, it is intended to get us to think more deeply about the issues and relations of power that affect our lives and the lives of others. Like those progressive educators that inspired him along the way, he encouraged countless students to fight oppression in all of its forms as a scholar and activist.

In every country on every continent, young people have always played a pivotal role in struggles for social justice. In the last 500 years alone—certainly since the advent of the university in the Middle Ages – societies have witnessed social transformation on a grand scale mobilized, or at least in part energized, by young people. With the ratification of the Convention on the Rights of the Child on November 20, 1989 the United Nations took the first steps to institutionally realize the active participation of youth in global affairs:

> Article 12: States Parties shall assure to the child who is capable of forming his or her own views the right to express those views freely in all matters affecting the child, the views of the child being given due weight in accordance with the age and maturity of the child.

> Article 15: States Parties recognize the rights of the child to freedom of association and to freedom of peaceful assembly. Retrieved from: http://www2.ohchr.org/english/law/crc.htm#art15

Given that public schools in any democracy are always intended to be agencies of civic mindedness and responsibility, and that the well-being of young people is the pretext for almost every political movement on the planet, educators should use these public institutions to encourage youth to recognize their power to act upon the world via critical awareness.

There are certainly plenty of reasons for young people to work for social change in the United States, a country that continues to have the highest child poverty rate among major industrialized nations. Nationally, one-in-five children grow up poor. The nation ranks seventeenth of all industrialized countries in efforts to eradicate poverty among the young, and twenty-third in infant mortality. In addition, young people are experiencing a great deal of discrimination along the lines of race, language, disability, religion, gender, and sexuality. The government's response to the growing problems that youth in this country face is the implementation of a standardized curriculum, high stakes testing, accountability schemes, English-only mandates, strict zero-tolerance policies, and Draconian budget cuts. In this era of

'No Child Left Behind'—conversely referred to as "the war against the young"—millions of children have thus far been left in its wake.

Meanwhile, of the over seven billion people that currently live on this planet, almost half of them are under the age of 25. Half the world's 1 billion poor are children. Victims of the residue of a brutal history of colonial rule, sustained racism and patriarchy, and now the neoliberal mandates of deregulation, structural adjustment, and austerity measures, 11 million of these kids under the age of 5 die annually because of malnutrition, dirty water (or a lack of water altogether), disease, and substandard housing. Hundreds of millions of youth around the world are not getting a formal education and millions are trapped in the sex trade and sweat shops or caught up in military conflicts where they are often forced into fighting someone else's economic and ideological wars.

As Howard understood, the youth of the world can be looked to as a democratizing force capable of dismantling the structured inequalities in societies. It is for this very reason that conservatives and capitalists fear them so and vigilantly work to contain and control them; as they worked to control Howard when the FBI, considering him a national security risk, kept a close eye on and documented his movements. As students at all levels of schooling are currently being distracted or lured away from critically reading historical and existing social formations, especially those that maintain abuses of power, they often become the newest wave of exploited labor power and reproducers, whether they are conscious of it or not, of oppressive social practices. It is precisely this lack of inquiry, analysis, and agency that a critical and activist-based philosophy of learning and teaching should work to reverse.

Students could gain a great deal of insight from social movement and action research. Social movement research documents the power of activist efforts and their impact on people, public discourse, policy, institutions, and governments. It looks at the ways in which activists understand and make use of the cracks of agency made possible by shifting economic, political, and cultural relations, and how organizations and networks develop, mobilize, and change. As part of their formal education, students could be encouraged to critically appropriate from examples of activist efforts, intercultural and intergenerational cooperation, and international solidarity. For example, the public school curriculum could include an exploration and analysis of the labor movement in the U.S. and youth participation therein: investigating important events like the Newsboy Strike in 1899, the 1903 "Children's Crusade," and the development of the American Youth Congress in the 1930s. Students could also examine efforts to desegregate schools in the 1950s and the work of the Student Nonviolent Coordinating Committee. They could find a great deal of inspiration in the Civil Rights Movement of the 1960s and the college campus activism that was mobilized by groups such as Students for a Democratic Society. There are also lessons to be learned from government efforts to mobilize youth and to have their voices heard in drafting public policy, such as what happened with the National Commission on Resources for Youth in the 1970s. There have been a plethora of recent and informative youth protests against discriminatory and abusive social and educational policies, such as in California against the passage of Propositions 187, 209, and 21 led by organizations like Critical Resistance, Youth Force, and Youth Organizing Communities. In fact, there is a vast array of organizations that merit investigation by kids and young adults in schools, like Youth on Board, the Youth Activism Project, the Freechild Project, and the National Youth Rights Association. And of course there's the Zinn Education Project, started by one of Howard's former students, designed to help teachers and learners develop a critical sense of history and knowledge.

Public schools could also engage students in conducting Action Research, which has always had a political and transformative agenda explicitly woven into its theoretical and empirical fabric. Advocates of this exploratory model embrace the idea of doing research in the community with others rather than on them in an effort to collaboratively understand and consequently change any given situation.

When encouraged to think and speak, youth are more than willing and able—as they have always been – to analyze social injustice and come up with solutions. Youth movements in the past two decades provide a great deal of evidence of this: students of all ages and grade levels have taken up such causes as education and media reform; immigrant and labor rights; AIDS awareness; environmental protection; animal rights; anti-war activism; civil liberties; and gay, disability and women's rights. They have battled against sweatshop labor, racism, police brutality, the rise in incarceration, and poverty.

In this era of globalization, in which no society is entirely isolated and untouched by undemocratic, neoliberal policies and practices, and any local action has a global impact and vice versa, constructive approaches to youth activism should have an international scope. In this way, youth in the U.S. can more effectively work in solidarity with other young people from around the world and realize substantive social, political, economic, and institutional change. As Howard Zinn exemplified, this is what can happen when ordinary people – such as teachers – have the epistemological curiosity and the pedagogical courage to do, and inspire others to do, extraordinary things.

Dr. Leistyna

REFERENCES

Zinn, H. (1980). *A People's History of the United States: 1492 to Present*. New York, NY: HarperCollins
Zinn, H. (1994). *You can't be neutral on a moving train: A personal history of our times*. Boston, MA: Beacon Press.

AFFILIATION

Pepi Leistyna
Department of Applied Linguistics
The University of Massachusetts Boston

PAULINE SAMESHIMA

51. SLOW LOVE

Living and Teaching Through Rilke's Letters

Based on Rainier Rilke's letters to Franz Xaver Kappus in 1903 and 1908 and written for Rosalyn Heyman, a community leader, philanthropist, lifelong teacher, principal, assistant superintendent, and inspiring friend.

Pullman, WA. October, 29, 2011

MY DEAR ROSALYN,

I received your letter of August 29th in Vancouver, BC, and it is only now that I am responding. I'm very sorry for the long delay—but I wanted to return home before writing. I wanted to spend some time with your words and answer you while looking out at the garden. Like me, the flowers and shrubs have at last found their rhythm and dwelling places, after five years at this address. Perhaps this is the first summer I really feel at home, and I'm sure it's because the garden is starting to grow in. I suppose nature needs time to find home as well. We put in a winding dry riverbed and flowing shrubs, and the perennials are settling into their spaces. The gazing ball fountain outside the open window makes the inside air restful while refreshing. I like the solitude of my home work space with the distant barking dog, the birds, and the trickling water. Jane Piirto (2011), a creativity researcher, encourages this necessary space of meditative solitude. The kaleidoscope of golden pale crescent butterflies seem to have settled in and around the Echinacea—simply lovely.

We returned from Vancouver about six weeks ago. The city, an attractive tourist destination location, is difficult for me to cope with after living in the serene Palouse these past years. I am no longer used to traffic and the feverish energies in the air. The city asphalt seems to exhale a drumbeat urgency, a jarring juxtaposition trapped between the stunning mountain line and ocean air. And yet, the Vancouver air in the rain, is like no other—the moist freshness settling inside me with each deep breath. As in any place, as Rilke says of Rome, "there is no more beauty here than elsewhere . . . there is much beauty here, because there is much beauty everywhere" (1934, p. 42). The atmosphere we create for ourselves and the way we meld our bodies into the land reveals what we see and develops the embracing we feel.

Rilke reminds me to find those flowings of presentness in order to see the beauty. He says "Through such impressions one collects oneself, wins oneself back again out

T. M. Kress and R. Lake (Eds.), We Saved the Best for You: Letters of Hope, Imagination and Wisdom for 21st Century Educators, 231–238.
© *2013 Sense Publishers. All rights reserved.*

of the pretentious multiplicity that talks and chatters there, (and how talkative it is!), and one learns slowly to recognize the very few things in which the eternal endures that one can love and something solitary in which one can quietly take part" (p. 43).

Pullman, in Eastern Washington, where I now live, is a small town historically rooted in agriculture. This is a restful place. Most of our commuting is within 5-minutes. I "rejoice in the great quiet" (p. 43), the expansive undulating hills, wheat fields in all their glorious colors, the multitude of bright stars, and the soft dawn and twilight of the Palouse. I am at home here now. Our exchanges remind me of the importance of intentionally setting up the classroom environment—to create safe, comforting spaces which allow for quiet work and mindful solitude.

I wanted to tell you that the book you sent has not arrived yet. I hope it is not lost. I so look forward to your writings. Please know my appreciation for your letters. This poem is in response to your query. Don't worry. Everything takes time.

MAKING FARES

I wait inside the Sacramento airport
outside, taxi cabs fill and refill at the curb
eyes drawn to that stepping in and out space
frenetic on the sizzling asphalt
sounds swirl inside tight and loose in flow
with the synthetic breeze of air conditioning

then a lyrical lapse in time settles

through the window
a driver waits for a fare
he is sprawled, eyes closed
leg hanging out
of the passenger seat
door wide open
in the open the sun

he waits a long time
perhaps he has a dream
because when he awakes
he gets out and walks around
to the driver's seat and pulls away

the cab behind him inches forward
as a cacophonous crowd walks past me
through the automatic double doors
straight to the cab pulling up

With wishes and greetings,
Yours,
Pauline

****

Pullman, WA. December 23, 2011

MY DEAR ROSALYN,

I think often of you in your solitude while my house is busy with bustling children in this Christmas season. I hear you speak of your loneliness and wish we lived closer. Sometimes I envy your space, that deep and necessary solitude for growing seeds for creating and writing. Rilke notes,

> Only the individual who is solitary is like a thing placed under profound laws, and when he goes out into the morning that is just beginning, or looks out into the evening that is full of happening, and if he feels what is going on there, then all status drops from him as from a dead man, though he stands in the midst of sheer life. (p. 47)

The challenges you speak of in teaching are issues we all face. Teachers seldom share teaching insecurities so I thank you for your courage. There are no easy answers. There is always so much and more to do.

> This feeling of constraint would not have been spared you.—It is everywhere; but that is no reason for fear or sorrow; if there is nothing in common between you and other people, try being close to things, they will not desert you; there are the nights still and the winds that go through the trees and across many lands; among things and with the animals everything is still full of happening, in which you may participate. (p. 48)

"For do you not see how everything that happens keeps on being a beginning . . . [and] beginning is in itself always so beautiful" (p. 49). Take your months into weeks and into days, hours, and minutes until you can feel your lungs expanding and contracting when you breathe that vibrant air into your lungs. Spend your time writing. You should finish your book. Rilke suggests that "Prose needs to be built like a cathedral: there, one is truly without a name, without ambition, without help: on scaffoldings, alone with one's consciousness" (p. 112). Be glad and confident.

Have you seen Jeff Harris, the Toronto photographer's self-portrait project? You can see his photos at jeffharris.org. He has a photograph of himself since 1999. His life is both beautiful and poignant. He talks about how the project has inspired him to "seek out interesting things" (Matutschovsky, 2012, n.p.). This intentionality is key for living well as a teacher.

233

Christmas is so precious with a toddler. Noelle is two and a half now and times with her two older sisters are the most joyful experiences reflected on her face. She says "happy" purely, with glowing eyes, and I know that she is referring to the adult's painful pressing of tightness in the lungs which is that fullness of utter delight. Her joy is not simply in decorations and twinkling lights, her enchantment is the air full of love.

I'm glad you are going to spend the new year with Peter and his family. These are the relationships and memories to collect and define from our daily preoccupations.

MISSED BIRTHDAYS

splash us
out of this living
a rebellion of the impossible
where there is
no skin
no armor
no barriers
only exposed nerves
urgency and pivotal moments
of bursting and crashing
showing us the surrender
we talk about
this middle age stillness
my birthdays have forgotten

Merry Christmas, my dear friend,
Pauline

****

Pullman, WA. December 26, 2011

MY DEAR ROSALYN,

Thank you so much for your kind letter which arrived yesterday. Your letters are always so wonderful to receive. Thank you for buying that tree in my name from the Arbor Day Foundation. What a wonderful gift idea! Our letters may have crossed paths en route as I just mailed you a letter a few days ago. A Christmas poem for you:
SAILING WINDS

So many days, past and forward
dissolve and disperse

heartache and history
swept through tides
washed and cleansed by an outlook
Contented she rests
in a schooner, carried by love,
gales and gentle winds, the natural
encounters she trusts

The clouds ballet
overhead in a
silent choreographed cacophony
of languorous musings
in unharried charms
but also dissonance

She watches and knows this landscape
above the earth, above the sea
understands her place
islands and lands
Now questions who
can accompany her
hushed lonesome journey
into beauty?
Who can sail
sail the sky?

My daily newspaper has a weekly section called Public Records, where the local county sheriffs and police department list days, times, and incidents of all their reports. There are about three or four citations four days a week (our town size is about 30,000). The citations are troubling – not brutal gang-related murders or drug busts but such things as a wedding ring stolen at a public restroom, a domestic violence dispute, a vehicle driven into the yard of a residence, fraudulent use of a credit card, a neighbor urinating in his front yard, or titanium screws stolen from a university engineering building. I remind myself that these incidences involve a very small portion of our town's population, and yet, these are the incidences that shape perceptions around fear and safety here.

When I first moved to this small town, I was astounded that there seemed to be so many car accidents and deaths here. I realized quickly that accidents and deaths are not prominent news stories in big cities because they happen all the time and are not dramatic headline news. Pullman criminal citations would probably be considered irrelevant in a major city. The Public Records remind me to question what is being reported and what is being left out. We don't consciously do this, and I think our perceptions are skewed by what is and what is not made visible (In our classrooms, how is the culture shaping learning?). These incident reports also raise concerns about my own morality—how are we shaped by Costco culture or how are my goals for my family shaped? If I lived in a large city, would I forget that "irrelevant" incidences are occurring on a larger scale?

Jane Piirto (2011) also says creativity comes with a high tolerance for ambiguity. Well, a new year's poem with no answers.

LESSONS ON USING CUTLERY

they sat at the table next to us
for the free deluxe breakfast
in the downtown Spokane hotel

the stories on their faces speak of an
overworked accountant and an
exhausted mother waiting for
the notion that the pending new birth
would give her silence
the freedom to dream in stillness while
nourishing a suckling newborn

violated ceasefires and marching militants
blare from the morning TV news
Silas, their 3-year old
kneels on his chair
using his knife as a fork

none of my business
why should I care?
ruin my own breakfast?
ruin my joy with my family?
we're far from perfect

Silas stabs his pancake pieces
with his knife and raises the
dripping portions to his mouth
sucking the thick syrupy sweetness
off the blade as he slides the knife
through his tightly closed lips
over and over

and the air won't take notice

the fork on the table as
invisible as he is
to his parents

the flavor of fear is unsavory
I can't taste my food
we watch war on the screen

I am comatose as my children laugh
delighting in freshly made waffles

how do I live without caring?
how can I speak without judgment?
how do I step out without separating myself?
how can I scream softly?
I hold the sharpness
tightly behind my lips

Silas begins to comb his hair
with his sugary knife
he's good with cutlery for his age
fluidly keeping the sharp end
away from his eyes

do I remain silent?
not feel the TV
not notice the headline gloss

who has the guidebook for living?

who can shake the truth in my face
that I see in these parents
the enviable blind freedom
I sometimes covet

who can tell me my
own children need me more
than I can be?

Pauline Sameshima

REFERENCES

Matutschovsky, N. (2012, January 3). Jeff Harris: 4,748 Self-portaits and counting. *Time LightBox*. Retrieved on January 3, 2010, from http://lightbox.time.com/2012/01/03/jeff-harris-self-portraits/.

Piirto, J. (2011). *Creativity for 21st century skills: How to embed creativity into the curriculum*. Rotterdam, The Netherlands: Sense.

Rilke, R. M. (1934). *Letters to a young poet*. (M. D. Herter Norton, Trans., Revised ed.). New York, NY: Norton & Company.

AFFILIATION

Pauline Sameshima
Department of Teaching & Learning
Washington State University

M. CATHRENE CONNERY

52. TO BE A TEACHER

A Desiderata for the 21st Century Educator

My dear students:

I stand before you and my breath catches in my throat. I marvel at your beauty and bravery.

You are the big-hearted inclusiveness of the fearless undergraduate. You are the spunk of an emerging professional. You are the raised eyebrow of a resolute veteran, the shimmering inquiries of a graduate assistant, and the silk-like assurance of a scholar in the field. You are the courageous contemplation of a mid-life career changer valiantly realizing their dreams. As emerging, novice, and expert educators, you are the fresh-faced hope, wisdom, and imagination of our society.

Within you, I see the promise of spring. You are the arc of a dancer, crouched in a position of trembling uncertainty. In time, you will twist and rise into a tower of confidence. With arms outstretched, you are as rooted as an ancient pine, as graceful as a growing birch, as elegant as the weighty magnolia certain to blossom in the sun's new warmth. Inside you, I glimpse the massive strength of mountains, the prudence of a seed, the steel girds of a glass-faced sky scraper, and the agile quicksilver of wild, running streams.

Listen closely, and you will hear the call of silver trumpets faintly in the distance. Peer carefully, and you will see that I brandish a celebratory flag on your behalf. The banner waves in your name, a rainbow of color announcing your vitality, significance, and strength. I gift you a blueprint of resilience hidden within my assignments, comments, and stories. I seek to provide for you an ornamented cloak of protection for colder days when you depart these warm rooms and venture onto the landscape of the world.

A wise person once said that women hold up three quarters of the sky. They forgot to mention that teachers function as the fourth and essential pillar.

To be a teacher is the hardest job in the world: at one and the same time, you must represent the best of humanity while serving as a human Kleenex.

To be a teacher is to lead learners into the shadowed chambers of Egyptian royalty and poisonous spiders. It is to explore the Marian Trench with heavy oxygen tanks strapped to your back, to jump out of a plane into the steamy jungle of the Amazon, or share breakfast with a princess, president, or penguin. To be a teacher is to shoot a

T. M. Kress and R. Lake (Eds.), We Saved the Best for You: Letters of Hope, Imagination and Wisdom for 21st Century Educators, 239–242.
© *2013 Sense Publishers. All rights reserved.*

class VI, white water rapid, all without leaving your classroom. For, to be a teacher is to wield imagination as one's greatest tool and ethical responsibility. Children will learn about themselves and their place in the cosmos through the colorful rendering you bestow them. Through your guidance, they will discover beauty, excitement, and resilience in the face of ugliness, apathy, and defeat.

To be a teacher is to facilitate super-heroic accomplishments by learners who don't even know they are wearing a cape. It is to be intellectually generous enough to stand back from those who are already flying high. To be a teacher is to inconspicuously hang a safety net for both types of aeronauts.

To be a teacher is to continually brandish a giant mirror to reflect the best of a learner back at themselves, even when they are sticking out their tongue or giving you the finger.

To be a teacher is to be humble enough to understand that, ultimately, you can't teach anyone anything. But like leading the proverbial horse to water, there is a great deal a teacher can do to inspire thirst to drink.

To be a teacher is to glimpse behind the masks of inexperience, uncertainty and fear. It is to validate the intelligence and talent that lurk beneath, authenticating their place in the sun. To be a teacher is to allow the learner to remove their own protection, knowing nothing is more terrifying than the threat of someone else tearing off your own scab.

To be a teacher is to be inspired by defiance and determination in the face of horrific dysfunction. It is to have the courage to sort through charred remains for that which is indestructible or left unbroken. To be a teacher is to gracefully accept the gift of loss. Fortunately, to be a teacher is to witness profound acts of kindness that reach primordial wells of emotion, only to bathe, bless, and transform the learner's soul.

To be a teacher is to dance simultaneously in and with the past, present, and future. They trade in the currency of what comes before, within, and after the teaching-learning moment, midwifing what is yet unborn.

To be a teacher is to simultaneously labor as a social sculptor and political architect. Manipulating an invisible medium, teachers organize attention, cultivate wonder, shape self-esteem, focus vision, and foster priority and care. Teachers discover the song inside the instrument and the words inside the pen. They coax, wheedle, invite, encourage, and sometimes even yank out the voice that hides and grows within the caverns of the heart.

Teachers are the champions and defenders of our birthright to know, to not know, and the journey to begin to find out, all initiated by a pat on the floor beside them.

To be a teacher is to embrace a life committed to civil rights, fully aware of the marginalizing consequences assigned to the secular bodhisattva.

As a young teacher, Max Ehrman's (1948) "*Desiderata*" graced a wall in my tiny apartment. The poem proved to be ancient map that helped me to safely navigate the high seas of the educational profession. In the five a.m. darkness, digging the sleep from my eyes, I silently anticipated my day, my week, my month, my school year through the prism of his insight. I offer you his crystalline words as a semiotic talisman:

Go placidly amidst the noise and haste, and remember what peace there may be in silence.

As far as possible, without surrender, be on good terms with all persons.

Speak your truth quietly and clearly; and listen to others, even the dull and the ignorant; they too have their story.

Avoid loud and aggressive persons, they are vexations to the spirit.

If you compare yourself with others, you may become vain or bitter; for always there will be greater and lesser persons than yourself.

Enjoy your achievements as well as your plans. Keep interested in your own career, however humble; it is a real possession in the changing fortunes of time.

Exercise caution in your business affairs; for the world is full of trickery.

But let this not blind you to what virtue there is; many persons strive for high ideals; and everywhere life is full of heroism.

Be yourself. Especially, do not feign affection.

Neither be cynical about love; for in the face of all aridity and disenchantment it is as perennial as the grass.

Take kindly the counsel of the years, gracefully surrendering the things of youth.

Nurture strength of spirit to shield you in sudden misfortune.

But do not distress yourself with dark imaginings. Many fears are born of fatigue and loneliness.

Beyond a wholesome discipline, be gentle with yourself. You are a child of the universe, no less than the trees and the stars; you have a right to be here.

And whether or not it is clear to you, no doubt the universe is unfolding as it should.

Therefore be at peace.

Whatever your labors and aspirations, in the noisy confusion of life keep peace with your soul.

With all its sham, drudgery, and broken dreams, it is still a beautiful world.

Be cheerful. Strive to be happy (Ehrmann, 1948, p. 10–11).

In your palms, you cradle the pristine gem of the future. So, tend your own home fires. Exercise self-care and self-love. Remember that, no matter what, kindness always, always, always matters. Only with that which we have in ourselves, can we inspire in others.

To be a teacher is to keep on keeping on. It is to run the extra mile in a sparsely populated stadium with the torch of childhood in one hand and flame of social justice in the other. To be a teacher is to weave emotions and ideas on the loom of promise. It is to exercise an artistry of compassion. It is to gently touch the best of what it means to be human: the inherent need to make sense of the world, to find our place within it, and to share that space with those we often come to love.

My dear students, as you face my podium, behind you I see the exponential collective of children, families, and communities impacted by your hope, imagination, and wisdom. I marvel at your beauty and bravery. And my breath catches in my throat.

Best wishes,
Dr. C.

REFERENCE

Ehrmann, M. (1948). *The desiderata of happiness: A collection of philosophical poems.* New York, NY: Crown Publishers.

AFFILIATION

M. Cathrene Connery
Department of Education
Ithaca College

ABOUT THE AUTHORS

Jennifer D. Adams is an assistant professor of science education at Brooklyn College, the City University of New York. Prior to this she was a classroom teacher of biology, field instructor for New York City Outward Bound and then a manager of professional development and curriculum initiatives at the American Museum of Natural History. Her current research interests lie in place-based science education and informal science education in urban contexts and pre-service teacher education in settings beyond the traditional classroom. Her recent work examines sense-of-place and identity of diverse youth in urban contexts, and youth identity development and motivation through science participation in informal science education settings.

Carolyne Ali-Khan is an Assistant Professor at the University of North Florida. Prior to this, she spent twenty years as an educator in New York City, and has also been involved in numerous international educational projects. Her research interests include critical pedagogy, multicultural education, youth studies, and visual studies.

Peter Appelbaum is President of The American Association for the Advancement of Curriculum Studies and Professor of Education, Director-at-Large of Undergraduate Curriculum, and the Director of the sTRANGELY fAMILIAR mUSIC gROUP at Arcadia University, Philadelphia, USA.

Rick Ayers is a Professor of Education at the University of San Francisco in the Urban Education and Social Justice cohort. He taught in the Communication Arts and Sciences small school at Berkeley High School. He is the co-author of Teaching the Taboo: Courage and Imagination in the Classroom (2010).

Gillian U. Bayne earned her doctorate in Urban Education Department (Science, Math and Technology) from the City University of New York's Graduate Center. She combines her expertise and commitment to excellence with innovative teaching philosophies and practices in order to create greater possibilities for students and teachers as they embark on the complex journey that is science education.

Andy Blunden is a Melbourne writer, who works with the Independent Social Research Network. Andy developed an interest in Hegel in 1980, has held a Hegel Summer School since 1998, and runs the Hegel-by-HyperText website. He is a joint Editor of *Mind, Culture & Activity* a journal of cultural psychology.

Joan Braune is a doctoral candidate in Philosophy at University of Kentucky. Her dissertation is on Erich Fromm's defense of hope and "prophetic messianism" as a radical philosophy of history. She is preparing to publish her dissertation and is currently researching Fromm's contribution to critical pedagogies and his dialogue with monk Thomas Merton.

M. Cathrene Connery is an Assistant Professor of Education at Ithaca College. A bilingual educator, researcher and advocate, she has drawn on her visual arts education as a painter to inform her research and professional activities in language, literacy, and sociocultural studies. Dr. Connery has presented on theoretical, pedagogic, and programmatic concerns surrounding the education of culturally and linguistically diverse children in the United States for the past 25 years. Her current research interests include multicultural teacher education, biliteracy and the development of first and second languages, semiotics, sociopolitical issues in development, learning, and education as well as the social construction of feminist identities by female artists and teachers. She has utilized Vygotskian theory to articulate ethnographic accounts in *Profiles in Emergent Biliteracy: Children Making Meaning in a Chicano Community* (2011) and as an editor and contributor to *Vygotsky and Creativity: A Cultural-historical Approach to Play, Meaning-making, and the Arts* (2010) published by Peter Lang.

Clyde Coreil holds a Ph.D. in linguistics from the City University of New York, and an M.F.A. in playwriting from Carnegie Mellon University. His most recent long play, completed in the summer of 2012, is entitled *Laredo*. He has edited some 10 annual volumes of *The Journal of the Imagination in Language Learning*. At present, he is completing a 100-page book, *Coreil's Way to Write Academic "Term" Papers*. He is also engaged in writing the music and lyrics to approximately 20 songs.

Ana Cruz was born in Manaus, the heart of Amazonas, Brazil and, thanks to a committed teacher/sociologist/activist, was exposed to the work of Paulo Freire already in high school. Proud of her multiracial identity, Cruz embraces her black/native Indian/white heritage. She was raised in a middle-class family, but was not isolated from the unique environment of Manaus, with its distinctive ecological setting, conspicuous cultural diversity, oppression, and instances of utter poverty. Cruz has taught elementary school, high school, adult education, and College/University in Brazil and in the U.S. In her current position, she prepares two-year college students to become teachers. Cruz's research is strongly influenced by Freire's work (e.g., the oppressor-oppressed relationship, the internalization of the oppressor's views by the oppressed, and the process of gaining consciousness). Critical pedagogy/critical theory inform her research in Music and Deafness, where she investigates the power relationships within the Deaf community and the relationships to the hearing world.

Robert Danberg is a Visiting Assistant Professor in the Writing Initiative at Binghamton University. His essays have appeared in *Composition Studies* and *Writing on the Edge*; his poetry has appeared in *Ploughshares, The Sun, The Cortland Review* and other journals on line and in print. His scholarship focuses on ways to design writing courses that facilitate the acquisition of habits of mind and experiential knowledge.

Donna DeGennaro is an assistant professor of Instructional Technology at the University of Massachusetts, Boston. Her research draws on theories from cultural sociology and critical pedagogy to examine the interrelationship between culture, history, and social interactions and how they inform emergent learning designs.

Rosalina Diaz is employed at Medgar Evers College as an Associate Professor in the Department of Education, where she focuses on culturally responsive pedagogical practices. She earned a Ph.D. from the CUNY Graduate Center in Urban Education with a concentration in Anthropology and a certificate in Women's Studies. She has taught at the Borough of Manhattan Community College, City College, and Hunter College in the areas of Anthropology, Geography, Women's Studies, and Education. She worked as an interdisciplinary (English, Social Studies, & Science) teacher at several New York City public high schools for over 15 years. Most recently, she completed work on a co-edited volume titled *Beyond Stereotypes, Children of Immigration in Urban Schools*. She is a mother of 4 girls ranging in ages from six to twenty seven.

Riane Eisler is internationally known for her work as a systems scientist and for influential books such as *The Chalice and the Blade* (now in 24 foreign editions), *Tomorrow's Children: A Blueprint for Transforming Education,* and *The Real Wealth of Nations* (hailed by Archbishop Tutu as "a template for the better world we have been so urgently seeking"). She is president of the Center for Partnership Studies, www.partnershipway.org, has taught at the University of California and now teaches at the California Institute of Integral Studies, keynotes conferences worldwide, and consults for governments and businesses. She has received many honors, including honorary Ph.D. degrees, for her contributions to scholarship and human advancement, and numerous awards, including the Nuclear Age Peace Foundation's 2009 Distinguished Peace Leadership Award, for her groundbreaking work to advance social and economic development, human rights, and peace. She can be contacted at center@partnershipway.org.

Christopher Emdin is a faculty member in the Department of Mathematics, Science and Technology at Teachers College, Columbia University, where he also serves as Director of Secondary School Initiatives at the Urban Science Education Center.

Roser Giné is a Clinical Assistant Professor at the University of Massachusetts Lowell. She holds an Ed.D. from the University of Massachusetts Boston, a Masters in Teaching Mathematics from Harvard University, and a B.A. in Mathematics from Dartmouth College. Her research focus is on student learning of mathematics in classroom contexts.

Sandy Grande is an Associate Professor and Chair of the Education Department at Connecticut College. She is currently working on developing an indigenous think tank, *The Tecumseh Institute,* based in New York City. Her research and teaching are profoundly inter- and cross-disciplinary and interfaces critical and Indigenous theories of education with the concerns of Indigenous education. Her book, *Red Pedagogy: Native American Social and Political Thought* (Rowman and Littlefield, 2004) has been met with critical acclaim. She is also working as principle evaluator of The American Indian College Fund's project *Wakanyeja* "Sacred Little Ones" Project, a Tribal College Readiness and Success by Third Grade Initiative funded by the W. K. Kellogg Foundation. She has also published several book chapters and articles including: 'Confessions of a Fulltime Indian,' *Journal of Curriculum Studies, The Journal of Curriculum and Pedagogy*; "Red Land, White Power: A Pedagogy for the Dispossessed," *The Havoc of Capitalism:Education for Social and Environmental Justice*, J. Suoranta, D. Houston, G. Martin, P.McLaren (Eds.); and "American Indian Geographies of Identity and Power: At the Crossroads of Indigena and Mestizaje," *Harvard Educational Review.*

Lois Holzman is a cofounder with Fred Newman of the East Side Institute for Group and Short Term Psychotherapy in New York City and is the Institute's current director. She is a leading proponent of cultural approaches to learning, development and psychotherapy. Holzman is a leading methodologist of social therapy, an approach to human development and learning created by Fred Newman and has been Newman's chief collaborator since the 1970's. She is considered the leading expert on Newman's work and on social therapy, having published 9 books and dozens of academic articles on social therapeutic methodology. Her books include *Performing Psychology: A Postmodern Culture of the Mind; Schools for Growth: Radical Alternatives to Current Educational Models* and *Lev Vygotsky: Revolutionary Scientist* (with Fred Newman).

James C. Jupp works as Assistant Professor of Curriculum at Georgia Southern University and previously worked at Arkansas State University as Assistant Professor of Educational Foundations. He worked in rural and inner-city Title I settings for eighteen years before accepting a university position training teachers and administrators at the university level. A veteran of teaching children of color in rural and inner-city Title I schools, one line of his research focuses on white teachers' understandings of race, diversity, and difference pedagogy. Drawing on his experiences as teacher of Mexican immigrant, Mexican-American, and

Latino students, and as administrator in Title I schools, he is the author of "Culturally Relevant Pedagogy: One Teacher's Journey Through Theory and Practice," a piece which adds to discussions on White teachers that has been anthologized several times. He has published more than twenty scholarly articles in a variety of journals including the *International Journal of Qualitative Research in Education, Curriculum Inquiry, Urban Education, the Journal of the American Association for the Advancement of Curriculum Studies, the Journal of Curriculum and Pedagogy, the English Journal*, and *Multicultural Review*.

Tricia M. Kress is an Assistant Professor at the University of Massachusetts Boston in the Leadership in Urban Schools doctoral program. She received her Ph.D. in Urban Education from the Graduate Center, City University of New York. Her areas of expertise are critical pedagogy, ethnography, and socio-cultural perspectives on education. She has published in numerous educational volumes and journals. Of note is her recent work as a guest editor of a special edition of *The International Journal of Qualitative Studies in Education*, which focused on using critical research for educational and social change, and her recently published textbook *Critical Praxis Research: Breathing New Life into Research Methods for Teachers,* which applies critical pedagogy to research methods in order to bridge the scholar-practitioner divide that is so often prevalent in typical research methodologies.

Robert Lake is an Associate Professor at Georgia Southern University. He teaches both undergraduate and graduate courses in multicultural education from both a local and global perspective. Robert is the author of *Vygotsky on Education* for the Peter Lang Primer Series. His other books include *Dear Maxine: Letters from the Unfinished Conversation with Maxine Greene (2010)* and *Dear Nel: Opening the Circles of Care* (Letters to Nel Noddings 2012) published by Teachers College Press.

Thomas Lake is a senior writer for *Sports Illustrated* and the co-founder of the Auburn Chautauqua, an annual writers' conference. He is the third of Dr. Robert Lake's six children, who also include a teacher, a social worker, a nurse, an electrical lineman and a graduate student in Spanish.

Megan J. Laverty is Associate Professor in the Philosophy and Education Program at Teachers College, Columbia University. Her main area of interest is in moral philosophy and its significance for education.

Carl Leggo is a poet and professor in the Department of Language and Literacy Education at the University of British Columbia. His research focuses on the experiences of educators, especially how to promote heartful and hopeful relationships in educational communities. His poetry, fiction, and scholarly essays have been published in many journals in North America and around the world. He has written three collections of poems: *Growing Up Perpendicular on the Side of* *a Hill* (Killick Press, 1994); *View from My Mother's House* (Killick Press, 1999); *Come-By-Chance* (Breakwater Books, 2006). He has also written a book about reading and teaching poetry, titled *Teaching to Wonder: Responding to Poetry in the Secondary Classroom* (Pacific Educational Press, 1997).

Pepi Leistyna received his Masters and Doctorate from Harvard University, and is an Associate Professor of Applied Linguistics Graduate Studies at the University of Massachusetts Boston, where he coordinates the research program, teaches courses in cultural studies, critical pedagogy, media literacy, and language acquisition, and is the Director of the Center for World Languages and Cultures.

Dennis Littky is the co-founder and co-director of *Big Picture Learning* and the *Met Center* in Providence. He is nationally known for his extensive work in secondary education in urban, suburban, and rural settings, spanning over 40 years. As an educator, Dennis has a reputation for working up against the edge of convention and out of the box, turning tradition on its head and delivering concrete results. Presently, Dennis's focus is to expand the *Big Picture Learning* design to include college-level accreditation through *College Unbound*, where students will have the opportunity to earn a B.A. and advanced certifications through a critically challenging, real-world based, and entrepreneurial course of study. Dr. Littky holds a double Ph.D. in psychology and education from the University of Michigan.

Kurt Love is an assistant professor at Central Connecticut State University in the Teacher Education Department. His interest is working directly with teachers in their classroom on building teaching practices that use place-based contexts and cultural and ecological investigations. He also teaches courses at the Sustainable Farm School of Connecticut at the Flamig Farm.

Curry Stephenson Malott is an Assistant professor of educational foundations in the Department of Professional and Secondary Education at West Chester University of Pennsylvania. As a critical pedagogue and scholar of critical pedagogy Dr. Malott is particularly interested in the role critical theory and critical education can and are playing in transgressing the ravages of global capitalism and settler-state societies.

Rebecca Martusewicz has been a teacher educator at Eastern Michigan University for 23 years, teaching courses that integrate ecojustice content into social foundations courses. She is the Director of the Southeast Michigan Stewardship Coalition, working to develop EcoJustice Education in schools. She is editor and co-founder of *The EcoJustice Review: Educating for the Commons,* an internationally juried online journal, and *Educational Studies: Journal of AESA.* She is author *EcoJustice Education: Toward Diverse, Democratic and Sustainable Communities,* co-authored with Jeff Edmundson and Johnny Lupinacci (2012), and *Seeking Passage: PostStructuralism, Pedagogy, Ethics* (2001).

Julie Maudlin is an associate professor in Department of Teaching and Learning, College of Education, Georgia Southern University and co-director of the *Curriculum Studies Summer Collaborative*. She teaches courses in Elementary Education Methods, Curriculum and Instruction . She also works with doctoral candidates and is the Program Chair, of the American Educational Research Association, Critical Issues in Curriculum and Cultural Studies SIG. Her research is focused on Early Childhood Education, Curriculum and Cultural Studies, Consumerism, Creativity and Imagination. She has published on these topics in numerous journals and books.

Susan Jean Mayer is a learning and curriculum theorist who currently lectures at Brandeis and Northeastern Universities. Her recent book, *Classroom Discourse and Democracy: Making Meanings Together* analyzes questions of intellectual agency and authority; other published work has treated issues related to democratic K-12 practice and social science method.

Greg McClure is an Assistant Professor in the Department of Curriculum and Instruction at Appalachian State University where he teaches courses that prepare teachers for working with linguistically and culturally diverse learners. His research interests examine the ways language, culture, and power intersect to influence teaching and learning. His work can be found in *Pedagogies: An International Journal, TESOL Journal,* and *Equity & Excellence in Education.*

Jennifer L. Milam is an assistant professor in Early Childhood/Elementary Curriculum at The University of Akron. Her primary areas of interest and research are curriculum and cultural studies, specifically the intersections of teacher education and autobiography. She is partner to John, mother to Alexandra and Keith, and seeker of joy and wisdom.

Sonia Nieto is Professor Emerita of Language, Literacy, and Culture, School of Education, University of Massachusetts, Amherst. Her publications and more about her may be found at http://www.sonianieto.com/index.html

Nel Noddings is Professor Emerita of Philosophy and Education at Teachers College, Columbia University, and Lee L. Jacks Professor of Child Education Emerita at Stanford University. She has 10 children and has been married for 63 years. She credits her early educational experiences and her close relationships as key in her development of her philosophical position. She is the author of numerous books and articles and still in great demand around the globe as a presenter on care theory, moral philosophy and democratic education.

Patricia Paugh, a K-12 teacher for 20 years, is currently an Associate Professor at the University of Massachusetts Boston. Her research interests include school-university research partnerships, equitable access to academic literacy for students in linguistically and culturally diverse communities, critical literacy, and the value of practitioner research in teachers' professional development.

William M. Reynolds teaches in the Department of Curriculum, Foundations and Reading at Georgia Southern University. His two most recent books are *Expanding Curriculum Theory: Dis/positions and Lines of Flight* (2004) and *The Civic Gospel: A Political Cartography of Christianity* (2009).

Mike Rose was born in Altoona, Pennsylvania, and raised in Los Angeles, California. He is a graduate of Loyola University (B.A.), the University of Southern California (M.S.), and the University of California, Los Angeles (M.A. and Ph.D.). Over the last forty years, he has taught in a range of educational settings, from kindergarten to job training and adult literacy programs. He is currently on the faculty of the UCLA Graduate School of Education and Information Studies.

Pauline Sameshima's work centres on curriculum, arts and technology integration, collaborative and creative scholarship, eco-responsive pedagogies, and innovative forms of knowledge production and acknowledgment. Her books include: *Seeing Red, Climbing the Ladder with Gabriel* (with Roxanne Vandermause, Stephen Chalmers, and Gabriel), and *Poetic Inquiry* (with Monica Prendergast and Carl Leggo).

William H. Schubert is Professor Emerita of education and coordinator of the Graduate Curriculum Studies Programs at the University of Illinois at Chicago.

Brian D. Schultz is Associate Professor and Chair of the Department of Educational Inquiry & Curriculum Studies at Northeastern Illinois University in Chicago. His research focuses on students and teachers theorizing together, developing integrated curriculum based on the students' priority concerns, and curriculum as social action and public pedagogy.

Robert W. Simmons III is an Assistant Professor in the School of Education at Loyola University Maryland and a member of the social justice collaborative Edchange (edchange.com). Twice nominated as the Walt Disney National Teacher of the Year and once for the Whitney and Elizabeth MacMillan Foundation Outstanding Educator Award, Robert's research currently focuses on urban education and the experiences of African American male students and teachers.

Christina Siry is an Associate Professor in Educational Sciences at the University of Luxembourg, where she teaches in the area of science education. Her research foci include the use of participatory approaches for working together with teachers and students around the learning of science at the primary school level.

Kevin Smith (Ph.D, Miami University, 2010; M.Ed, Miami University, 2005; B.S, Utah State University, 2004) currently lives in Ha'ateiho, Tonga where he works as the Fellow in Curriculum at the Institute of Education. Prior to working in Tonga, he also taught for six years in public schools in Cincinnati, Ohio.

Christopher Darius Stonebanks is an Associate Professor in the School of Education and Chair of the Research Ethics Board at Bishop's University. His research regarding the Other has been published in *Studies of Symbolic Interaction* and *Cultural Studies ↔ Critical Methodologies* and within *The Handbook of Critical and Indigenous Methodologies.*

Barbara J. Thayer-Bacon, Ph.D. (Indiana University, Bloomington, IN), Professor, teaches graduate courses on philosophy and history of education, social philosophy, and cultural diversity for the University of Tennessee. Her primary areas of scholarship as a philosopher of education are feminist theory and pedagogy, pragmatism, and cultural studies in education.

Eve Tuck is a new mother, and Assistant Professor of Educational Foundations at the State University of New York at New Paltz. She is the author of *Urban Youth and School Pushout: Gateways, Get-aways, and the GED* (Routledge, 2012). Eve's family is from St. Paul Island, Alaska. The language that appears in her letter is *Unangam Tunuu.*

Susan Verducci is an Associate Professor of Humanities and coordinator of the Liberal Studies program at San José State University. She co-edited *Democracy, Education and the Moral Life* (2009) and *Taking Philanthropy Seriously: Beyond Noble Intentions to Responsible Giving* (2006). Her fields of interest include educational philosophy, ethics and philanthropy.

Tina Wagle, Ph.D. is currently Associate Professor and Chair of Teacher Education in the School for Graduate Studies at SUNY-Empire State College. Her research areas include sociological identity development especially among peoples from underrepresented groups, bilingual education, teacher education, and urban education and has published and done professional presentations in those areas. She is actively engaged in several initiatives with the Buffalo Public Schools and has provided professional services to educational and civic organizations serving bilingual communities. She is the recipient of the SUNY Chancellor's Award for Excellence in Faculty Service.

Melissa Winchell is an instructor of English at Massasoit Community College in Brockton, MA. A doctoral candidate in the Leadership in Urban Schools program at The University of Massachusetts Boston, Melissa's research interests include critical pedagogy, critical race theory, co-teaching, and participatory action research.

Helena Worthen is a Visiting Scholar at the Center for Labor Research and Education at UC Berkeley. She holds a PhD in Education from UC Berkeley. Previously, she was a labor educator at the University of Illinois and at UNITE in Philadelphia and worked for the California Federation of Teachers. Her research focus is activist learning for equity and justice on the job.

Tianlong Yu is an Associate Professor of Social Foundations of Education at Southern Illinois University Edwardsville. His research interest is focused on political and social issues in moral education. He also writes on multicultural education. During 2011–2012 when this essay was written, he was on sabbatical leave from SIUE and taught at Shandong Normal University in Shandong, China where Confucius was born, lived, and taught.

CPSIA information can be obtained at www.ICGtesting.com
Printed in the USA
LVOW011349151212

311828LV00001B/2/P

9 789462 091207